Praise for *Holot*

"*Holotropic Breathwork* elucidates a map expanded beyond the biographical and psychological realms of Western psychology into the perinatal and transpersonal realms identified by modern consciousness research and the study of ancient and tribal rituals and their cosmologies ... The wonder of this book ... is that this is not just a book, a map, a set of theories, or someone's research results, but that it also describes a very concrete and currently available technique one can employ for transformation."

— *Journal of Transpersonal Psychology*

"For anyone interested in Holotropic Breathwork this book offers a very extensive and detailed overview ... [and] offers a number of practical details of how to conduct a session."

— *Network Review*

"Stanislav and Christina Grof are modern pioneers of consciousness and this book is their map of the territory. *Holotropic Breathwork* reveals how the Grofs developed their revolutionary healing techniques, often told through fascinating stories of people being transformed by the breathwork process. The Grofs are at the center of the current psycho-spiritual revolution in the West, and this book is a testament to their role in our collective healing."

— Wes Nisker, author of *The Essential Crazy Wisdom* and *Buddha's Nature: A Practical Guide to Discovering Your Place in the Cosmos*

"The Grofs offer the first comprehensive text of the theory and practice of their pioneering and integrative model of experiential psychotherapy and self-exploration. This 'psychology of the future,' with its extended cartography of the psyche, provides irrefutable evidence that spontaneous episodes of nonordinary states of consciousness have great healing, transformative, and even evolutionary potential for humankind. History will record that *Holotropic Breathwork* and the certification training and program designed by the Grofs advanced the field of psychotherapy far beyond the contributions of Freud and Jung."

— Angeles Arrien, author of *The Four-Fold Way: Walking the Paths of the Warrior, Teacher, Healer, and Visionary*

"In this remarkable book Stanislav and Christina Grof summarize their pathbreaking discoveries of the past thirty years. They make two significant contributions, one to science, the other to our shared future. The first, by showing that altered states of consciousness have a dimension that is veridical—'imaginal' rather than 'imaginary'—and thereby transcend the outdated but still persistent belief that our experience of the world is limited to information conveyed by our senses. The second, by demonstrating that the altered states achieved inter alia through their holotropic breathwork method reduce aggression and enhance tolerance, compassion, ecological sensitivity, and a sense of planetary citizenship. Since these are the very qualities we urgently need to cope with the global emergency in which we presently find ourselves, their contribution to the future of humankind matches their contribution to the future of psychology."

— Ervin Laszlo, author of *The Connectivity Hypothesis: Foundations of an Integral Science of Quantum, Cosmos, Life, and Consciousness*

"Holotropic Breathwork appears to have the potential for facilitating psychological insights and transformations that can be remarkably rapid and deep."

— Roger Walsh, coeditor of *Higher Wisdom: Eminent Elders Explore the Continuing Impact of Psychedelics*

"You hold in your hands a visionary book, one that offers a new understanding of healing, mental health, and human potential, along with powerful techniques to bring about these transformations. Developing such an integrated understanding, which combines science, experience, and spirit is critical for the twenty-first century."

— from the Foreword by Jack Kornfield

"The long-awaited volume by Stanislav and Christina Grof is the first comprehensive text on the theory and practice of their new strategy of psychotherapy and self-exploration ... this is sure to be a cherished addition to the libraries of intelligent seekers around the world and one of the most influential books of the decade."

— Renn Butler, member of the Holotropic Breathwork Community

HOLOTROPIC BREATHWORK

SUNY series in Transpersonal and Humanistic Psychology

Richard D. Mann, editor

HOLOTROPIC BREATHWORK

A New Approach to Self-Exploration and Therapy

STANISLAV GROF &
CHRISTINA GROF

Foreword by Jack Kornfield

excelsior editions

State University of New York Press
Albany, New York

Published by
STATE UNIVERSITY OF NEW YORK PRESS
ALBANY

Excelsior Editions is an imprint of State University of New York Press

For information, contact
State University of New York Press, Albany, NY
www.sunypress.edu

Production, Ryan Morris
Marketing, Fran Keneston

Library of Congress Cataloging-in-Publication Data

Grof, Stanislav, 1931–
    Holotropic breathwork : a new approach to self-exploration and therapy / Stanislav Grof and Christina Grof.
        p. ; cm. — (SUNY series in transpersonal and humanistic psychology)
    Includes bibliographical references and index.
    ISBN 978-1-4384-3393-6 (hardcover : alk. paper)
    ISBN 978-1-4384-3394-3 (pbk. : alk. paper)
    1. Holotropic Breathwork (Trademark)   I. Grof, Christina.
II. Title. III. Series: SUNY series in transpersonal and humanistic psychology.
    [DNLM: 1. Breathing Exercises.   2. Holistic Health.
3. Psychoanalytic Theory.   4. Psychotherapy—methods.
WB 543 G874h 2010]

    RZ403.H65G76 2010
    615.8'36—dc22   2010002382

10 9 8 7 6 5 4

CONTENTS

FOREWORD

You hold in your hands a visionary book, one that offers a new understanding of healing, mental health, and human potential, along with powerful techniques to bring about these transformations. Developing such an integrated understanding, which combines science, experience, and spirit is critical for the twenty-first century.

The prevailing materialistic culture has created a divided world where the sacred is relegated to churches and temples, the body to the gym, mental health to pills from the pharmacy. Economic growth is pursued as if it had nothing to do with the environment and ignorance, racism, and warfare continue to separate people and nations. These divisions and the great suffering they produce result from a restricted and limited human consciousness.

Through decades of their work, Christina and Stan have developed a psychology that reintegrates the fractured consciousness of the world. They offer a psychology of the future, one that expands our human possibility and reconnects us with one another and the cosmos. In forging this new paradigm, they exemplify the courageous and prophetic spirit of pioneers and join a handful of remarkable figures who have helped the field of psychology grow in revolutionary new ways.

This book is foremost a detailed guide to the experience and practice of Holotropic Breathwork, but it is more than that. It outlines the radical vision of this new psychology. To begin with, it includes one of the widest possible maps of the human psyche I have ever encountered. Within it the full breadth of human experience is valued and integrated. Just the knowledge of this map, presented in the beginning of their workshops by Stan and Christina, has a beneficial effect on those present. It includes, validates, and integrates such a wide range of experience that healing takes place in the hearts of some who simply hear this map.

The holotropic map of human experience is not just theoretical, it is born out of extensive clinical and experimental experience. To witness a

large group practicing Holotropic Breathwork is to see a remarkable range
of experiences, with practitioners reliving any stage of their own history
or entering the realms of archetypes, of animals, of birth and death. Being
present at a group breathwork session is like entering into Dante's *Divine
Comedy*, with the realms of Paradiso, Purgatorio, and Inferno all on display
as breathers go through the profound process of breathing, healing, and
awakening.

In Holotropic Breathwork the field of mental health and therapy is
expanded. Most of the medical modes of Western psychology have been
limited to the study of pathology. While new understandings of psychopathology are discovered in this work, the Grofs offer a comprehensive vision
of mental health and of human growth potential that extends the range of
psychology to dimensions of the perinatal, the transpersonal, the transcultural,
and mystical. Their work organically incorporates the indigenous wisdom
of shamanism and the natural world, the cultural and historical basis of
consciousness, and the far-reaching breadth of modern physics and systems
theory. In it, the personal and the universal are equally valued, the physical
and the biographical, the cultural, evolutionary, and spiritual dimensions of
our humanity are included.

The vision behind Holotropic Breathwork also radically redefines the
role of healer, shifting from "the healer as expert," the doctor who knows
best treating the ignorant patient, to the "healer as midwife." In this role,
the healer safeguards, facilitates, and supports the patient's own profound
natural healing process. In this revision it is not the therapist or psychiatrist
or healer who is wise, but the psyche of the individual whose wisdom is
tended and brought to flower.

The therapeutic benefits of Holotropic Breathwork are remarkable, as
the cases written here attest. The healing of illness, anxiety, depression and
conflict, the release and healing of trauma and abuse, the reintegration with
family and community, the opening of compassion, forgiveness, courage and
love, the reclaiming of purpose, the finding of our lost soul and the highest
insights of spiritual understanding all come spontaneously from the unfolding
of this powerful process.

While visionary, this is also a guide for people experiencing and practicing Holotropic Breathwork. In a hands-on way, Stan and Christina offer the
simple directions for Holotropic Breathwork, how to introduce the practice,
how to nurture and safeguard the participants, how to deal with unexpected
difficulties, and how to integrate these experiences into everyday life. They
articulate the importance of release and healing through the complementary practice of bodywork, and detail the roles of music, creative art, and
storytelling that are essential to the breathwork.

For thirty-five years I have had the privilege of learning from and col-
laborating with Stan and Christina. My own training as a Buddhist monk in

Burma, Thailand, and India first introduced me to powerful breath practices and visionary realms of consciousness. I have felt blessed to find in their work a powerful match for these practices in the Western world. I have valued being part of the growth of Holotropic Breathwork, from its inception to its current form, and come to deeply respect the international community of practitioners that has grown with it.

In Holotropic Breathwork, Stan and Christina have blended scientific and intellectual understanding, masculine and feminine, and ancient and postmodern wisdom, and made their work and training available on every continent. In time, I believe their contributions will be seen as a major gift to the field of psychology and to the healing of the world.

—Jack Kornfield
Spirit Rock Meditation Center
Woodacre, California
2010

PREFACE

This book describes the theory and practice of Holotropic Breathwork, a new approach to self-exploration and psychotherapy developed by the two of us in the mid- to late 1970s. Holotropic Breathwork brings together and integrates elements from various avenues of depth psychology—the theory and practice of the Freudian, Reichian, Rankian, and Jungian schools—adding insights from modern consciousness research, anthropology, Eastern spiritual practices, and mystical traditions of the world (for explanation of the word *holotropic*, see pages pp. 9ff.). While we have been practicing Holotropic Breathwork for more than thirty-five years within the context of our work-shops, international conferences, and training of facilitators all around the world, this volume is our first comprehensive text on the theory and practice of this new strategy of psychotherapy and self-exploration.

The book opens with a brief review of the historical roots of Holotropic Breathwork. In chapter 1, we acknowledge the influence of the groundbreaking work of Sigmund Freud, the founder of depth psychology, and of his followers who further advanced the understanding of the human psyche. Holotropic Breathwork also shares certain elements with the experiential therapies that appeared on the scene in the 1960s in the context of humanistic psychology. The discovery of the powerful psychoactive effects of LSD-25 and our experience with psychedelic therapy made it possible for us to chart the deep recesses of the psyche and appreciate the remarkable therapeutic potential of non-ordinary states of consciousness. The chapter closes with the description of the origins of transpersonal psychology, the discipline that provides the theoretical basis for Holotropic Breathwork.

Chapter 2 discusses the changes that the work with non-ordinary states of consciousness introduces to our understanding of the nature of consciousness and of the human psyche in health and disease. This "psychology of the future" (Grof 2000), necessary for the practice of Holotropic Breathwork, features a vastly extended map of the psyche, which is not limited to post-natal biography and the Freudian individual unconscious as is the model of academic psychology. It includes two important additional domains—*perinatal* (related to the memory of biological birth) and *transpersonal* (the historical and archetypal collective unconscious). According to the new understanding of the "architecture of psychopathology," the roots of emotional and psychosomatic disorders are not only in infancy and childhood, but reach deep into these two previously unrecognized domains of the unconscious. This seemingly discouraging finding is outweighed by the discovery of new, powerful therapeutic mechanisms that become available on the perinatal and transpersonal levels of the psyche in non-ordinary states of consciousness.

The new insights concerning the strategy of self-exploration and therapy represent probably the most radical innovation of the new psychology. The rich spectrum of psychotherapeutic schools and the astonishing lack of agreement among them, concerning the most fundamental aspects of theory and practice, reflect the erroneous strategy that they all share (with the exception of Jungian analysis). They attempt to obtain an intellectual understanding of how the psyche operates and to develop from it a technique that makes it possible to correct its functioning. The work with non-ordinary states of consciousness offers a radical alternative that greatly simplifies the therapeutic process. These states mobilize an "inner radar" that automatically finds the material with strong emotional charge and brings it into consciousness for processing. The therapist is not an active agent in this process, but a "co-adventurer" who intelligently supports what is happening.

An important part of chapter 2 addresses the problem of spirituality and religion. While traditional psychiatrists and psychologists subscribe to a monistic materialistic worldview and have no place for spirituality or religion of any kind, Holotropic Breathwork facilitators use in their work transpersonal psychology, a discipline that sees spirituality based on direct personal experience as a legitimate and important dimension of the human psyche and of human life. Many observations from Holotropic Breathwork and other approaches using non-ordinary states of consciousness are so radical that they undermine not only the conceptual framework of mainstream psychology and psychiatry, but also the basic metaphysical assumptions of Western science concerning the nature of the universe and the relation between consciousness and matter.

Chapter 3 discusses the basic components of Holotropic Breathwork and traces them to their roots in the ritual life of native cultures and to the spiritual practices of the great religions of the world and of various mystical traditions. We explore here the essential role that breathing and music have played throughout human history as important elements in various "technologies of the sacred" and healing ceremonies. Similarly, the body-work and nourishing physical contact employed in Holotropic Breathwork have antecedents in various native rituals. Painting mandalas to assist the process of integration of holotropic experiences also has a long history in the ritual life of native cultures, the spiritual life of ancient civilizations, and the religious traditions of the East.

Chapter 4 gives a detailed account of the practice of Holotropic Breathwork—how to create a safe physical setting and interpersonal support system for participants, how to prepare them theoretically and practically for the session, and how to screen them for emotional and physical contraindications. It discusses the basic principles of conducting the breathwork sessions, the role of sitters and facilitators, and the nature of Holotropic Breathwork experiences. Another important topic of this section is the work with mandala drawing and the strategy of conducting the processing groups.

The outcome of the Holotropic Breathwork sessions depends critically on good integration of the experience. Chapter 5 describes important aspects of this process—how to create the best possible conditions for successful integration, what to do to ease the transition to everyday life, how to successfully handle the interface with the culture at large, and how to conduct follow-up interviews. We give special attention to various therapeutic approaches that represent a good complement to the breathwork and can facilitate integration of the holotropic experience, such as Gestalt practice, good bodywork, expressive painting and dancing, Jacob Moreno's psychodrama, Dora Kalff's sandplay, Francine Shapiro's EMDR (eye movement desensitization and reprocessing), Bert Hellinger's family constellation, among others.

Holotropic Breathwork is a radical innovation of psychotherapy that in many ways differs from conventional approaches. It has certain features—induction of non-ordinary states of consciousness, use of uncommon music played at a high volume, expression of strong emotions, intense physical manifestations, and close physical contact—that tend to elicit strong reaction in people who are not familiar with it. Chapter 6, entitled "Trials and Tribulations of Holotropic Breathwork Facilitators," is a collection of stories describing various adventures we have experienced and challenges we have encountered as we were conducting Holotropic Breathwork workshops in different parts of the world and in various cultural milieus.

Chapter 7 is dedicated to the therapeutic potential of Holotropic Breathwork and to the mechanisms of healing and transformation that become available in non-ordinary states of consciousness. We discuss the positive effects that this approach can have on a variety of emotional and psychosomatic disorders and even some diseases that current medical theory considers to be organic. Another important aspect of the action of Holotropic Breathwork is its effect on personality, life strategy, and hierarchy of values. Using as examples the experiences of individuals with Native American and Australian Aboriginal heritage, we show the potential that Holotropic Breathwork can have for the healing of cultural wounds and resolution of historical conflict.

Chapter 8 explores the therapeutic mechanisms operating in Holotropic Breathwork. This approach greatly intensifies all the mechanisms known from traditional verbal therapies—softening of psychological defense mechanisms, remembering of forgotten or repressed traumatic events, reconstructing the past from dreams or neurotic symptoms, attaining intellectual and emotional insights, and analysis of transference. In addition, it makes available a large number of processes of extraordinary healing and transformative power as yet unrecognized by academic circles—actual reliving of traumatic memories in full age regression, reliving of biological birth and prenatal traumas, the experience of psychospiritual death and rebirth, past life memories, encounter with archetypal figures, feelings of cosmic unity, among others.

According to medical handbooks of respiratory physiology, faster breathing tends to result in the "hyperventilation syndrome" character-ized by tetany of hands and feet (carpopedal spasms), anxiety, and various forms of physical discomfort. These symptoms are generally considered to be mandatory physiological reactions to the chemical changes induced by hyperventilation. In chapter 9, which describes the physiological changes during Holotropic Breathwork, we show that this is a myth that has been dispelled by observations from breathwork sessions. These observations show that the reaction to faster breathing reflects the psychosomatic history of the breather and covers a very wide spectrum of manifestations—including occasional complete absence of physical symptoms—rather than being a rigid stereotype. In addition, the symptoms induced by faster breathing rhythm represent a therapeutic opportunity rather than pathology. Of special interest are also the new insights that the work with holotropic states brings into the understanding of psychosomatic disorders, currently plagued by disagree-ments between conflicting theories.

The concluding section of the book (chapter 10) focuses on the past, present, and future of Holotropic Breathwork. It traces its history back to its origins at the Esalen Institute in Big Sur, California, and to the early years when the two of us offered it in workshops in different parts of the world. We then describe the development of the training for Holotropic Breathwork facilitators from its early form to the present, in which the number of trained practitioners worldwide amounts to more than a thousand, with additional hundreds currently in training. Since the growing interest in Holotropic Breathwork in paraprofessional circles and the general public has not so far been matched by an equally warm reception by academic institutions and practicing clinicians, we discuss at some length the reasons for this resistance.

We then outline the advantages and benefits that await those practi-tioners who are capable of accepting the radical changes in thinking and in therapeutic practice brought about by the holotropic perspective. Among them are deeper understanding of emotional and psychosomatic disorders, better and faster therapeutic results, ability to reach many clients who do not respond to traditional forms of therapy, and illuminating insights into religion, politics, and art. The beneficial effect of Holotropic Breathwork and of responsible work with holotropic states of consciousness, in general, brings more than alleviation or resolution of symptoms. It is accompanied by spiritual opening; development of compassion, tolerance, and ecological sensitivity; and radical changes in the hierarchy of values. These changes are beneficial not only for the individuals involved, but also for human society at large. If they could occur on a large enough scale, they could increase the chances of humanity to survive the rapidly escalating global crisis.

The book has two appendixes. The first, "Special Situations and Interventions in Breathwork Sessions," describes in some detail the challenges that facilitators can encounter in assisting the breathers and the most effective ways of dealing with them. The second appendix focuses on the similarities and differences between Holotropic Breathwork and other forms of experiential therapy using breathing techniques, such as various neo-Reichian approaches, Leonard Orr's Rebirthing, and Gay and Kathleen Hendricks' Radiance Breathwork.

As we have seen so far, this book offers a comprehensive and detailed description of the theory and practice of Holotropic Breathwork. This brings with it *a great potential danger*: it can easily be mistaken for an instruction manual that provides, in and of itself, adequate information for readers to embark on their own self-exploration or—even worse—to begin conducting breathwork sessions with others. It is very easy to induce a non-ordinary state of consciousness, however, dealing with all the situations that might emerge and bringing the session to a good closure requires extensive experience with non-ordinary states of consciousness, both one's own and those of others.

We therefore urge those who wish to experience Holotropic Breathwork to do it in the context of workshops offered by trained facilitators. Those who plan to conduct sessions with others should first undergo adequate training, which will give them ample opportunity to alternate in the roles of breathers, "sitters" (personal assistants to breathers), and "floaters" (facilitators available for the entire group) under expert supervision. People who are in Holotropic Breathwork training or have already completed it can gain additional hands-on practice by assisting (apprenticing) in the workshops of experienced senior facilitators. The necessary information can be found on our websites holotropic.com or stanislavgrof.com.

ACKNOWLEDGMENTS

Where to start? Over many years, as we developed, practiced, and taught Holotropic Breathwork and took our work to various countries of the world, we have received inestimable emotional, physical, and financial support from many friends, colleagues, and participants in our programs. We would need another volume in which to mention them all by name; here, we offer heartfelt and humbling gratitude to each of these individuals.

However, there are a few persons whose contributions to our work have been so essential and vital that they deserve special notice. Kathy Altman and Lori Saltzman provided much-needed organizational direction and gentle guidance as we formed and began our training program. They offered encouragement and practical structure as we stepped into new territories, and for that, we are forever thankful.

We are profoundly grateful to Tav Sparks and Cary Sparks, our close friends and coworkers, who have, over the years, played crucial roles in helping to organize and run many of our conferences, workshops, and trainings. Both Cary and Tav became certified breathwork facilitators in 1988 in our very first training program. In the following years, they became very active in Grof Holotropic Training (GTT), Tav as coleader in many of the workshops and training modules worldwide, Cary as the director and administrator of most of these events.

In 1998, we passed GTT into the Sparks' capable hands, and they have been owners and directors of this organization ever since, with Tav as principal teacher. We also transferred to them the trademark that, since 1990, limits the practice of Holotropic Breathwork to those practitioners who have successfully completed the GTT training and have become certified. The purpose of this trademark is to provide legal protection for Holotropic Breathwork in cases of unauthorized use of the name and practice by untrained, noncertified individuals.

Diane Haug and Diana Medina, senior members of the GTT staff, have played crucial roles in numerous training modules; for years, they have been leading some modules on their own. Diane Haug especially deserves thanks for the amount of time and energy she selflessly gave to the breathwork training in South America, during a period when the economic crisis in that part of the world would not have otherwise allowed the training to continue there. We would like to express our deep gratitude and thanks to Tav, Cary, Diane, and Diana for the dedication and integrity with which they preserve the original spirit of our work.

Over the years, GTT has received much support from Glenn Wilson, who helped to organize many GTT events and has run its bookstore, and, more recently, from Cary's administrative assistant, Stacia Butterfield. The trainings and other GTT events in various countries of the world would not have been possible without many certified breathwork practitioners who have helped to arrange and manage them, or assisted in them as facilitators. Some have been able to develop trainings in their own countries and teach the majority of the modules. Vladimir Maykov, president of the Russian Transpersonal Association, has created an offshoot GTT program for Russia (also open to participants from other Eastern European countries), and Alvaro Jardim initiated and heads a filial training program in Brazil. For several years, Ingo Jahrsetz and Brigitte Ashauer offered a similar curriculum in Germany. We appreciate very much the important contributions of all of these former students.

Kylea Taylor deserves particular thanks for her role in training and for publishing activity that has helped to disseminate information about Holotropic Breathwork. For many years, she was editor of *The Inner Door*, the breathwork newsletter started in 1988 by Cary Sparks. With her partner Jim Schofield, Kylea created Hanford Mead Publishers, Inc., that, among others, has been publishing books related to Holotropic Breathwork; Kylea has also written several books on this subject. We are also very grateful to the founders of the Association for Holotropic Breathwork International (AHBI)—Cary Sparks, Kylea Taylor, and Laurie Weaver—and its past presidents, board members, and current president Ken Sloan for everything they have done to support and expand the global Holotropic Breathwork network.

We extend our gratitude to pioneers in the areas of transpersonal psychology, consciousness research, and various fields of new paradigm science, many of whom are our friends and colleagues. They have provided inestimable support for our work by laying the foundations for a new worldview within which the theory and practice of Holotropic Breathwork loses its otherwise controversial nature and becomes acceptable to open-minded members of the academic community. We greatly value their groundbreaking contributions.

State University of New York Press deserves accolades for the interest of its staff members in publishing, as part of their series in transpersonal and humanistic psychology, many books with themes that lie on the cutting edge of the traditional scientific worldview. We particularly appreciate Jane Bunker, associate director and editor-in-chief at SUNY Press, for her deep knowledge of the transpersonal field, in general, and of our work, in particular. We feel deeply grateful for the support she has granted our work over the years and especially for her keen interest in the present book. We very much appreciate the encouragement and patience she has shown as she guided us through various stages of the publication process. She has played an essential role in the birth of this book in its present form. Elizabeth Gibson deserves special thanks for the many ways in which she contributed to the publication of this book.

Over the years, we have received sorely needed financial support for our various endeavors from friends who have appreciated the potential relevance of the work we have been doing. We are profoundly thankful to John Buchanan, Betsy Gordon, Bokara Legendre, Michael Marcus and Janet Zand, Robert Schwartz, Ken and Petra Sloan, Alexey Kupcov, and Eduard Sagalaev.

Unfortunately, the persons whose contributions to this book are most essential must remain anonymous, with the exception of a few who explicitly agreed to have their names used in the book. We are talking here about many thousands of participants in our workshops and training modules who have explored with admirable courage the ordinarily hidden realms of their psyches and of reality itself. Their verbal reports about what they experienced, and the art with which they illustrated their adventures in the inner world, have been for us essential sources of information. Our indebtedness and gratitude to these individuals of many cultures can hardly be adequately expressed in words. Without them this book could not have been written.

CHAPTER ONE

Historical Roots of Holotropic Breathwork

1. Sigmund Freud and the dawn of depth psychology

Holotropic Breathwork is one of the more recent contributions to depth psychology, a discipline initiated at the beginning of the twentieth century by the Austrian neurologist Sigmund Freud. Since Freud single-handedly laid the foundations of this new field, depth psychology has had a complex and stormy history. Freud's contributions to psychology and psychiatry were truly groundbreaking. He demonstrated the existence of the unconscious and described its dynamics, developed the technique of dream interpretation, identified the psychological mechanisms involved in the genesis of psychoneuroses and psychosomatic disorders, discovered infantile sexuality, recognized the phenomenon of transference, invented the method of free association, and outlined the basic principles of psychotherapy (Freud and Breuer 1936; Freud 1953, 1962).

Although initially Freud's interest was primarily clinical—to explain the etiology of psychoneuroses and to find a way of treating them—in the course of his explorations his horizons expanded enormously. The range of phenomena that he studied included, besides the content of dreams and psychodynamics of neurotic symptoms, such themes as the mechanism of jokes and slips of the tongue and a number of cultural and sociopolitical phenomena—problems of human civilization, history, wars and revolutions, religion, and art (Freud 1955a and b, 1957a and b, 1960a and b, 1964a and b).

Freud surrounded himself with a group of unusually talented and imaginative thinkers (the "Viennese circle"), several of whom had their own unique perspectives and developed renegade schools of psychotherapy.

While Freudian psychoanalysis became an important part of thinking in mainstream psychology and psychiatry, the so-called renegade schools—Adlerian, Rankian, Reichian, and Jungian—have never been accepted by official academic circles. However, as we will see later, in the last several decades some of them have become increasingly popular and influential as alternative approaches to psychotherapy and many ideas of their founders have been integrated into the theory and practice of Holotropic Breathwork.

2. Humanistic psychology and experiential therapies

In the middle of the twentieth century, American psychology was dominated by two major schools—behaviorism and Freudian psychoanalysis. Increasing dissatisfaction with these two orientations as adequate approaches to the understanding of the human psyche led to the development of humanistic psychology. The main spokesman and most articulate representative of this new field was the well-known American psychologist Abraham Maslow. He offered an incisive critique of the limitations of behaviorism and psychoanalysis, or the First and the Second Force in psychology as he called them, and formulated the principles of a new perspective in psychology (Maslow 1962, 1964. and 1969).

Maslow's main objection against behaviorism was that the study of animals, such as rats and pigeons, could only clarify those aspects of human functioning that we share with these animals. It thus has no relevance for the understanding of higher, specifically human qualities that are unique to human life, such as love, self-consciousness, self-determination, personal freedom, morality, art, philosophy, religion, and science. It is also largely useless in regard to some specifically human negative characteristics, such as greed, lust for power, cruelty, and tendency to "malignant aggression." He also criticized the behaviorists' disregard for consciousness and introspection and their exclusive focus on the study of behavior.

By contrast, the primary interest of humanistic psychology, Maslow's Third Force, was in human subjects, and this discipline honored the interest in consciousness and introspection as important complements to the objective approach to research. The behaviorists' exclusive emphasis on determination by the environment, stimulus/response, and reward/punishment was replaced by emphasis on the capacity of human beings to be internally directed and motivated to achieve self-realization and fulfill their human potential.

In his criticism of psychoanalysis, Maslow pointed out that Freud and his followers drew conclusions about the human psyche mainly from the study of psychopathology and he disagreed with their biological reductionism and their tendency to explain all psychological processes in terms of base instincts. By comparison, humanistic psychology focused on healthy populations, or even individuals who show supernormal functioning in various areas (Maslow's "growing tip of the population"), on human growth and potential, and on higher functions of the psyche. It also emphasized that it is important for psychologists to be sensitive to practical human needs and to serve important interests and objectives of human society.

Within a few years after Abraham Maslow and Anthony Sutich launched the Association for Humanistic Psychology (AHP) and its journal, the new movement became very popular among American mental health professionals and even in the general public. The multidimensional perspective of humanistic psychology and its emphasis on the whole person provided a broad umbrella for the development of a rich spectrum of new, effective therapeutic approaches that greatly expanded the range of possibilities when addressing emotional, psychosomatic, interpersonal, and psychosocial problems.

Among the important characteristics of these new approaches was a decisive shift from the exclusively verbal strategies of traditional psychotherapy ("talking therapies") to the direct expression of emotions. The therapeutic strategy also moved from exploration of individual history and of unconscious motivation to the feelings and thought processes of the clients in the here and now. Another important aspect of this therapeutic revolution was the emphasis on the interconnectedness of the psyche and the body and overcoming the taboo against touching that previously dominated the field of psychotherapy. Various forms of work with the body thus formed an integral part of the new treatment strategies; Fritz Perls' Gestalt therapy, Alexander Lowen's bioenergetics and other neo-Reichian approaches, encounter groups, and marathon sessions can be mentioned here as salient examples of humanistic therapies.

3. The advent of psychedelic therapy

A serendipitous discovery of Albert Hofmann, a Swiss chemist conducting research of ergot alkaloids in the Sandoz laboratories in Basel, introduced into the world of psychiatry, psychology, and psychotherapy a radically new element—the heuristic and healing potential of non-ordinary states of consciousness. In April 1943, Hofmann discovered the psychedelic effects of LSD-25, or diethylamide of lysergic acid, when he accidentally intoxicated himself during the synthesis of this substance. After the publication of the first clinical paper on LSD by Zurich psychiatrist Walter A. Stoll in the late 1940s (Stoll 1947), this new semisynthetic ergot alkaloid, active in incredibly minute quantities of micrograms or *gammas* (millionths of a gram), became overnight a sensation in the world of science.

In clinical research and self-experimentation with LSD, many professionals discovered that the current model of the psyche, limited to postnatal biography and the Freudian individual unconscious, was superficial and inadequate. The new map of the psyche that emerged out of this research (Grof 1975) added to the current model of the psyche two large transbiographical domains—the perinatal level, closely related to the memory of biological birth, and the transpersonal level, harboring among others the historical and archetypal domains of the collective unconscious as envisioned by C. G. Jung (Jung 1959a). Early experiments with LSD also showed that the sources of emotional and psychosomatic disorders were not limited to traumatic memories from childhood and infancy, as traditional psychiatrists assumed, but that their roots reached much deeper into the psyche, into the perinatal and transpersonal regions (Grof 2000). This surprising revelation was accompanied by the discovery of new, powerful therapeutic mechanisms operating on these deep levels of the psyche.

Using LSD as a catalyst, it became possible to extend the range of applicability of psychotherapy to categories of patients that previously had been difficult to reach, such as alcoholics and drug addicts, and even positively influence the behavior of sexual deviants and criminal recidivists (Grof 2006c). Particularly valuable and promising were the early efforts to use LSD psychotherapy in the work with terminal cancer patients. Research with this population showed that LSD was able to relieve severe pain, often even in patients who had not responded to medication with narcotics. In a large percentage of these patients, it was also possible to ease or even eliminate difficult emotional and psychosomatic symptoms, such as depression, general tension, and insomnia, alleviate the fear of death, increase the quality of their life during their remaining days, and positively transform the experience of dying (Cohen 1965; Kast and Collins 1966; Grof 2006b).

4. Abraham Maslow, Anthony Sutich, and the birth of transpersonal psychology

In the 1960s, the observations from the research of non-ordinary states of consciousness—analysis of experiences from psychedelic sessions and Maslow's study of spontaneous mystical experiences ("peak experiences")—revolutionized the image of the human psyche and inspired a radically new orientation in psychology. In spite of the popularity of humanistic psychology, its founders Abraham Maslow and Anthony Sutich grew dissatisfied with the discipline that they had themselves fathered. They became increasingly aware that they had left out an extremely important element—the spiritual dimension of the human psyche (Sutich 1976).

Maslow's own research of "peak experiences," the therapeutic use of psychedelics, widespread psychedelic experimentation of the young generation during the stormy 1960s, and the renaissance of interest in Eastern spiritual philosophies, various mystical traditions, meditation, and ancient and aboriginal wisdom, made the current conceptual framework in psychology untenable. It became clear that a comprehensive and cross-culturally valid psychology needed to include observations from such areas as mystical states; cosmic consciousness; psychedelic experiences; trance phenomena; creativity; and religious, artistic, and scientific inspiration.

In 1967, a small working group, including Abraham Maslow, Anthony Sutich, Stanislav Grof, James Fadiman, Miles Vich, and Sonya Margulies, met repeatedly in Menlo Park, California, with the purpose of creating a new psychology that would honor the entire spectrum of human experience, including various non-ordinary states of consciousness. During these discussions, Maslow and Sutich accepted Grof's suggestion and named the new discipline "transpersonal psychology." This term replaced their own original name, "transhumanistic" or "reaching beyond humanistic concerns." Soon afterward, they launched the Association of Transpersonal Psychology (ATP) and started the *Journal of Transpersonal Psychology*. Several years later, in 1975, Robert Frager founded the (California) Institute of Transpersonal Psychology in Palo Alto, which has remained at the cutting edge of transpersonal education, research, and therapy for more than three decades.

CHAPTER TWO

Theoretical Foundations of Holotropic Breathwork

Holotropic Breathwork is a powerful method of self-exploration and therapy that uses a combination of seemingly simple means—accelerated breathing, evocative music, and a type of bodywork that helps to release residual bioenergetic and emotional blocks. The sessions are usually conducted in groups; participants work in pairs and alternate in the roles of breathers and "sitters." The process is supervised by trained facilitators, who assist participants whenever special intervention is necessary. Following the breathing sessions, participants express their experiences by painting mandalas and share accounts of their inner journeys in small groups. Follow-up interviews and various complementary methods are used, if necessary, to facilitate the completion and integration of the breathwork experience.

In its theory and practice, Holotropic Breathwork combines and integrates various elements from depth psychology, modern consciousness research, transpersonal psychology, Eastern spiritual philosophies, and native healing practices. It differs significantly from traditional forms of psychotherapy, which use primarily verbal means, such as psychoanalysis and various other schools of depth psychology derived from it. It shares certain common characteristics with the experiential therapies of humanistic psychology, such as Gestalt practice and the neo-Reichian approaches, emphasizing direct emotional expression and work with the body. However, the unique feature of Holotropic Breathwork is that it utilizes the intrinsic healing potential of non-ordinary states of consciousness.

1. Holotropic states of consciousness

The remarkable healing power of non-ordinary states of consciousness, which was known and used in ancient civilizations and native cultures since

7

time immemorial, was confirmed by modern consciousness research and therapeutic experimentation conducted in the second half of the twentieth century. This research has also shown that the phenomena occurring during non-ordinary states and associated with them cannot be accounted for by the conceptual frameworks currently used by academic psychiatry and psychology. Because this issue is essential for understanding the Holotropic Breathwork, we will precede our discussion of this method with a survey of the theoretical challenges that non-ordinary states of consciousness pose not only for psychiatry, psychology, and psychotherapy, but also for the basic metaphysical assumptions of Western science.

Let us start with a few semantic comments. Our primary interest in this book is to explore the healing, transformative, and evolutionary potential of non-ordinary states of consciousness and their great value as a source of new revolutionary data about consciousness, the human psyche, and the nature of reality. From this perspective, the term *altered states of consciousness* commonly used by mainstream clinicians and theoreticians is not appropriate, because of its one-sided emphasis on the distortion or impairment of the "correct way" of experiencing oneself and the world. (In colloquial English and in veterinary jargon, the term *alter* is used to signify castration of domestic dogs and cats.) Even the somewhat better term *non-ordinary states of consciousness* is too general, since it includes a wide range of conditions that are not relevant from the point of view of our discussion.

Consciousness can be profoundly changed by a variety of pathological processes—by cerebral traumas, by intoxication with noxious chemicals, by infections, or by degenerative and circulatory processes in the brain. Such conditions can certainly result in profound psychological changes that would be included in the category of *non-ordinary states of consciousness*. However, they cause what can be called "trivial deliria" or "organic psychoses." People suffering from delirious states are typically disoriented; they do not know who and where they are and what the date is. In addition, their mental functioning is significantly impaired. They typically show a disturbance of intellectual functions and have subsequent amnesia for these experiences. For these conditions, the term *altered states of consciousness* is certainly fitting. These states are very important clinically, but are not interesting from the therapeutic and heuristic point of view.

In this book, we will focus on a large and important subgroup of non-ordinary states of consciousness that are radically different from those just described. These are the states that novice shamans experience during their initiatory crises and later induce in their clients. Ancient and native cultures have used these states in rites of passage and in their healing ceremonies. They were described by mystics of all ages and initiates in the ancient mysteries of death and rebirth. Procedures inducing these states were also developed and used in the context of the great religions of the world—Hinduism, Buddhism, Taoism, Islam, Judaism, and Christianity.

The importance of non-ordinary states of consciousness for ancient and aboriginal cultures is reflected in the amount of time and energy that the members of these human groups dedicated to the development of *technologies of the sacred*, various procedures capable of inducing them for ritual and spiritual purposes. These methods combine in various ways drumming and other forms of percussion, music, chanting, rhythmic dancing, changes of breathing, and cultivation of special forms of awareness. Extended social and sensory isolation, such as a stay in a cave, desert, arctic ice, or in high mountains, also play an important role as means of inducing this category of non-ordinary states. Extreme physiological interventions used for this purpose include fasting, sleep deprivation, dehydration, use of powerful laxatives and purgatives, and even infliction of severe pain, body mutilation, and massive bloodletting. By far the most effective tool for inducing healing and transformative non-ordinary states has been ritual use of psychedelic plants.

Mainstream psychiatrists initially dismissed and even ridiculed native ritual events as products of primitive superstition based on ignorance and magical thinking. They relegated non-ordinary states of consciousness of any kind into the domain of psychopathology. This situation gradually changed in the course of the twentieth century, particularly in its second half, when Western scientists actually made some major contributions to the armamentarium of the technologies of the sacred. Clinical and experimental psychiatrists and psychologists had the opportunity to acquire firsthand experience with chemically pure psychedelic substances and with a variety of laboratory mind-altering procedures from sensory deprivation to biofeedback. They also witnessed the effect of non-ordinary states of consciousness in various forms of experiential therapeutic techniques using breathwork and bodywork, such as neo-Reichian approaches, Rebirthing, and Holotropic Breathwork. Those open-minded enough to take on the challenge of these revolutionary tools thus had a chance to discover their power and their great therapeutic potential.

When we recognized the unique nature of this category of non-ordinary states of consciousness, we found it difficult to believe that contemporary psychiatry does not have a specific category and term for these theoretically and practically important experiences. Because we felt strongly that they deserve to be distinguished from altered states of consciousness and not be seen as manifestations of serious mental diseases, we started referring to them as *holotropic* (Grof 1992). This composite word means literally "oriented toward wholeness" or "moving toward wholeness" (from the Greek *holos* = whole and *trepein* = moving toward or in the direction of something). The word *holotropic* is a neologism, but it is related to a commonly used term *heliotropic*—the property of plants to always turn in the direction of the sun.

The name *holotropic* suggests something that might come as a surprise to an average Westerner—that in our everyday state of consciousness we identify with only a small fraction of who we really are and do not experience the full extent of our being. Holotropic states of consciousness have the potential to help us recognize that we are not "skin-encapsulated egos"—as British philosopher and writer Alan Watts called it—and that, in the last analysis, we are commensurate with the cosmic creative principle itself. Or that—using the statement by Pierre Teilhard de Chardin, French paleontologist and philosopher—"we are not human beings having spiritual experiences, we are spiritual beings having human experiences" (Teilhard de Chardin 1975).

This astonishing idea is not new. In the ancient Indian Upanishads, the answer to the question "Who am I?" is "Tat tvam asi." This succinct Sanskrit sentence means literally: "Thou art That," or "You are Godhead." It suggests that we are not *namarupa*—name and form (body/ego), but that our deepest identity is with a divine spark in our innermost being (*Atman*) that is ultimately identical with the supreme universal principle (*Brahman*). And Hinduism is not the only religion that has made this discovery. The revelation concerning the identity of the individual with the divine is the ultimate secret that lies at the mystical core of all great spiritual traditions. The name for this principle could thus be the Tao, Buddha, Cosmic Christ, Allah, Great Spirit, Sila, and many others. Holotropic experiences have the potential to help us discover our true identity and our cosmic status (Grof 1998).

Psychedelic research and the development of intensive experiential techniques of psychotherapy moved holotropic states from the world of healers of preliterate cultures into modern psychiatry and psychotherapy. Therapists who were open to these approaches and used them in their practice were able to confirm the extraordinary healing potential of holotropic states and discovered their value as goldmines of revolutionary new information about consciousness, the human psyche, and the nature of reality. However, since the very beginning, the mainstream academic community has shown a strong resistance to these radical innovations and has not accepted them either as treatment modalities or as a source of critical conceptual challenges.

In a sense, this resistance is understandable, considering the scope and radical nature of the conceptual revisions that would be necessary to account for the rich array of "anomalous phenomena" encountered in the study of holotropic states. These extraordinary observations could not be handled by minor adjustments of the existing theories (technically called "ad hoc hypotheses"), but would require radical revision of the most fundamental concepts and basic metaphysical assumptions. The resulting conceptual cataclysm would be comparable to the revolution that physicists had to face in the first three decades of the twentieth century when they had to move from Newtonian to quantum-relativistic physics. In a sense, it would represent a logical completion of the radical change in understanding reality that has already happened in physics.

We will briefly describe the conceptual challenges posed by the experiences and observations in holotropic states and outline the revisions in thinking about consciousness and the human psyche that they urge us to make. Michael Harner, an anthropologist of good academic standing, who also underwent a shamanic initiation during his fieldwork in the Amazonian jungle and practices shamanism, suggested that Western psychiatry and psychology are seriously biased in at least two significant ways—they manifest what he called the *ethnocentric and cognicentric bias* (Harner 1980).

Mainstream academicians and clinicians consider the understanding of the human psyche and of reality developed by Western materialistic science to be the only correct one and superior to all others. They attribute the ritual and spiritual life of pre-industrial cultures to primitive superstition, magical thinking, or outright psychopathology (ethnocentric bias). In their theoretical speculations, they also take into consideration only experiences and observations made in the ordinary state of consciousness and ignore or misinterpret data from the research of holotropic states (cognicentric or pragmacentric bias).

Michael Harner's criticism raises some interesting questions: What would psychiatry and psychology look like if it could overcome its ethnocentric bias—stop pathologizing all experiences and behaviors that cannot be understood in the narrow context of the monistic-materialistic paradigm—and treat with respect ritual and spiritual life of other cultures? What changes would have to be introduced into psychiatric theory and practice if the findings from the research of holotropic states were subjected to serious scientific scrutiny and recognized for what they are—a rich array of "anomalous phenomena" that present theories can not explain and that represent formidable conceptual challenges?

When we practice Holotropic Breathwork, conduct psychedelic therapy, or support individuals undergoing spiritual emergencies, using a conceptual framework of traditional psychiatry and psychology would be inappropriate, ineffective, and counterproductive. We have to use the understanding of consciousness, of the human psyche, and of the nature and function of emotional and psychosomatic disorders that has emerged from modern consciousness research or, more specifically, from the study of holotropic states of consciousness.

The changes introduced into our thinking by research of holotropic states are radical and fall into several large categories. To account for the observations from modern consciousness research, the model of the psyche currently used by psychiatrists and psychologists needs to be vastly expanded and include new areas previously unrecognized or misinterpreted by academic circles. This is associated with a new understanding of the nature of emotional and psychosomatic disorders and with the recognition of the depth of their roots. This sobering finding is balanced by the discovery of new mechanisms of healing and positive personality transformation operating on deep levels of the unconscious.

Probably the most exciting innovation that has emerged from the study of holotropic states is the shift from verbal to experiential approaches to self-exploration and psychotherapy and from the guiding role of the therapist or facilitator to the utilization of innate healing intelligence of the client's own psyche. The recognition of the critical role of cosmic consciousness (C. G. Jung's *anima mundi*) in the universal scheme of things and acceptance of the existence of the collective unconscious logically lead to the conclusion that the spiritual quest based on direct experience is a legitimate and vitally important aspect of human life.

2. Dimensions of the human psyche

Traditional academic psychiatry and psychology use a model of the human psyche that is limited to postnatal biography and to the individual unconscious as described by Sigmund Freud. According to Freud, our psychological history begins after we are born; the newborn is a *tabula rasa*, a clean slate. Our psychological functioning is determined by an interplay between biological instincts and influences that have shaped our life since we came into this world—the quality of nursing, the nature of toilet training, various psychosexual traumas, development of the superego, our reaction to the Oedipal triangle, and conflicts and traumatic events in later life. Who we become and how we psychologically function is determined by our postnatal personal and interpersonal history.

The Freudian individual unconscious is also essentially a derivative of our postnatal history; it is a repository of what we have forgotten, rejected as unacceptable, and repressed. This underworld of the psyche, or the *id* as Freud called it, is a realm dominated by primitive instinctual forces. Freud described the relationship between the conscious psyche and the unconscious using his famous image of the submerged iceberg. What we thought to be the totality of the psyche is just a small part of it, like the section of the iceberg showing above the surface. Psychoanalysis discovered that a much larger part of the psyche, comparable to the submerged part of the iceberg, is unconscious and, unbeknown to us, governs our thought processes and behavior. This model, modified and refined, has been adopted by mainstream psychology and psychiatry.

In the work with holotropic states of consciousness induced by psychedelics and various non-drug means, as well as those occurring spontaneously, this model proves to be painfully inadequate. To account for all the phenomena occurring in these states, we must drastically revise our understanding of the dimensions of the human psyche. Besides the *postnatal biographical level* that it shares with the traditional model, the new expanded cartography includes two additional large domains.

The first of these domains can be referred to as *perinatal*, because of its close connection with the trauma of biological birth. This region of the unconscious contains the memories of what the fetus experienced in the consecutive stages of the birth process, including all the emotions and physical sensations involved. These memories form four distinct experiential clusters, each of which is related to one of the stages of the birth process. We can refer to them as *Basic Perinatal Matrices* (BPM I–IV).

BPM I consists of memories of the advanced prenatal state just before the onset of the delivery. BPM II is related to the first stage of the delivery when the uterus contracts, but the cervix is not yet open. BPM III reflects the struggle to be born after the uterine cervix dilates. And finally, BPM IV holds the memory of emerging into the world, the birth itself. The content of these matrices is not limited to fetal memories; each of them also represents a selective opening into the areas of the historical and archetypal collective unconscious, which contain motifs of similar experiential quality. We will return to the concept of BPMs later in this book; interested readers can find detailed discussion of perinatal matrices in several earlier publications (Grof 1975, 1987, and 2000).

The second transbiographical domain of the new cartography can best be called *transpersonal*, because it contains matrices for a rich array of experiences in which consciousness transcends the boundaries of the body/ego and the usual limitations of linear time and three-dimensional space. This results in experiential identification with other people, groups of people, other life forms, and even elements of the inorganic world. Transcendence of time provides experiential access to ancestral, racial, collective, phylogenetic, and karmic memories.

Yet another category of transpersonal experiences can take us into the realm of the collective unconscious that the Swiss psychiatrist C. G. Jung called *archetypal*. This region harbors mythological figures, themes, and realms of all the cultures and ages, even those of which we have no intellectual knowledge (Jung 1959a). In its farthest reaches, individual consciousness can identify with the Universal Mind or Cosmic Consciousness, the creative principle of the universe. Probably the most profound experience available

in holotropic states is identification with the Supracosmic and Metacosmic
Void (Sanskrit *sunyata*), primordial Emptiness and Nothingness that is conscious of itself. The Void has a paradoxical nature; it is a *vacuum*, because
it is devoid of any concrete forms, but it is also a *plenum*, since it seems to
contain all of creation in a potential form.

In view of this vastly expanded model of the psyche, we could now
paraphrase Freud's simile of the psyche as an iceberg. We could say that
everything Freudian analysis has discovered about the psyche represents
just the top of the iceberg showing above the water. Research of holotropic
states has made it possible to explore the colossal rest of the iceberg hidden
under water, which has escaped the attention of Freud and his followers,
with the exception of the remarkable renegades Otto Rank and C. G. Jung.
Mythologist Joseph Campbell, known for his incisive Irish humor, used a
different metaphor: "Freud was fishing while sitting on a whale." Detailed
discussion of the transpersonal domain, including descriptions and examples
of various types of transpersonal experiences, can be found in other publications (Grof 1975, 1987, and 2000).

3. The nature, function, and architecture of emotional and psychosomatic disorders

To explain various emotional and psychosomatic disorders that do not have
an organic basis ("psychogenic psychopathology"), traditional psychiatrists
use the superficial model of the psyche described earlier. They believe that
these conditions originate in infancy and childhood as a result of various
psychosexual traumas and interpersonal dynamics in the family. There
seems to be general agreement in dynamic psychotherapy that the depth
and seriousness of these disorders depends on the timing of the original
traumatization.

Thus, according to classical psychoanalysis, the origin of alcoholism, drug
addiction, and manic-depressive disorders can be found in the oral period of
libidinal development; obsessive-compulsive neurosis has its roots in the anal
stage; phobias and conversion hysteria result from traumas incurred in the
"phallic phase" and at the time of the Oedipus and Electra complexes, and
so on (Fenichel 1945). Later developments in psychoanalysis linked some
very deep disorders—autistic and symbiotic infantile psychoses, narcissistic
personality, and borderline personality disorders—to disturbances in the early
development of object relations (Blanck and Blanck 1974 and 1979).

These conclusions have been drawn from observations of therapists
using primarily verbal means. The understanding of psychogenic disorders
changes radically if we employ methods that involve holotropic states of

consciousness. These approaches engage levels of the unconscious, which are out of reach of most forms of verbal therapy. Initial stages of this work typically uncover relevant traumatic material from early infancy and childhood that is meaningfully related to emotional and psychosomatic problems and appears to be their source. However, when the process of uncovering continues, deeper layers of the unconscious unfold and we find additional roots of the same problems on the perinatal level and even on the transpersonal level of the psyche.

Various avenues of work with holotropic states, such as psychedelic therapy, Holotropic Breathwork, or psychotherapy with people experiencing spontaneous psychospiritual crises, have shown that emotional and psychosomatic problems cannot be adequately explained as resulting exclusively from postnatal psychotraumatic events. The unconscious material associated with them typically forms multilevel dynamic constellations—*systems of condensed experience* or *COEX systems* (Grof 1975 and 2000). A typical COEX system consists of many layers of unconscious material that share similar emotions or physical sensations; the contributions to a COEX system come from different levels of the psyche. More superficial layers contain memories of emotional or physical traumas from infancy, childhood, and later life. On a deeper level, each COEX system is typically connected to a certain aspect of the memory of birth, a specific BPM; the choice of this matrix depends on the nature of the emotional and physical feelings involved. If the theme of the COEX system is victimization, this would be BPM II, if it is a fight with a powerful enemy, the connection would be with BPM III, and so on.

The deepest roots of COEX systems underlying emotional and psychosomatic disorders reach into the transpersonal domain of the psyche. They have the form of ancestral, racial, collective, and phylogenetic memories, experiences that seem to be coming from other lifetimes (*past life memories*), and various archetypal motifs. Thus therapeutic work on anger and disposition to violence can, at a certain point, take the form of experiential identification with a tiger or a black panther, the deepest root of serious antisocial behavior can be a demonic archetype, the final resolution of a phobia can come in the form of reliving and integration of a past life experience, and so on.

The overall architecture of the COEX systems can best be shown using a clinical example. A person suffering from psychogenic asthma might discover in serial breathwork sessions a powerful COEX system underlying this disorder. The biographical part of this constellation might consist of a memory of near drowning at the age of seven, memories of being repeatedly strangled by an older brother between the ages of three and four, and a memory of severe whooping cough or diphtheria at the age of two. The perinatal contribution to this COEX would be, for example, suffocation experienced during birth because of strangulation by the umbilical cord twisted around the neck. A typical transpersonal root of this breathing disorder would be an experience of being hanged or strangled in what seems to be a previous lifetime. A detailed discussion of COEX systems, including additional examples, appears in several earlier publications (Grof 1975, 1987, and 2000).

4. Effective therapeutic mechanisms

Traditional psychotherapy knows only therapeutic mechanisms operating on the level of the biographical material, such as weakening of the psychological defense mechanisms, remembering of forgotten or repressed traumatic events, reconstructing the past from dreams or neurotic symptoms, attaining intellectual and emotional insights, and analysis of transference. As we will discuss in detail in a later section of this book (pages 147ff.), psychotherapy using holotropic states of consciousness offers many additional highly effective mechanisms of healing and personality transformation, which become available when experiential regression reaches the perinatal and transpersonal levels. Among these are actual reliving of traumatic memories from infancy, childhood, biological birth, and prenatal life, past life memories, emergence of archetypal material, experiences of cosmic unity, and others.

5. Strategy of psychotherapy and self-exploration

The most astonishing aspect of modern psychotherapy is the number of competing schools and the lack of agreement among them. They have vast differences of opinion concerning the most fundamental issues, such as: what are the dimensions of the human psyche and what are its most important motivating forces; why do symptoms develop and what do they mean; which issues that the client brings into therapy are central and which are less relevant; and, finally, what technique and strategy should be used to correct or improve the emotional, psychosomatic, and interpersonal functioning of the clients.

The goal of traditional psychotherapies is to reach intellectual understanding of the human psyche, in general, and that of a specific client, in particular, and then use this knowledge in developing an effective therapeutic technique and strategy. An important tool in many modern psychotherapies is "interpretation"; it is a way in which the therapist reveals to the client the "true" or "real" meaning of his or her thoughts, emotions, and behavior. This method is widely used in analyzing dreams, neurotic symptoms, behavior, and even seemingly trivial everyday actions, such as slips of the tongue or other small errors, Freud's "Fehlleistungen" (Freud 1960a). Another area in which interpretations are commonly applied is interpersonal dynamics, including transference of various unconscious feelings and attitudes on the therapist.

Therapists spend much effort trying to determine what is the most fitting interpretation in a given situation and what is the appropriate timing of this interpretation. Even an interpretation that is "correct" in terms of its content can allegedly be useless or harmful for the patient if it is offered prematurely, before the client is ready for it. A serious flaw of this approach to psychotherapy is that individual therapists, especially those who belong to diverse schools, would attribute very different value to the same psychological manifestation or situation and offer for it diverse and even contradictory interpretations.

This can be illustrated by a humorous example from psychoanalytic training of one of us. As a beginning psychiatrist, Stan was in training analysis with the nestor of Czechoslovakian psychoanalysis and president of the Czechoslovakian Psychoanalytic Association, Dr. Theodor Dosuzkov. Dr. Dosuzkov was in his late sixties and it was known among his analysands—all young psychiatrists—that he had a tendency to occasionally doze off during analytical hours. Dr. Dosuzkov's habit was a favorite target of jokes of his students. Besides individual sessions of training psychoanalysis, Dr. Dosuzkov also conducted seminars, where his students shared reviews of books and articles, discussed case histories, and could ask questions about the theory and practice of psychoanalysis. In one of these seminars, a participant asked a "purely theoretical" question: "What happens if during analysis the psychoanalyst falls asleep? If the client continues free-associating, does therapy continue? Is the process interrupted? Should the client be refunded for that time, since money is such an important vehicle in Freudian analysis?"

Dr. Dosuzkov could not deny that such a situation could occur in psychoanalytic sessions. He knew that the analysands knew about his foible and he had to come up with an answer. "This can happen," he said. "Sometimes, you are tired and sleepy—you did not sleep well the night before, you are recovering from a flu, or are physically exhausted. But, if you have been in this business a long time, you develop a kind of "sixth sense"; you fall asleep only when the stuff that is coming up is irrelevant. When the client says something really important, you wake up and you are right there!"

Dr. Dosuzkov was also a great admirer of I. P. Pavlov, the Russian Nobel Prize-winning physiologist who derived his knowledge of the brain from his experiments with dogs. Pavlov wrote much about the inhibition of the cerebral cortex that occurs during sleep or hypnosis; he described that sometimes there could be a "waking point" in the inhibited brain cortex. His favorite example was a mother who can sleep through heavy noises, but wakes up immediately when her own child is moaning. "It is just like the situation of the mother Pavlov wrote about," explained Dr. Dosužkov, "with enough experience, you will be able to maintain connection with your client even when you fall asleep."

There was clearly a problem with Dr. Dosužkov's explanation. What a therapist considers to be relevant in the client's narrative reflects his or her training and personal bias. Had Stan had an Adlerian, Rankian, or Jungian therapist instead of a Freudian one, they would have awakened at different times of his session, each at the moment when Stan's narrative would bring something that, according to their judgment, was "relevant." Because of the great conceptual differences between the schools of depth psychology, the question naturally arises which of them has a more correct understanding of the human psyche in health and disease.

If it were true that correct and properly timed interpretations are a significant factor in psychotherapy, there would have to be great differences in the therapeutic success achieved by various schools. Their therapeutic results could be mapped on a Gaussian curve; therapists of the school with the most accurate understanding of the psyche and, therefore, most fitting interpretations would have the best results and those belonging to orientations with less accurate conceptual frameworks would be distributed on the descending parts of the curve.

To our knowledge, there are not any scientific studies showing clear superiority of some schools of psychotherapy over others. If anything, the differences are found within the schools rather than between them. In each school there are better therapists and worse therapists. And, very likely, the therapeutic results have very little to do with what the therapists think they are doing—the accuracy and good timing of interpretations, correct analysis of transference, and other specific interventions. Successful therapy probably depends on factors that do not have much to do with intellectual brilliance and are difficult to describe in scientific language, such as the "quality of the human encounter" between therapists and clients or the feeling of the clients that they are unconditionally accepted by another human being, frequently for the first time in their life.

The lack of a generally accepted theory of psychotherapy and of basic agreement concerning therapeutic practice is very disconcerting. Under these circumstances, a client who has an emotional or psychosomatic disorder can choose a school by flipping a coin. With each school comes a different explanation of the problem he or she brought into therapy and a different technique is offered as the method of choice to overcome it. Similarly, when a beginning therapist seeking training chooses a particular therapeutic school, it says more about the personality of the applicant than the value of the school.

It is interesting to see how therapy using holotropic states of consciousness can help us to avoid the dilemmas inherent in this situation. The
alternative that this work brings actually confirms some ideas about the
therapeutic process first outlined by C. G. Jung. According to Jung, it is
impossible to achieve intellectual understanding of the psyche and derive
from it a technique that we can use in psychotherapy. As he saw it in his
later years, the psyche is not a product of the brain and is not contained in
the skull; it is the creative and generative principle of the cosmos (*anima
mundi*). It permeates all of existence and the individual psyche of each
of us is teased out of this unfathomable cosmic matrix. The intellect is a
partial function of the psyche that can help us orient ourselves in everyday
situations. However, it is not in a position to understand and manipulate
the psyche.

There is a wonderful passage in Victor Hugo's *Les Misérables*: "There is
one spectacle grander than the sea, that is the sky; there is one spectacle
grander than the sky; that is the interior of the soul." Jung was aware of
the fact that the psyche is a profound mystery and approached it with great
respect. It was clear to him that the psyche is infinitely creative and cannot be described by a set of formulas that can then be used to correct the
psychological processes of the clients. He suggested an alternative strategy
for therapy that was significantly different from using intellectual constructs
and external interventions.

What a psychotherapist can do, according to Jung, is to create a supportive environment, in which psychospiritual transformation can occur; this
container can be compared to the hermetic vessel that makes alchemical
processes possible. The next step then is to offer a method that mediates
contact between the conscious ego and a higher aspect of the client, the
Self. One of Jung's tools for this purpose was *active imagination*, continuation
of a dream in the analyst's office (Jung 1961; Franz 1997). The communica-
tion between the ego and the Self occurs primarily by means of symbolic
language. In this kind of work, healing is not the result of brilliant insights
and interpretations of the therapist; the therapeutic process is guided from
within by the Self.

In Jung's understanding, the Self is the central archetype in the collective unconscious and its function is to lead the individual toward order,
organization, and unity. Jung referred to this movement toward highest
unity as the *individuation process*. The use of holotropic states for therapy
and self-exploration essentially confirms Jung's perspective and follows the
same strategy. The facilitators create a protective and supportive environment
and help the clients enter a holotropic state. Once that occurs, the healing
process is guided from within by the clients' own inner healing intelligence
and the task of the facilitators is to support what is happening.

This process automatically activates unconscious material, which has strong emotional charge and is available for processing on the day of the session. This saves the facilitators the hopeless task of sorting out what is "relevant" and what is not that plagues verbal therapies. They simply support whatever is spontaneously emerging and manifesting from moment to moment, trusting that the process is guided by intelligence that surpasses the intellectual understanding that can be obtained by professional training in any of the schools of psychotherapy.

6. The role of spirituality in human life

The leading philosophy of Western science has been monistic materialism. Various scientific disciplines have described the history of the universe as the history of developing matter and accept as real only what can be measured and weighed. Life, consciousness, and intelligence are seen as more or less accidental by-products of material processes. Physicists, biologists, and chemists recognize the existence of dimensions of reality that are not accessible to our senses, but only those that are physical in nature and can be revealed and explored with the use of various extensions of our senses, such as microscopes, telescopes, and specially designed recording devices.

In a universe understood this way, there is no place for spirituality of any kind. The existence of God, the idea that there are invisible dimensions of reality inhabited by nonmaterial beings, the possibility of survival of consciousness after death, and the concepts of reincarnation and karma have been relegated to fairy tales and handbooks of psychiatry. From a psychiatric perspective to take such things seriously means to be ignorant, unfamiliar with the discoveries of science, superstitious, and subject to primitive magical thinking. If the belief in God or Goddess occurs in intelligent persons, it is seen as an indication that they have not come to terms with infantile images of their parents as omnipotent beings they had created in their infancy and childhood. And direct experiences of spiritual realities are considered manifestations of serious mental diseases—psychoses.

The study of holotropic states has thrown new light on the problem of spirituality and religion. The key to this new understanding is the discovery that in these states it is possible to encounter a rich array of experiences that are very similar to those that inspired the great religions of the world—visions of God and various divine and demonic beings, encounters with discarnate entities, episodes of psychospiritual death and rebirth, visits to Heaven and Hell, past life experiences, and many others. Modern research has shown beyond any doubt that these experiences are not products of pathological processes afflicting the brain, but manifestations of archetypal material from the collective unconscious, and thus normal and essential constituents of the human psyche. Although these mythic elements are accessed intrapsychically, in a process of experiential self-exploration and introspection, they are ontologically real, have objective existence. To distinguish transpersonal experiences from imaginary products of individual fantasy or psychopathology, Jungians refer to this domain as *imaginal*.

French scholar, philosopher, and mystic Henri Corbin, who first used the term *mundus imaginalis*, borrowed this idea from his study of Islamic mystical literature (Corbin 2000). Islamic theosophers call the imaginal world, where everything existing in the sensory world has its analogue, *'alam al-mithal*, or the "eighth climate," to distinguish it from the "seven climates," regions of traditional Islamic geography. The imaginal world possesses extension and dimensions, forms and colors, but these are not perceptible to our senses as they would be if they were properties of physical objects. However, this realm is in every respect as fully ontologically real and susceptible to consensual validation by other people as the material world perceived by our sensory organs.

In view of these observations, the fierce battle that religion and science have fought over the last few centuries appears ludicrous and completely unnecessary. Genuine science and authentic religion do not compete for the same territory; they represent two approaches to existence, which are complementary, not competitive. Science studies phenomena in the material world, the realm of the measurable and weighable, spirituality and true religion draw their inspiration from experiential knowledge of the imaginal world as it manifests in holotropic states of consciousness. The conflict that seems to exist between religion and science reflects a fundamental misunderstanding of both. As Ken Wilber has pointed out, there cannot possibly be a conflict between science and religion, if both of these fields are properly understood and practiced. If there seems to be a conflict, we are likely dealing with "bogus science" and "bogus religion." The apparent incompatibility is due to the fact that either side seriously misunderstands the other's position and very likely represents also a false version of its own discipline (Wilber 1882).

The only scientific endeavor that can make any relevant and valid judgments about spiritual matters is consciousness research studying holotropic states, since it requires intimate knowledge of the imaginal realm. In his groundbreaking essay, *Heaven and Hell*, Aldous Huxley suggested that concepts such as Hell and Heaven represent subjective realities experienced in a very convincing way during non-ordinary states of consciousness induced by psychedelic substances, such as LSD and mescaline, or various powerful non-drug techniques (Huxley 1959). The seeming conflict between science and religion is based on the erroneous belief that these abodes of the Beyond are located in the physical universe—Heaven in interstellar space, Paradise somewhere in a hidden area on the surface of our planet, and Hell in the interior of the earth.

Astronomers have used extremely sophisticated devices, such as the Hubble telescope, to explore and map carefully the entire vault of heaven. Results of these efforts, which have of course failed to find God and heaven replete with harp-playing angels and saints, have been taken as proof that such spiritual realities do not exist. Similarly, in cataloguing and mapping every acre of the planetary surface, explorers and geographers have found many areas of extraordinary natural beauty, but none of them matched the descriptions of paradises found in spiritual scriptures of various religions. Geologists have discovered that the core of our planet consists of layers of solid and molten nickel and iron, and that its temperature exceeds that of the sun's surface. This certainly is not a very plausible location for the caves of Satan.

Modern studies of holotropic states have brought strong supportive evidence for Huxley's insights. They have shown that Heaven, Paradise, and Hell are ontologically real; they represent distinct and important states of consciousness that all human beings can under certain circumstances experience during their lifetime. Celestial, paradisiacal, and infernal visions are a standard part of the experiential spectrum of psychedelic inner journeys, near-death states, mystical experiences, as well as shamanic initiatory crises and other types of "spiritual emergencies." Psychiatrists often hear from their patients about experiences of God, Heaven, Hell, archetypal divine and demonic beings, and about psychospiritual death and rebirth. However, because of their inadequate superficial model of the psyche, they misinterpret them as manifestations of mental disease caused by a pathological process of unknown etiology. They do not realize that matrices for these experiences exist in deep recesses of the unconscious psyche of every human being.

An astonishing aspect of transpersonal experiences occurring in holotropic states of various kinds is that their content can be drawn from the mythologies of any culture of the world, including those of which the individual has no intellectual knowledge. C. G. Jung demonstrated this extraordinary fact for mythological experiences occurring in the dreams and psychotic experiences of his patients. On the basis of these observations, he realized that the human psyche has access not only to the Freudian individual unconscious, but also to the collective unconscious, which is a repository of the entire cultural heritage of humanity. Knowledge of comparative mythology is thus more than a matter of personal interest or an academic exercise. It is a very important and useful guide for individuals involved in experiential therapy and self-exploration and an indispensable tool for those who support and accompany them on their journeys (Grof 2006b).

The experiences originating on deeper levels of the psyche, in the collective unconscious, have a certain quality that Jung referred to as *numinosity*. The word *numinous* is relatively neutral and thus preferable to other similar expressions, such as religious, mystical, magical, holy, or sacred, which have often been used in problematic contexts and are easily misleading. The term *numinosity* used in relation to transpersonal experiences describes direct perception of their extraordinary nature. They convey a very convincing sense that they belong to a higher order of reality, a realm that is sacred and radically different from the material world.

In view of the ontological reality of the imaginal realm, spirituality is a very important and natural dimension of the human psyche and spiritual quest is a legitimate and fully justified human endeavor. However, it is necessary to emphasize that this applies to genuine spirituality based on personal experience and does not provide support for ideologies and dogmas of organized religions. To prevent misunderstanding and confusion that in the past compromised many similar discussions, it is critical to make a clear distinction between spirituality and religion.

Spirituality is based on direct experiences of ordinarily invisible numinous dimensions of reality, which become available in holotropic states of consciousness. It does not require a special place or officially appointed persons mediating contact with the divine. The mystics do not need churches or temples. The context in which they experience the sacred dimensions of reality, including their own divinity, is provided by their bodies and nature. And instead of officiating priests, they need a supportive group of fellow seekers or the guidance of a teacher who is more advanced on the inner journey than they are themselves.

Direct spiritual experiences appear in two different forms. The first of these, the experience of *the immanent divine*, involves subtly but profoundly transformed perception of the world of everyday reality. A person having this form of spiritual experience sees people, animals, and inanimate objects in the environment as radiant manifestations of a unified field of cosmic creative energy and realizes that the boundaries between them are illusory and unreal. This is a direct experience of God in nature or God as nature. Using the analogy with television, this experience could be likened to a situation where a black and white picture would suddenly change into one in vivid, "living color." As in the experience of the immanent divine, many of the features of the TV image remain the same, but they are radically enhanced by the addition of a new dimension.

The second form of spiritual experience, the experience of *the transcendental divine*, involves manifestation of archetypal beings and realms that are not available to perception in the everyday state of consciousness. In this type of spiritual experience, entirely new elements seem to "unfold" or "explicate"—to borrow terms from David Bohm—from another level or order of reality. When we return to the analogy with television mentioned earlier, this would be like discovering that there exist other channels that are different from the one we have been previously watching.

Spirituality involves a special kind of relationship between the individual and the cosmos and is, in its essence, a personal and private affair. By comparison, organized religion is institutionalized group activity that takes place in a designated location, a temple or a church, and involves a system of appointed officials who might or might not have had personal experiences of spiritual realities themselves. Once a religion becomes organized, it often completely loses the connection with its spiritual source and becomes a secular institution that exploits human spiritual needs without satisfying them.

Organized religions tend to create hierarchical systems focusing on the pursuit of power, control, politics, money, possessions, and other worldly concerns. Under these circumstances, religious hierarchy as a rule dislikes and discourages direct spiritual experiences in its members, because they foster independence and cannot be effectively controlled. When this is the case, genuine spiritual life continues only in the mystical branches, monastic orders, and ecstatic sects of the religions involved. People who have experiences of the immanent or transcendent divine open up to spirituality found in the mystical branches of the great religions of the world or in their monastic orders, not necessarily in their mainstream organizations. A deep mystical experience tends to dissolve the boundaries between religions and reveals deep connections between them, while dogmatism of organized religions tends to emphasize differences between various creeds and engender antagonism and hostility.

There is no doubt that the dogmas of organized religions are generally in fundamental conflict with science, whether this science uses the mechanistic-materialistic model or is anchored in the emerging paradigm. However, the situation is very different in regard to authentic mysticism based on spiritual experiences. The great mystical traditions have amassed extensive knowledge about human consciousness and about the spiritual realms in a way that is similar to the method that scientists use in acquiring knowledge about the material world. It involves methodology for inducing transpersonal experiences, systematic collection of data, and intersubjective validation.

Spiritual experiences, like any other aspect of reality, can be subjected to careful, open-minded research and studied scientifically. There is nothing unscientific about unbiased and rigorous study of transpersonal phenomena and of the challenges they present for materialistic understanding of the world. Only such an approach can answer the critical question about the ontological status of mystical experiences: Do they reveal deep truth about some basic aspects of existence, as maintained by various systems of perennial philosophy, or are they products of superstition, fantasy, or mental disease, as Western materialistic science sees them?

Western psychiatry makes no distinction between a mystical experience and a psychotic experience and sees both as manifestations of mental disease. In its rejection of religion, it does not differentiate between primitive folk beliefs or the fundamentalist literal interpretations of religious scriptures and sophisticated mystical traditions or the great Eastern spiritual philosophies based on centuries of systematic introspective exploration of the psyche. Modern consciousness research has brought convincing evidence for the objective existence of the imaginal realm and has thus validated the main metaphysical assumptions of the mystical worldview, of the Eastern spiritual philosophies, and even certain beliefs of native cultures.

7. The nature of reality: Psyche, cosmos, and consciousness

Some observations from the study of holotropic states are so radical that they not only challenge the theory and practice of psychiatry, psychology, and psychotherapy, but also undermine some of the most fundamental metaphysical assumptions of Western science. None of these conceptual challenges are more drastic and far-reaching than the new insights regarding the nature of consciousness and its relationship to matter. According to Western neuroscience, consciousness is an epiphenomenon of matter, a by-product of the complex neurophysiological processes in the brain and thus an intrinsic and inseparable part of the body. Modern consciousness research conducted in the last five decades has made this hypothesis highly questionable.

Very few people, including most scientists, realize that we have absolutely no proof that consciousness is actually produced in the brain and by the brain. There is no doubt that there exists vast clinical and experimental evidence showing significant interconnections and correlations between the anatomy, physiology, and biochemistry of the brain, on the one hand, and states of consciousness, on the other. However, it represents a major logical jump to infer from the available data that these correlations represent a proof that the brain is actually the source of consciousness. Such a deduction would be tantamount to the conclusion that the TV program is generated in the TV set, because there is a close correlation between functioning or malfunctioning of its components and the quality of the sound and picture. It should be obvious from this example that the close connection between cerebral activity and consciousness does not exclude the possibility that the brain mediates consciousness, but does not actually generate it. The research of holotropic states has amassed ample evidence for this alternative.

There exist no scientific theories explaining how consciousness is generated by material processes, nor does anybody have even a remote idea how something like that could possibly happen. The gap between consciousness and matter is so formidable that it is impossible to imagine how it could be bridged. In spite of the lack of convincing evidence that consciousness is an epiphenomenon of matter, this basic metaphysical assumption remains one of the leading myths of Western materialistic science. While there exists no scientific proof for the fact that the brain generates consciousness, there are numerous observations indicating that consciousness can under certain circumstances function independently of the brain and of the world of matter.

In holotropic states, our consciousness can reach far beyond the boundaries of the body/ego and obtain accurate information about various aspects of the material world that we have not obtained in this lifetime through the mediation of our sensory organs. We have already mentioned reliving of birth, of prenatal memories, and of conception. In transpersonal experiences our consciousness can identify with other people, with members of various species of the animal kingdom from primates to unicellular organisms, with plant life, and even with inorganic materials and processes. We can also transcend linear time and experience vivid ancestral, racial, karmic, and phylogenetic sequences, and episodes from the collective unconscious.

Transpersonal experiences can provide not only accurate new information about various aspects of the material world, including those that we are unfamiliar with, but also about various figures and realms of the archetypal domain of the collective unconscious. We can witness or even participate in mythological sequences from any culture of the world and any historical period accurately portrayed in every detail. It is absurd to attribute this rich array of experiences accurately portraying various present and past aspects of the material world and figures, realms, and themes from world mythology to some yet unknown pathology afflicting the brain.

The most convincing evidence that consciousness is not produced by the brain and can function independently of it comes from the young scientific discipline of thanatology, the study of death and dying. It is now an established fact, confirmed by many independent observations, that disembodied consciousness of people in near-death situations is able to accurately observe the environment and various near or remote locations and events. Individuals, who are clinically dead (in a state of cardiac death and even brain death), are able to observe their bodies and the rescue procedures from above and "travel" freely to other parts of the same building or various remote places. Independent research has repeatedly confirmed the accuracy of observations made by disembodied consciousness (Ring and Valarino 1998; Sabom 1982 and 1998).

Such experiences are strikingly reminiscent of the descriptions of the *bardo body* found in the Tibetan Book of the Dead (*Bardo Thödol*). This famous spiritual text states that, after having fainted from fear in the *Chönyid Bardo*, the dying person awakens in the *Sidpa Bardo* in a new form—the *bardo body*. This body differs from the gross body of everyday life. It is not composed of matter and has many remarkable qualities, such as the power of unimpeded motion, the ability to penetrate through solid objects, and the capacity to perceive the world without the mediation of the senses. Those who exist in the form of the *bardo body* can travel instantaneously to any place on earth and even to the sacred cosmic mountain Mount Meru. Only two places are not accessible to this form: the maternal womb and Bodh Gaya, clear references to leaving the *bardo* state at the time of conception or enlightenment (Evans-Wentz 1957).

An extensive study conducted by Ken Ring and his colleagues has added a fascinating dimension to these observations: people who are congenitally blind for organic reasons and have never been able to see anything in their entire lives can perceive the environment when their consciousness detaches from their bodies during various life-threatening situations. The veracity of many of these visions has been confirmed by consensual validation; Ring refers to such visions as *veridical OBEs* (out-of-body experiences) (Ring and Valarino 1998; Ring and Cooper 1999). Various aspects of the environment accurately perceived by disembodied consciousness of blind subjects ranged from details of electrical fixtures on the ceiling of the operating room to the surroundings of the hospital observed from bird's-eye view. Modern thanatological research has thus confirmed an important aspect of classical descriptions of OBEs, which can be found in spiritual literature and philosophical texts.

Veridical OBEs are not limited to near-death situations. We have seen them repeatedly in people undergoing psychospiritual crises ("spiritual emergencies") and in participants in Holotropic Breathwork workshops. Some of these individuals were able to observe the group from above and describe unusual behavior of some of its members, in spite of the fact that they themselves breathed with their eyes closed. The consciousness of others left the building and observed the environment from above or traveled to some remote locations and observed the events there. On occasion, these bird's-eye views appeared in the mandalas.

These observations demonstrate without any reasonable doubt that consciousness is not a product of the brain and thus an epiphenomenon of matter. It is more likely at least an equal partner of matter, or possibly superordinated to it. The matrices for many of the aforementioned experiences clearly are not contained in the brain, but are stored in some kinds of immaterial fields or in the field of consciousness itself. The most promising developments in hard science offering models for transpersonal experience are David Bohm's idea of the *implicate order* (Bohm 1980), Rupert Sheldrake's concept of *morphogenetic fields* (Sheldrake 1981 and 1988) and Ervin Laszlo's hypothesis of the *psi field* or *Akashic field* (Laszlo 1993 and 2004).

CHAPTER THREE

Essential Components of Holotropic Breathwork

The theory and practice of Holotropic Breathwork are based on the observations from modern consciousness research that we discussed in the previous chapter and on the revolutionary insights into the human psyche in health and disease they have engendered. This method of therapy and self-exploration combines very simple means to induce holotropic states of consciousness—faster breathing, evocative music, and releasing bodywork—and uses the healing and transformative power of these states.

Holotropic Breathwork provides access to biographical, perinatal, and transpersonal domains of the unconscious and thus to deep psychospiritual roots of emotional and psychosomatic disorders. It also makes it possible to utilize the powerful mechanisms of healing and personality transformation that operate on these levels of the psyche. The process of self-exploration and therapy in Holotropic Breathwork is spontaneous and autonomous; it is governed by the inner healing intelligence of the breather, rather than guided by a therapist following the principles of a particular school of psychotherapy.

However, most of the recent revolutionary discoveries concerning consciousness and the human psyche are new only for modern psychiatry and psychology. They have a long history as integral parts of ritual and spiritual life of many ancient and native cultures and their healing practices. They thus represent rediscovery, validation, and modern reformulation of ancient wisdom and procedures, some of which can be traced to the dawn of human history. As we will see, the same is true for the principal constituents used in the practice of Holotropic Breathwork—breathing, instrumental music, chanting, bodywork, and mandala drawing or other forms of artistic expression. They have been used since time immemorial in sacred practices of ancient and native cultures.

1. The healing power of breath

In ancient and pre-industrial societies, breath and breathing have played a very important role in cosmology, mythology, and philosophy, as well as a principal tool in ritual, spiritual, and healing practice. Various breathing techniques have been used in many historical periods and by many different cultures of the world to induce holotropic states of consciousness for religious and healing purposes. Since earliest history, virtually every major psychospiritual system seeking to comprehend human nature has viewed breath as a crucial link between the material world, the human body, the psyche, and the spirit. This is clearly reflected in the words many languages use for breath.

In the ancient Indian literature, the term *prana* meant not only physical breath and air, but also the sacred essence of life. Similarly, in traditional Chinese medicine, the word *chi* refers to the cosmic essence and the energy of life, as well as the natural air we breathe into our lungs. In Japan, the corresponding word is *ki*. Ki plays an extremely important role in Japanese spiritual practices and martial arts. In ancient Greece, the word *pneuma* meant both air or breath and spirit or the essence of life. The Greeks also saw breath as being closely related to the psyche. The term *phren* was used both for the diaphragm, the largest muscle involved in breathing, and for the mind (as in the term *schizophrenia* = literally, *split mind*).

In the old Hebrew tradition, the same word, *ruach*, denoted both breath and creative spirit, which were seen as identical. The following quote from Genesis shows the close relationship between God, breath, and life: "Then the Lord God formed man [Hebrew *adam*] from the dust of the ground and breathed into his nostrils the breath of life; and the man became a living being." In Latin the same name was used for breath and spirit—*spiritus*. Similarly, in Slavic languages, spirit and breath have the same linguistic root.

In the native Hawaiian tradition and medicine (*kanaka maoli lapa'au*), the word *ha* means the divine spirit, wind, air, and breath. It is contained in the popular Hawaiian *aloha*, an expression that is used in many different contexts and on many different occasions. It is usually translated as presence (*alo*) of the Divine Breath (*ha*). Its opposite, *ha'ole*, meaning literally without breath or without life, is a term that native Hawaiians have applied to white-skinned foreigners since the arrival of the infamous British sea captain James Cook in 1778. The *kahunas*, "Keepers of Secret Knowledge," have used breathing exercises to generate spiritual energy (*mana*).

It has been known for centuries that it is possible to influence consciousness by techniques that involve breathing. The procedures that have been used for this purpose by various ancient and non-Western cultures cover a very wide range from drastic interference with breathing to subtle and sophisticated exercises of various spiritual traditions. Thus the original form of baptism practiced by the Essenes involved forced submersion of the initiate under water for an extended period of time. This resulted in a powerful experience of death and rebirth. In some other groups, the neophytes were half-choked by smoke, by strangulation, or by compression of the carotid arteries.

Profound changes in consciousness can be induced by both extremes of the breathing rate, hyperventilation and prolonged withholding of breath, as well as by using them in an alternating fashion. Very sophisticated and advanced methods of this kind can be found in the ancient Indian science of breath, or *pranayama*. William Walker Atkinson, an American writer who was influential in the turn-of-the-century (1890s–1900s) spiritual/philosophical movement, wrote under the pseudonym Yogi Ramacharaka a comprehensive treatise on the Hindu science of breath (Ramacharaka 1903). Specific techniques involving intense breathing or withholding of breath are also part of various exercises in Kundalini Yoga, Siddha Yoga, the Tibetan Vajrayana, Sufi practice, Burmese Buddhist and Taoist meditation, and many others. Indirectly, the depth and rhythm of breathing is profoundly influenced by such ritual artistic performances as the *Balinese monkey chant* or *Ketjak*, the Inuit Eskimo *throat music*, and singing of *kirtans*, *bhajans*, or Sufi *dhikrs*.

More subtle techniques, which emphasize special awareness in relation to breathing, rather than changes of the respiratory dynamics, have a prominent place in Buddhism. *Anāpānasati* is a basic form of meditation taught by the Buddha; it means literally "mindfulness of breathing" (from the Pali *anāpāna* = inhalation and exhalation and *sati* = mindfulness). Buddha's teaching of *anāpānasati* was based on his experience in using it as a means of achieving his own enlightenment. He emphasized the importance of not only being mindful of one's breath, but using the breath to become aware of one's entire body and of all of one's experience. According to the *Anāpānasati Sutta* (*sutra*), practicing this form of meditation leads to the removal of all defilements (*kilesa*). The Buddha taught that systematic practice of *anāpānasati* would lead to the final release (*nirvana* or *nibbāna*).

In materialistic science, breathing lost its sacred meaning and was stripped of its connection to the psyche and spirit. Western medicine reduced it to an important physiological function. The physical and psychological manifestations that accompany various respiratory maneuvers have all been pathologized. The psychosomatic response to faster breathing, the so-called *hyperventilation syndrome*, is considered a pathological condition, rather than what it really is, a process that has an enormous healing potential. When hyperventilation occurs spontaneously, it is routinely suppressed by administration of tranquilizers, injections of intravenous calcium, and application of a paper bag over the face to increase the concentration of carbon dioxide and combat the alkalosis caused by faster breathing.

In the last few decades, Western therapists rediscovered the healing potential of breath and developed techniques that utilize it. We have ourselves experimented in the context of our month-long seminars at the Esalen Institute in Big Sur, California, with various approaches involving breathing. These included both breathing exercises from ancient spiritual traditions under the guidance of Indian and Tibetan teachers and techniques developed by Western therapists. Each of these approaches has a specific emphasis and uses breath in a different way. In our own search for an effective method of using the healing potential of breath, we tried to simplify this process as much as possible.

We came to the conclusion that it is sufficient to breathe faster and more effectively than usual and with full concentration on the inner process. Instead of emphasizing a specific technique of breathing, we follow even in this area the general strategy of holotropic work—to trust the intrinsic wisdom of the body and follow the inner clues. In Holotropic Breathwork, we encourage people to begin the session with faster and somewhat deeper breathing, tying inhalation and exhalation into a continuous circle of breath. Once in the process, they find their own rhythm and way of breathing.

We have been able to confirm repeatedly Wilhelm Reich's observation that psychological resistances and defenses are associated with restricted breathing (Reich 1949, 1961). Respiration is an autonomous function, but it can also be influenced by volition. Deliberate increase of the pace of breathing typically loosens psychological defenses and leads to a release and emergence of unconscious (and superconscious) material. Unless one has witnessed this process or experienced it personally, it is difficult to believe on theoretical grounds alone the power and efficacy of this approach.

2. The therapeutic potential of music

In Holotropic Breathwork, the consciousness-expanding effect of breath is further enhanced by the use of evocative music. Like breathing, instrumental music and other forms of sound technology—monotonous drumming, rattling, and chanting—have been used for centuries, or even millennia, as principle tools in shamanic practice, healing rituals, and rites of passage in many different parts of the world. Quite independently, many pre-industrial cultures have developed drumming rhythms that in Western laboratory experiments have demonstrable effect on the electric activity of the brain (Jilek 1974, 1982; Neher 1961, 1962; Kamiya 1969; Maxfield 1990, 1994). The archives of cultural anthropologists contain countless examples of trance-inducing methods of extraordinary power combining music, percussion, human voices, and body movement.

In many cultures, music has been used specifically for healing purposes in the context of intricate ceremonies. The Navajo healing rituals conducted by trained singers have extraordinary complexity that has been compared to that of the scores of Wagnerian operas. The trance dance of the !Kung Bushmen of the African Kalahari Desert has unusual healing power, as has been documented in many anthropological studies and films (Lee and DeVore 1976; Katz 1976). The healing potential of the syncretistic religious rituals of the Caribbean and South America, such as the Cuban *Santería* or Brazilian *Umbanda* is recognized by many professionals in these countries who have traditional Western medical education. Remarkable instances of emotional and psychosomatic healing have also been described in the meetings of Christian groups using music, singing, and dance, such as the Snake Handlers (Holy Ghost People), and the revivalists or members of the Pentecostal Church.

Some spiritual traditions have developed sound technologies that not only induce a general trance state, but also have a specific effect on consciousness, the human psyche, and the body. Thus the Indian teachings describe specific connections between certain acoustic frequencies and the individual *chakras*. With systematic use of this knowledge, it is possible to influence the state of consciousness in a predictable and desirable way. The ancient Indian tradition called *nada yoga*, or "the way to union through sound," has the reputation of maintaining, improving, and restoring emotional, psychosomatic, and physical health and well-being. According to the ancient Indian text *Swara Sastra*, singing certain chants with full devotion and proper pronunciation can affect the energy channels in the subtle body (*nadis* and *chakras*) and have a positive effect on the flow of life energy and on blood circulation. Representatives of the tradition called *Raga Chikitsa* ("healing with *ragas*") assert that certain *ragas* can be used for healing of specific diseases—*Pahadi Raga* has a positive influence on respiratory problems, *Raga Chandrakauns* on heart diseases, *Raga Bhupali* and *Raga Todi* can lower high blood pressure and, conversely, *Raga Asawari* can elevate low blood pressure.

Examples of extraordinary vocal performances used for ritual, spiritual, and healing purposes are the multivocal chanting of the Tibetan Gyotso monks and of the Mongolian and Tuva shamans, the Hindu *bhajans* and *kirtans*, the Santo Daime chants (*Ikaros*) used in the *ayahuasca* ceremonies, the throat music of the Inuit Eskimo people, or the sacred chants of various Sufi orders. These are just a few examples of the extensive use of instrumental music and chanting for healing, ritual, and spiritual purposes.

Carefully selected music serves several important functions in holotropic states of consciousness. It mobilizes emotions associated with repressed memories, brings them to the surface, and facilitates their expression. It helps to open the door into the unconscious, intensifies and deepens the healing process, and provides a meaningful context for the experience. The continuous flow of music creates a carrier wave that helps the individual move through difficult experiences and impasses, overcome psychological defenses, surrender, and let go. In Holotropic Breathwork sessions, which are usually conducted in groups, music has an additional important function: it masks the noises made by the participants and merges with them into a complex aesthetic form.

To use music as a catalyst for deep self-exploration and experiential work, it is necessary to learn a new way of listening to music and relating to it that is alien to our culture. We often employ music as an acoustic background that has little emotional relevance. Typical examples are the use of popular music in cocktail parties or piped music (Muzak) in shopping areas and work spaces. A different approach used by sophisticated audiences is the disciplined and attentive listening to music in theaters and concert halls. The dynamic and elemental way of using music characteristic of rock concerts comes closer to the use of music in Holotropic Breathwork. However, the attention of participants in such events is usually extroverted and the experience lacks an element that is essential in holotropic self-exploration or therapy—sustained, focused introspection.

In the work with holotropic states of consciousness, it is essential to surrender completely to the flow of music, let it resonate in one's entire body, and respond to it in a spontaneous and elemental fashion. This includes manifestations that would be unthinkable in a concert hall, where even crying or coughing is seen as a disturbance and causes annoyance and embarrassment. In Holotropic Breathwork, one has to give full expression to whatever the music is bringing out, whether it is loud screaming or laughing, baby talk, animal noises, shamanic chanting, or talking in tongues. It is also important not to control any physical impulses, such as bizarre grimacing, sensual movements of the pelvis, violent shaking, or intense contortions of the entire body. Naturally, there are exceptions to this rule; destructive behavior directed toward oneself, others, and the physical environment is not permissible.

We also encourage participants to suspend any intellectual activity, such as trying to guess the composer of the music or the culture from which the music comes. Other ways of avoiding the emotional impact of the music involve engaging one's professional expertise—judging the performance of the orchestra, guessing which instruments are playing, and criticizing the technical quality of the recording or the music equipment in the room. When we can avoid these pitfalls, music can become a very powerful tool for inducing and supporting holotropic states of consciousness. For this purpose, the music has to be of superior technical quality and sufficient volume to drive the experience. The combination of music with faster breathing has remarkable activating effect on the psyche and consciousness-expanding power.

The basic principles of the use of music in Holotropic Breathwork and the criteria for the selection of specific pieces for various stages of the sessions were formulated by Christina. Her father was a musician and music has been an important part of her life since her early childhood; she inherited her father's ear and his deep interest in this universal language. If breathwork is used without music, the experience follows a natural trajectory that resembles the curve of an orgasm; the intensity of the emotions and physical feelings builds up to a culmination point and then gradually subsides, even if the person continues to breathe faster. This provides the guiding principle for the selection of music for the sessions.

The general rule for the choice of music is to respond sensitively to the phase, intensity, and content of the participants' experiences, rather than trying to program them in any way. This is in congruence with the general philosophy of Holotropic Breathwork, particularly the deep respect for the wisdom of the inner healer, for the collective unconscious, and for the autonomy and spontaneity of the healing process. If we conduct private breathwork sessions, it is not difficult to apply this principle. The experiences of participants in group sessions follow various individual patterns in terms of their nature and timing of the stages. Here the choice of music cannot be individualized; the best we can do is to select pieces that reflect and support the overall emotional atmosphere in the room.

Over the years, Christina collected a large number of recordings from different parts of the world. They cover a wide range of genres from lesser-known classical compositions, religious music, movie scores, and good electronic pieces to selections of trance-inducing and ethnic performances. During the sessions, she likes to stay in touch with the group and respond sensitively to the energy in the room, even if it means playing only one track from an audiotape or a CD at a time. Many of the facilitators who have completed our training have changed this practice and use prerecorded sets of music. This practice is not ideal, since the dynamics varies from session to session. Having prerecorded music for the entire session prevents us from choosing pieces that reflect the momentary changes of emotional atmosphere in the room. However, this practice has become very popular, since it saves facilitators the energy and money necessary to create their own extensive collections and frees them for the work with the participants during the session.

As far as the specific choice of music is concerned, we will outline only the general principles and give a few suggestions based on our experience. We prefer to use stereophonic music that is evocative, has a steady rhythm and consistent intensity, and has no lapses between pieces. We try to avoid selections that are jarring, dissonant, and anxiety provoking. We also do not recommend playing songs and other vocal pieces in languages that participants can understand and that would through their verbal content convey a specific message or suggest a specific theme. When we play vocal compositions, we prefer those that are sung in foreign languages, so that the human voice is perceived as just another musical instrument. For the same reason, we try to avoid pieces that are well known, evoke specific intellectual associations, or program the content of the session, such as Richard Wagner's or Felix Mendelssohn-Bartholdy's wedding marches and overtures to Georges Bizet's *Carmen* or Giuseppe Verdi's *Aida*.

The session typically begins with activating music that is dynamic, flowing, and emotionally uplifting and reassuring. As the session continues, it gradually increases in intensity and moves to powerful rhythmic pieces—creations of contemporary musicians, lesser-known classical compositions, or recordings of ethnic, ritual, and spiritual music from various cultures of the world. About an hour and a half into the session of Holotropic Breathwork, when the experience typically culminates, we introduce what we call "peak" or "breakthrough music." The selections used at this time range from sacred music—masses, oratoria, requiems, or Sufi *dhikrs*—and powerful orchestral pieces to excerpts from dramatic movie soundtracks. In the second half of the session, the intensity of the music gradually decreases and we bring in uplifting and emotionally moving pieces ("heart music"). Finally, in the termination period of the session, the music has a soothing, flowing, timeless, and meditative quality.

In selecting the music for the session, we try to provide a wide range of styles, instruments, and genres and find a good balance between masculine and feminine selections. Soft and sweet-sounding music with female voices is particularly important in the final stages of the sessions; it helps integration and positive closure of the experience. In holotropic states of consciousness, people are usually extremely sensitive to music and tend to prefer natural sounds, such as human voices, or instruments played by human beings. Electronic music might sound cold and artificial, unless it has rich higher harmonics that make it sound less technical. Of particular interest for Holotropic Breathwork are compositions that combine a fast rhythmic beat with drawn-out melodic sounds. This makes it possible for individual breathers to focus on the aspect of music that best reflects the nature of their experience—high activity and struggle or movement toward relaxation and opening.

Equally important as the selection of music is the quality of the music equipment. When we are planning a breathwork workshop, we have learned to make sure that we have a high-quality amplifier and set of speakers, two

CD-players or tape decks, and a mixer. This makes it possible to play our selections with sufficient volume and high acoustic quality and achieve smooth transition from one piece of music to another. Ideally, we would also have back-up equipment that we could use in case of technical failure. Music is an essential component of the Holotropic Breathwork experience. The ability of the workshop leader to choose the right music often determines whether the session will be a deeply meaningful or even life-transforming experience or a frustrating waste of time.

3. The use of releasing bodywork

The physical response to Holotropic Breathwork varies considerably from one person to another. Most commonly, faster breathing brings, at first, more or less intense psychosomatic manifestations. The textbooks of respiratory physiology refer to this response to accelerated breathing as the "hyperventilation syndrome." They describe it as a stereotypical pattern of physiological responses that consists primarily of tensions in the hands and feet (carpopedal spasms). We have now conducted over thirty-five thousand holotropic breathing sessions and have found the current medical understanding of the effects of faster breathing to be incorrect (for a more detailed discussion of the controversy surrounding the problem of the hyperventilation syndrome in medical literature, see pages 163ff.).

There exist many people in whom fast breathing carried over a period of three to four hours does not lead to a classical hyperventilation syndrome, but to progressive relaxation, intense sexual feelings, or even mystical experiences. Others develop tensions in various parts of the body, but do not show signs of the carpopedal spasms. Moreover, in those who develop tensions, continued faster breathing does not lead to progressive increase of the tensions, but tends to be self-limited. It typically reaches a climactic culmination followed by profound relaxation. The pattern of this sequence has a certain resemblance to sexual orgasm.

In repeated holotropic sessions, this process of intensification of tensions and subsequent relaxation tends to move from one part of the body to another in a way that varies from person to person. The overall amount of muscular tensions and of intense emotions associated with them decreases with the number of sessions. What happens in this process is that faster breathing extended for a long period of time changes the chemistry of the organism in such a way that blocked physical and emotional energies associated with various traumatic memories are released and become available for peripheral discharge and processing. This makes it possible for the previously repressed content of these memories to emerge into consciousness and be integrated.

It is thus a healing process that we want to encourage and support and not a pathological process that needs to be suppressed, as it is commonly practiced in mainstream medicine.

Physical manifestations that develop during the breathing in various areas of the body are not simple physiological reactions to hyperventilation. They have a complex psychosomatic structure and usually have specific psychological meaning for the individuals involved. Sometimes, they represent an intensified version of tensions and pains, which the person knows from everyday life, either as a chronic problem or as symptoms that appear at times of emotional or physical stress, fatigue, lack of sleep, weakening by an illness, or the use of alcohol or marijuana. Other times, they can be recognized as reactivation of old latent symptoms that the individual suffered from in infancy, childhood, puberty, or some other time of his or her life.

The tensions that we carry in our body can be released in two different ways. The first of them involves *catharsis* and *abreaction*—discharge of pent-up physical energies through tremors, twitches, various movements, coughing, gagging, and vomiting. Both catharsis and abreaction also typically include release of blocked emotions through crying, screaming, or other types of vocal expression. The Greek philosopher Aristotle coined the term *katharsis*, meaning literally "purification" or "cleansing," to describe the emotional release experienced by the audiences of Greek tragedies and by initiates participating in ancient mysteries (Aristotle 2006). In modern psychiatry, it is used for situations where emotional and physical release is not associated with emergence of any specific unconscious material. The name *abreaction* is reserved for situations, where such specific connection can be made.

Abreaction is a mechanism that is well known in traditional psychiatry since the time when Sigmund Freud and Joseph Breuer published their studies in hysteria (Freud and Breuer 1936). Various abreactive techniques have been successfully used in the treatment of traumatic emotional neuroses, and abreaction also represents an integral part of the new experiential psychotherapies, such as neo-Reichian work, Gestalt practice, and primal therapy. Later in this book, we will discuss at some length the controversy surrounding therapeutic value of abreaction in mainstream psychiatry and psychotherapy the (pages 148ff.).

The second mechanism that can release physical and emotional tensions plays an important role in Holotropic Breathwork and other forms of therapy using breathing techniques. It represents a new development in psychiatry and psychotherapy and equals or even surpasses the efficacy of abreaction. Here the deep tensions surface in the form of unrelenting muscular contractions of various duration (tetany). By sustaining these muscular tensions for extended periods of time, the breathers consume large amounts of previously pent-up energy and simplify the functioning of their bodies by disposing of them. The deep relaxation that typically follows the temporary intensification of old tensions or full manifestation of previously latent ones bears witness to the healing nature of this process.

These two mechanisms have their parallels in sport physiology; it is well known that it is possible to train and build the muscles in two different ways: by *isotonic* and *isometric exercises*. As the name suggests, during isotonic exercises the tension of the muscles remains constant while their length oscillates. During isometric exercises, the tension of the muscles changes, but their length remains the same all the time. Good examples of isotonic activity are boxing and aerobic exercises, while weight lifting or bench-pressing are distinctly isometric activities. Both of these mechanisms are extremely effective in releasing and resolving deep-seated chronic muscular tensions. In spite of their superficial differences, they serve the same purpose and in Holotropic Breathwork they complement each other very effectively.

In many instances, the difficult emotions and physical manifestations that emerge from the unconscious during holotropic sessions get automatically resolved and the breathers end up in a deeply relaxed meditative state. In that case, no external interventions are necessary and the breathers remain in this state until they return to an ordinary state of consciousness. After a brief check with the facilitators, they move to the art room to draw a mandala. If the breathing, in and of itself, does not lead to a good completion and there are residual tensions or unresolved emotions, facilitators offer participants a specific form of bodywork, which helps them reach a better closure for the session.

The general strategy of this work is to ask the breather to focus his or her attention on the area where there is a problem and do whatever is necessary to intensify the existing sensations. The facilitator then helps to intensify these feelings even further by appropriate physical intervention from the outside. While the attention of the breathers is focused on the energetically charged problem areas, we encourage them to find spontaneous motor or vocal reactions to this situation. This response should not reflect a conscious choice of the breather, but be fully determined by the unconscious process. It often takes an entirely unexpected and surprising form—talking in tongues or in an unknown foreign language, baby talk, gibberish, voice of a specific animal, a shamanic chant or another form of vocal performance from a particular culture unknown to the breather.

Equally frequent are completely unexpected physical reactions, such as strong tremors, jolts, coughing, gagging, and vomiting, as well as various characteristic animal movements—climbing, flying, digging, crawling, slithering, and others. It is essential that the facilitators encourage and support what is spontaneously emerging, rather than apply some technique offered by a particular school of therapy. This work continues until the facilitator and the breather reach an agreement that the session has been adequately closed.

Even if the breathers gave us the permission to do bodywork with them, or even asked for it, they remain in complete control of the process during the entire time by using the agreed upon signal "stop." When we hear this word, we interrupt everything we are doing and find out why they used this word. Sometimes the reason is that they do not think the intervention is correct or effective. More frequently, the bodywork is correctly applied, but it is bringing up more unconscious material than the breather is ready to handle. In both instances, the work will stop and we receive the feedback from the breather. After finding out why the signal was used, we decide how to proceed.

Under no circumstances do we continue with the bodywork after the breather asked us to stop, even if we are convinced that our intervention is appropriate and would be helpful. This could lead to a serious breach of trust on a very deep and critical level and permanently undermine our relationship with the person involved. However, we inform participants in advance that we will not interrupt the work unless they specifically use the word "stop." Commands, such as "leave me alone, get away from me, you are killing me, get off my back you bastard, or fuck off," would be considered part of the breather's dialogue with the protagonists of an inner drama and not valid signals for the facilitators.

4. Supportive and nourishing physical contact

In Holotropic Breathwork, we also use a different form of physical intervention, one that is designed to provide support on a deep preverbal level. This is based on the observation that there exist two fundamentally different forms of traumas that require diametrically different approaches. The first of these can be referred to as *trauma by commission*. It is the result of external influences that had damaging impact on the future development of the individual. Here belong such insults as physical, emotional, or sexual abuse, frightening situations, destructive criticism, or ridicule. These traumas represent foreign elements in the unconscious that can be brought into consciousness, energetically discharged, and resolved.

Although this distinction is not recognized in conventional psychotherapy, the second form of trauma, *trauma by omission*, is radically different. It actually involves the opposite mechanism—absence or lack of positive experiences that are essential for a healthy emotional development. Infants, as well as older children, have strong primitive needs for instinctual satisfaction and security that pediatricians and child psychiatrists call *anaclitic* (from the Greek *anaklinein* = to lean upon). These involve the need to be held and experience skin contact, be caressed, comforted, played with, and be the center of human attention. When these needs are not met, it has serious consequences for the future of the individual.

Many people have a history of emotional deprivation, abandonment, and neglect that resulted in serious frustration of the anaclitic needs. The only way to heal this type of trauma is to offer a corrective experience in the form of supportive physical contact in a holotropic state of consciousness. For this approach to be effective, the individual has to be deeply regressed to the infantile stage of development, otherwise the corrective measure would not reach the developmental level on which the trauma occurred. Depending on circumstances and on previous agreement, this physical support can range from simple holding of the hand or touching the forehead to full body contact.

Use of nourishing physical contact is a very effective way of healing early emotional trauma. However, it requires following strict ethical rules. We have to explain to the participants before the session the rationale of this technique and get their approval to use it. Under no circumstances can this approach be practiced without previous consent and no pressures can be used to obtain this permission. For many people with a history of sexual abuse, physical contact is a very sensitive and charged issue. Very often those who need it most have the strongest resistance to it. It can sometimes take a long time before a person develops enough trust toward the facilitators and the group to be able to accept this form of help and benefit from it.

Supportive physical contact has to be used exclusively to satisfy the needs of the breathers and not those of the sitters or facilitators. By this we do not mean only sexual needs or needs for intimacy, which, of course, are the most obvious issues. Equally problematic can be the sitter's strong need to be needed, loved, or appreciated, unfulfilled maternal needs, and other less extreme forms of emotional wants and desires. An incident from one of our workshops at the Esalen Institute in Big Sur, California, can serve here as a good example.

At the beginning of our five-day workshop, one of the participants, a postmenopausal woman, shared with the group how much she had always wanted to have children and how much she suffered because this had not happened. In the middle of the Holotropic Breathwork session, in which she was sitting for a young man, she suddenly pulled the upper part of her partner's body into her lap and started to rock and comfort him. Her timing could not have been worse; as we found out later during the sharing, he was at the time in the middle of a past life experience that featured him as a powerful Viking warrior on a military expedition. He described with a great sense of humor how he initially tried to experience her rocking as the movements of the boat on the ocean; however, when she added comforting baby talk, that brought him back to reality.

It is usually quite easy to recognize when the breather is regressed to early infancy. In a really deep age regression, all the wrinkles in the face tend to disappear and the individual can actually look and behave like an infant. This can involve various infantile postures and gestures, as well as copious salivation and thumb-sucking. Other times, the appropriateness of offering physical contact is obvious from the context, for example, when the breather just finished reliving biological birth and looks lost and forlorn. The maternal needs of the woman in the Esalen workshop were so strong that they took over and she was unable to objectively assess the situation and act appropriately.

The use of nourishing physical contact in holotropic states of consciousness to heal traumas caused by abandonment, rejection, and emotional deprivation was developed by two London psychoanalysts, Pauline McCririck and Joyce Martin; they used this method with their LSD patients under the name of *fusion therapy* (Martin 1965; McCririck 1966). During their sessions, their clients spent several hours in deep age regression, lying on a couch covered with a blanket, while Joyce or Pauline lay by their side, holding them in close embrace, as a good mother would do to comfort her child.

Their revolutionary method effectively divided and polarized the community of LSD therapists. Some of the practitioners realized that this was a very powerful and logical way to heal "traumas by omission," emotional problems caused by emotional deprivation and bad mothering. Others were horrified by this radical "anaclitic therapy"; they warned that close physical contact between therapists and clients in a non-ordinary state of consciousness would cause irreversible damage to the transference/countertransference relationship.

In 1964, one of us (Stan) had a chance to hear Joyce and Pauline's lecture on fusion therapy at the First International Congress of Social Psychiatry in London and was among those who were fascinated by it. It was clear to him that the "trauma by omission" could not be healed by talking therapy. He asked Joyce and Pauline many questions about their unorthodox approach and when they saw his genuine interest, they invited him to spend some time at their clinic on Welbeck Street in London to meet their patients and have a personal experience with their approach. Stan was impressed when he found out how much their clients benefited from the nourishing physical contact they had received in their psychedelic sessions. Talking to the patients, it also became clear to him that Joyce and Pauline encountered considerably less transference problems than an average Freudian analyst with his or her detached "dead-pan" approach to therapy.

Having heard enthusiastic stories from Joyce and Pauline's LSD patients, Stan became deeply interested in having a firsthand experience of fusion therapy. Here is his account of this session:

> My own session with Pauline was truly extraordinary. Although both of us were fully dressed and separated by a blanket, I experienced a profound age regression into my early infancy and identified with an infant nursing on the breast of a good mother and feeling the contact with her naked body. Then the experience deepened, and I became a fetus in a good womb blissfully floating in the amniotic fluid.
>
> For more than three hours of clock time, a period that subjectively felt like eternity, I kept experiencing both of those situations—"good breast" and "good womb"—simultaneously or in an alternating fashion. I felt connected with my mother by the flow of two nourishing liquids—milk and blood—both of which felt at that point sacred. The experience culminated in an experience of a numinous union with the Great Mother Goddess, rather than a human mother. Needless to say, I found the session profoundly healing.

At the International Conference on LSD Psychotherapy held in May 1965 in Amityville, New York, Joyce and Pauline showed their fascinating film on the use of the fusion technique in psychedelic therapy (Martin 1965). In a heated discussion that followed, most of the questions revolved around the transference/countertransference issues. Pauline provided a very interesting and convincing explanation why this approach presented less problems in this regard than the orthodox Freudian approach. She pointed out that most patients who come to therapy experienced in their infancy and childhood lack of affection from their parents. The cold attitude of the Freudian analyst tends to reactivate the resulting emotional wounds and triggers desperate attempts on the part of the patients to get the attention and satisfaction that had been denied to them.

By contrast, according to Pauline, fusion therapy provided a corrective experience by satisfying the old anaclitic cravings. Having their emotional wounds healed, the patients recognized that the therapist was not an appropriate sexual object and were able to find suitable partners outside of the therapeutic relationship. Pauline explained that this paralleled the situation in the early development of object relationships. Individuals who receive adequate mothering in infancy and childhood are able to emotionally detach from their mothers and find mature relationships. By contrast, those who experienced emotional deprivation remain pathologically fixated and go through life craving and seeking satisfaction of primitive infantile needs.

As a result of his experience in London, Stan occasionally used fusion therapy in the psychedelic research program at the Maryland Research Center, particularly in work with terminal cancer patients. In the mid-1970s, when we developed Holotropic Breathwork, anaclitic support became an integral part of our workshops and training.

5. Mandala drawing: The expressive power of art

Mandala is a Sanskrit word meaning literally "circle" or "completion." In the most general sense, this term can be used for any design showing complex geometrical symmetry, such as a spider web, arrangement of petals in a flower or blossom, sea shell (e.g., a sand dollar), image in a kaleidoscope, stained-glass window in a Gothic cathedral or labyrinth design on its floor. The mandala is a visual construct that can be easily grasped by the eye, since it corresponds to the structure of the organ of optical perception. The iris of the eye is itself a simple mandala form.

In ritual and spiritual practice, mandalas are images, which can be drawn, painted, modeled, or danced. In the Tantric branches of Hinduism, Buddhism, and Jainism this word refers to elaborate cosmograms composed of elementary geometrical forms (points, lines, triangles, squares, and circles), lotus blossoms, and complex archetypal figures and sceneries. They are used as important meditation aids, which help practitioners to focus attention inside and lead them to specific states of consciousness.

Although the use of mandalas in the Tantric branches of Hinduism, Buddhism, and Jainism has been particularly refined and sophisticated, the art of mandala drawing as part of spiritual practice can be found in many other cultures. Examples of beautiful mandalas are the *nierikas*, yarn paintings of the Huichol Indians from Central Mexico portraying visions induced by ritual ingestion of peyote. Elaborate sand paintings used in the healing and other rituals of the Navajo people and the bark paintings of the Australian Aborigines also feature many intricate mandala patterns.

The use of mandalas in spiritual and religious practice of various cultures and in alchemy attracted the attention of the Swiss psychiatrist C. G. Jung, who noticed that similar patterns appeared in the paintings of his patients at a certain stage of their psychospiritual development. According to him, the mandala is a "psychological expression of the totality of the self." In his own words: "The severe pattern imposed by a circular image of this kind compensates for the disorder and confusion of the psychic state—namely, through the construction of a central point to which everything is related" (Jung 1959b).

Our own use of mandala drawing was inspired by the work of Joan Kellogg, who was a member of our psychedelic research team at the Maryland Psychiatric Research Center in Baltimore. When she had worked as an art therapist in psychiatric hospitals in Wycoff and Paterson, New Jersey, Joan had given hundreds of patients a piece of paper with an outline of a circle and painting utensils and asked them to paint whatever came to their mind. She was able to find significant correlations between their psychological problems and clinical diagnosis and specific aspects of their paintings, such as choice of colors, preference for sharp or round shapes, use of concentric circles, dividing the mandala into sections, and respecting or not respecting boundaries of the circle.

At the Maryland Psychiatric Research Center, Joan compared the mandalas the participants in the program painted before and after their psychedelic sessions, looking for significant correlations between the basic features of the mandalas, the content of psychedelic experiences, and the outcome of therapy. We have found her method to be extremely useful in our work with Holotropic Breathwork. Joan herself saw the mandala drawing as a psychological test and described in several papers the criteria for interpretation of their various aspects (Kellogg 1977a and b, 1978). In our work, we do not interpret the mandalas and do not draw diagnostic conclusions from them. We use them in the processing groups simply as a source of information about the breathers' experiences. We will describe the work with the mandalas in a later section of this book (pages 91ff).

CHAPTER FOUR

The Practice of Holotropic Breathwork

1. Use of Holotropic Breathwork in individual sessions and groups

Holotropic Breathwork can be conducted in the form of individual sessions and in small or large groups. Many certified Holotropic Breathwork practitioners offer individual sessions in their private practice, both for people who are interested in experiencing breathwork for personal growth and for clients with minor emotional and psychosomatic issues, who would otherwise be able to do their inner work in group settings. This is not the best use of the potential of Holotropic Breathwork, since conducting sessions in group settings has distinct advantages. The most obvious of these are of practical, economic, and financial nature. While an individual session requires constant presence of one or two people, at least one of whom is an experienced therapist, in groups the ratio is one fully trained facilitator to eight to ten participants.

In Holotropic Breathwork groups, participants do most of their inner work without needing any external help and many of the situations that require assistance can be handled by sitters, including those who do not have any previous experience with Holotropic Breathwork. With some help and guidance from trained facilitators, sitters are able to create a safe emotional and physical environment for breathers and prevent them from interfering with each other. If necessary, they also remind their partners to keep a faster pace of breathing, take them to and from the bathroom, provide nourishing physical contact, bring them a cup of water, hand them Kleenexes, cover them with a blanket, and provide some other basic care.

While in the groups it is not much of a problem if some participants' Holotropic Breathwork experiences last longer than usual, this can be very challenging for therapists, who have fixed rigid schedules. There is no way of predicting the length of an individual session; the duration of sessions varies and it is mandatory that the facilitators stay with the breathers until the process is completed for the day. The usual practice is therefore to schedule individual breathwork sessions at the end of the therapy day; this naturally limits the number of sessions a practitioner can offer at any particular time.

There are also psychological advantages to group Holotropic Breathwork sessions that make the work more profound and effective than individual sessions allow. Sharing a holotropic state of consciousness with a number of other people in a large room, listening to powerful music combined with the sounds of the other participants, generates a very intense experiential field. The resulting atmosphere makes it easier for breathers to let go of their usual psychological defenses and to allow their unconscious material to surface and find emotional and physical expression.

The opportunity of sharing an embarrassing or private experience with others represents another significant advantage of working in a group. In holotropic states of consciousness, people often encounter sensitive material that they consider ethically or aesthetically objectionable, such as violent, sexual, or blasphemous imagery; memories of incest; or antisocial tendencies. Breathers may have difficulties in confiding such experiences to another human being and typically expect a negative reaction—moral judgment, disgust, or rejection.

When such disclosures happen in private sessions and the therapists do not respond with critical judgment, clients may attribute the therapists' tolerance to their special training that prevents them from reacting the way they really feel, or to years of their clinical experience with abnormal individuals that have immunized them toward deviant aspects of human nature. Under these circumstances, the overtly nonjudgmental and accepting behavior of the therapists is thus easily perceived as a contrived professional stance and it does not bring the corrective experience that it would provide if it came from an ordinary member of the human community.

For this reason, participation in a sharing group featuring a representative sample of the general population can be extremely redeeming. Listening to the stories of others, we discover that they too harbor emotions, fantasies, and tendencies that we ourselves consider reproachable and manifest behaviors that in our own judgment make us uniquely immoral and despicable. This brings to a sharp relief the recognition that these are aspects of human nature that "flesh is heir to" and that we all are "in the same boat."

As a matter of fact, the reaction of the group to honest disclosure of the material from the deep unconscious tends to be exactly the opposite of what the individual expects. As a rule, others offer understanding, compassion, and warm emotional support. Sincere confession of a group member often encourages them to be more trusting and open about dark aspects of their own inner life. Group work using holotropic states of consciousness typically leads to meaningful bonding between participants and rapidly generates a sense of belonging. Scottish American cultural anthropologist Victor Turner spent his professional career studying rites of passage of native cultures. According to him, sharing non-ordinary states of consciousness in a ritual context leads to the development of a sense of community (*communitas*) (Turner 1969, 1974).

Under the right circumstances, Holotropic Breathwork can be used with psychiatric patients who have serious emotional and psychosomatic problems. However, for most of them it would be difficult or impossible to participate in groups, which require the ability to alternate in the roles of breathers and sitters and to participate constructively in the processing of the experiences of others. Such patients need the undivided attention of an experienced therapist or, ideally, a male/female team for the entire duration of the session and a special setting where twenty-four-hour supervision is available.

In the following sections, we focus on the steps and conditions necessary for safe and effective practice of Holotropic Breathwork in the context of small and large introductory groups. We describe how to create the physical setting and interpersonal support system for this work and how to prepare the participants theoretically and practically for the sessions. A special section of this chapter is dedicated to the physical and emotional contraindications and it outlines the basic criteria for the screening of participants. We then discuss how to start and conduct a Holotropic Breathwork session, describe the spectrum of holotropic experiences, and explain the roles of the facilitators and sitters. The last section of this chapter discusses the work with the mandalas and provides the basic principles of leading the processing sessions.

2. Setting and interpersonal support system

Finding a suitable place for Holotropic Breathwork workshops and training can be challenging. To be effective and evocative, the music used in breathwork sessions needs sufficient volume, particularly in the first part and during the culmination period of the sessions. In addition, many facilitators include in their repertoire shamanic, ethnic, ritual, and spiritual music—African, Indian, Tibetan, Balinese, and Aboriginal Australian recordings—that might sound strange, uncanny, or frightening to groups of people who are unfamiliar with it.

For example, during our three-year training in Europe, we received complaints from a group of Swiss farmers, who were convinced that our work was "from the devil." We later discovered that they heard through open windows of our breathing room pieces like the *ketjak* (the Balinese monkey chant) and the multivocal chanting of the Tibetan Gyoto monks and Tuva shamans. The 1992 conference of the International Transpersonal Association (ITA) in Prague was picketed by fundamentalist Christians, because the program included the shamanic Deer Dance of the Huichol Indians from Central Mexico. On other occasions, recordings of Sufi *dhikrs*, Tuareg chants, Moroccan trance music, throat music of the Inuit Eskimo people, or African Burundi drumming received similar reactions.

Participants in Holotropic Breathwork sessions need to have the freedom to fully express whatever is emerging in their sessions. We have regularly heard loud crying and screaming, as well as baby talk, gibberish, talking in tongues and foreign languages, a broad range of animal sounds, cursing, and chanting. This can create a very unusual acoustic atmosphere, where harmonious music coincides with a broad array of cacophony. On occasion, it is not easy to tell what is coming from the speakers and what originates in the room. For uninitiated audiences, this can be an additional source of wild fantasies and strong negative reactions.

Paradoxically, most people participating in Holotropic Breathwork as breathers may easily adjust to a wide range of sounds that are part of the session, yet they tend to have an adverse reaction to intrusions from the outside world. Over the years, we have experienced many instances of such interferences: competing music from another event, hotel personnel breaking into the room, demanding that we stop the music because it was louder than they expected, sounds of sirens from a nearby fire station, and others. Once lightning struck the building in which we were working and a fire inspector insisted that we evacuate the room full of vulnerable people in the midst of their experience, or "in process" as we call it. Even ordinary conversations can be disturbing, particularly during the ending period of the session when the music is quiet and the mood is mostly meditative.

When we are looking for a suitable place to conduct Holotropic Breathwork, we try to find a retreat center or a hotel with a large room, which is sufficiently isolated and removed from other activities. It is essential that we may play music at full volume and generate a considerable amount of noise and, at the same time, are not exposed to any external interferences ourselves. The size of the room or hall that is needed depends on the number of participants; a ballpark figure is about twenty-five square feet (two square meters) per participant.

Ideally, it should be possible to cover the windows and significantly reduce the amount of light in the room; this is particularly important if participants do not have eyeshades. There has to be sufficient light for the facilitators and sitters to see what the breathers are doing. However, bright light tends to interfere with the experiences of the breathers unless it comes from within. Intense holotropic experiences, particularly ecstatic ones, can generate visions of radiant light independent of the illumination of the room, even in complete darkness.

An additional critical requirement for a good setting during Holotropic Breathwork is the proximity of the restrooms. If the bathrooms are too far, or getting there involves stairs or an elevator, the breathers tend to come out of the holotropic state. Under the best of circumstances—convenient location of the bathrooms and experienced partners—the breathers do not have to open their eyes on the way to the bathroom; they continue to breathe faster and stay in the process. The breathers can walk behind the sitters with their hands on the sitters' shoulders, or the sitters can guide the breathers while walking with them side by side.

During their experience, for comfort and safety, the breathers lie on a soft surface. If the room has a thick rug, particularly one with an elastic pad, sleeping bags that the participants bring from home might be perfectly adequate. If the floor is hard, we provide mats or mattresses of sufficient size, which give breathers enough freedom to move. The mats are augmented with other soft and warm items, such as pillows, cushions, blankets, zabutons, and zafus. If the site of the seminar cannot provide them, we ask participants to bring them or use some other resources.

Ideally, Holotropic Breathwork is conducted in a residential facility. This creates a safe, familiar environment, particularly for those participants whose breathing sessions take place in the afternoon hours. These people need enough time to integrate the experience to the extent that they are able to safely operate outside the workshop setting. The travel to the place of their residence might be challenging, particularly if they have to drive a car, deal with city traffic, or brave an onslaught of bad weather. In addition, some of them may face at home a complex interpersonal situation for which they might not be ready after a profound emotional experience.

Occasionally, we have the good fortune to find beautiful facilities, where we are completely alone or in a sufficiently secluded area so that participants do not have to mix with people unfamiliar with what we are doing. More frequently, our group shares the facility with other groups or individual guests. This situation tends to present problems of two kinds. The appearance and demeanor of people in holotropic states of consciousness is often unusual and tends to baffle or even upset outsiders who witness it. Conversely, participants in our groups, who are sensitized by their deep experiences, need a quiet and meditative environment after the session. They might find it difficult and disturbing to face the busy and noisy hotel environment.

Whether our seminar site gives us complete privacy or we have to share it with other guests, previous to the workshop we face the task of explaining to the management and to the personnel what we are doing and what they need to expect: We will be playing loud music and the breathers will be making unfamiliar sounds. The management also needs assurance that the non-ordinary states of consciousness we work with are induced by natural means and that no psychoactive substances will be involved. An additional issue that needs explanation and clarification is the use of close physical contact.

Many problems related to the use of Holotropic Breathwork in hotels or conference centers can be avoided if the members of the staff have the opportunity to personally participate in the session and experience the process. In places that we repeatedly used for our workshops or for our training, we have always invited people running the facility to join the group in the breathwork sessions. The need to thoroughly familiarize all those witnessing our work is based on our past experiences. Examples of the problems that can arise at the interface with the outside world can be found in chapter 6, entitled "Trials and Tribulations of Holotropic Breathwork Practitioners" (pages 109ff.).

Some of the best places in which we have worked in the past had features that made them ideal for intense inner work. They were located in beautiful natural surroundings—near an ocean, a lake, or a river, in the mountains, meadows, or forests. The Esalen Institute in Big Sur, California, with its famous hot springs and proximity to the Pacific Ocean and the Santa Lucia Mountains, and the Hollyhock Farm situated on the spectacular shore of Vancouver Bay in Cortes Island in British Columbia deserve special notice in this regard.

Following powerful breathwork sessions, the sensory channels of the participants are wide open; to use William Blake's expression, their "doors of perception have been cleansed." Their experience of colors, sounds, smells, and tastes is greatly enhanced and enriched and they feel close to nature. A leisurely swim in the ocean, river, or a lake can bring echoes of memories of the beginning of our existence in the amniotic fluid of the womb or even of the beginning of life in the primeval ocean. This can greatly facilitate successful integration of the experience. Under more modest circumstances, a hot tub or a warm bath may have a similar effect.

Closeness to nature and refined sensory acuity is also reflected in the attitude toward food. After Holotropic Breathwork sessions, people are attracted to and appreciate healthy, carefully prepared natural food with interesting tastes, colors, and textures. They are put off by sloppily served, artificial "fast food," or heavy and oily meals to which they might not object in their ordinary life. We take this into consideration when we negotiate with the facility that hosts the workshop.

3. Theoretical preparation of participants

Good theoretical preparation is an essential prerequisite for effective work with Holotropic Breathwork. There is an important reason for it: using this approach to self-exploration and therapy involves work with holotropic states of consciousness. Since the Industrial and Scientific Revolutions, Western civilization has embraced and glorified reason and rejected holotropic experiences and everything connected with them as irrational. Materialistic science has relegated the perspective on life and the worldview revealed in spiritual practice and in ritual activities to the realm of fairy tales and psychopathology. As a result, people in industrial societies are unfamiliar with holotropic states and have many misconceptions about them that need to be dispelled and rectified.

We usually start the preparation by asking participants the question: "How many of you have experienced in your everyday life non-ordinary states of consciousness, such as intense experiences during spiritual practice, in psychedelic self-experimentation, in shamanic rituals, in sessions of experiential psychotherapy, in near-death situations, or during spontaneous psychospiritual crises ('spiritual emergencies')." We then draw their attention to the fact that traditional psychiatrists refer to non-ordinary states of consciousness of any kind as "altered states" and see them as manifestations of mental disease. This implies that the information conveyed by them is inauthentic and represents a distortion or impairment of the correct way of experiencing ourselves and the world.

We explain that this might be appropriate in relation to some pathological conditions, such as deliria associated with encephalitis, meningitis, typhoid fever and other infectious diseases, uremia, and cardiovascular and degenerative disorders of the brain. However, the state of consciousness induced by Holotropic Breathwork belongs to a large and important subgroup of non-ordinary states of consciousness ("holotropic states"), for which such a classification is wrong and misguided. Here consciousness is changed qualitatively, but is not impaired or compromised; under the right circumstances, experiences in this mode have a healing, transformative, and evolutionary potential and can convey new and useful information.

Here belong the experiences that shamans encounter during their initiatory crises and use in the work with their clients, trance states that people in native cultures induce in rites of passage, and the experiential adventures that the initiates underwent in ancient mysteries of death and rebirth. Additional examples are experiences induced by various "technologies of the sacred," procedures for inducing holotropic states developed by various religious groups—different schools of yoga, Theravada, Mahayana, Zen, and Tibetan Buddhism, Taoism, Sufism, and mystical Christianity. Western civilization encountered holotropic states on a mass scale during the psychedelic revolution of the 1960s. Unfortunately, the irresponsible and chaotic nature of this movement obscured the enormous positive value of these states.

Correctly understood and properly supported, holotropic states are not pathological and abnormal; they have a healing, transformative, and even evolutionary potential. They also have an invaluable heuristic value; work with them provides new and revolutionary insights concerning the nature of consciousness, the human psyche in health and disease, and some of the deepest philosophical and metaphysical questions (Grof 1998, 2000). Modern consciousness research conducted in the second half of the twentieth century showed the errors made in the course of the Industrial and Scientific Revolutions concerning holotropic states.

In their enthusiasm about the power of reason and its enormous potential, the fledgling materialistic scientists rejected everything that was not rational as embarrassing leftovers from the infancy of humanity and from the Dark Ages. In their juvenile hubris, they did not realize that not everything that is non-rational is irrational. The domain of holotropic states and of mystical experiences is not irrational and abnormal, it is transrational and in many ways supernormal; it includes and transcends the rational. In the last several decades, transpersonally oriented researchers from various disciplines have realized the critical importance of the baby that was thrown out with the bathwater in the era of the Enlightenment and the Scientific Revolution.

After clarifying the misconceptions that exist in our culture with regard to non-ordinary states of consciousness, we share with participants some of the things that we discussed in some detail earlier in this book. We explain the meaning of the name *holotropic* ("moving toward wholeness") that we have given to our form of breathwork, describe the basic characteristics of holotropic experiences, and outline the radical changes we have to make in our understanding of consciousness and of the human psyche to work effectively and successfully with Holotropic Breathwork and other approaches using holotropic states.

We describe briefly the extended cartography of the psyche, including the perinatal and transpersonal domains, and expound the multilevel nature of emotional and psychosomatic symptoms and the healing mechanisms operating on various levels of the psyche. We spend some time discussing spirituality as an important and legitimate dimension of the psyche and of the universal scheme of things. This includes making a clear distinction between genuine spirituality based on personal experience, which is universal, nondenominational, and all-inclusive, and organized religions with their dogmas, often plagued by sectarian chauvinism, extremism, and fundamentalism.

Probably the most important task of the preparation is discussion of inner healing intelligence and trust in the process, something that distinguishes work with holotropic states from verbal therapies using techniques based on specific psychological theories. Closely related to this basic principle is the emphasis on letting go of all programs for the session—what we would like to experience, what issues we should work on, and which areas we would like to avoid. We stress the importance of staying in the present moment, focusing on emotions and physical feelings, and refraining from intellectual analysis. It is useful to remind participants that in experiential work using holotropic states "the mind is the worst enemy." If we surrender to the process, the holotropic state will automatically bring to the surface unconscious contents associated with strong emotional charge which are ready for processing, and will determine the order in which they will emerge.

4. Screening for physical and emotional contraindications

An essential part of the preparation for breathwork sessions is discussion of physical and emotional contraindications for the work with holotropic states. Ideally, the screening of participants for contraindications would be done by correspondence before they come to the workshop. We have found out that it is very difficult to send people home when some serious health problems are discovered immediately before the session. By that time, they have made their decision and commitment and invested time and money into coming into the workshop. We will very likely hear many explanations and justifications as to why it is all right for them to stay and comments like: "Don't worry, I will take full responsibility for what happens," and "I will sign a release." This, of course, does not free the organizers and facilitators from moral or legal responsibility.

After some difficulties that we had encountered during onsite screening, we decided to send all applicants a medical questionnaire and ask them to fill it and return it before they make their travel arrangements. The questionnaire contains questions about the conditions and situations that we need to discuss before the applicant is accepted into the workshop. We inform the applicants that they would not be able to participate until all the problematic issues in their medical questionnaire are cleared.

Our primary concern is about serious cardiovascular disorders—high blood pressure, aneurysms, a history of heart attacks, brain hemorrhage, myocarditis, atrial fibrillation, or other similar problems. The reason for this is that the breathwork session can bring to the surface traumatic memories associated with powerful emotions, which could be dangerous for participants with such conditions. These memories are typically repressed and subjected to amnesia, so that it is impossible to anticipate their emergence in advance. Some of these memories can also involve considerable physical tensions and pressures. Reliving one's birth is typically associated with physical stress, as well as intense emotions, and could present risks for people with serious cardiac problems.

When the problem is high blood pressure, we require that it be medically controlled. Another factor on which we can base our decision whether such person would be able to participate is the highest level the blood pressure had reached before it was controlled. If we are not able to evaluate the situation ourselves, we can ask the applicants' attending physicians or cardiologists for the assessment of these individuals' physical condition. Since it is unlikely that these physicians would be familiar with Holotropic Breathwork, we can get the necessary information indirectly, by asking if their patients could do some heavier sports involving activities that would put them under comparable degree of stress as Holotropic Breathwork, such as bench-pressing and weight lifting.

The situation regarding cardiovascular problems is paradoxical. On the one hand, psychological factors, such as traumatic memories from the perinatal period, infancy, childhood, and later life, play an important role in the genesis of cardiovascular diseases. Holotropic Breathwork is a very valuable tool for clearing such traumatic imprints. It can therefore be used in the prevention of cardiovascular problems or even in their treatment when they are still in their early stages. However, once these diseases progress, the previously functional (energetic) changes become organic (structural) and constitute a contraindication for deep emotional work.

Another important consideration is pregnancy. It does not represent an absolute contraindication; the decision whether the pregnant woman can participate and in what way is made individually. One important factor is the stage of the pregnancy. Women who are reliving their birth in a holotropic state of consciousness tend to experience themselves also as delivering, either simultaneously, or in an alternating fashion. This is not just a psychological matter; it has very distinct physiological concomitants. It often involves intense contractions of the uterus that could trigger a premature delivery in advanced stages of pregnancy. Occasionally, we have seen non-pregnant women who started menstruating in the middle of their cycle after a powerful birth experience. This clearly reflected the degree to which the uterus can be physiologically engaged in this process.

Since the combined experience of reliving birth and delivering is the only situation that in Holotropic Breathwork sessions presents a danger for the pregnancy, pregnant women can safely have a wide range of other experiences. For this reason, we have often accepted pregnant women into the workshop after making a specific agreement with them. They had to promise that they would not continue with the accelerated breathing if it starts taking them to the birth/delivery experience. Although we have made this arrangement with a large number of pregnant women over the years (mostly in earlier stages of pregnancy), we have never seen any indication that the breathing posed danger to the fetus and to the continuation of pregnancy. Naturally, the work with pregnant women has to be careful and considerate; sitters and facilitators need to be aware of their vulnerable condition and protect them from external insults that could mechanically endanger their pregnancy. This is a consideration that applies equally to these women's everyday lives and is not specific to Holotropic Breathwork.

Another condition that requires attention is a history of convulsive disorders, particularly grand mal epilepsy. It is known that hyperventilation tends to accentuate epileptic brainwaves (spikes, sharp waves, and spike-and-wave discharges). This phenomenon is actually used by neurologists as a diagnostic test for epilepsy. We were thus justifiably concerned that in participants with a history of epilepsy faster breathing could induce a grand mal seizure. However, we have never refused participation in the workshop to individuals with this history. We have prepared the facilitators and sitters for what might happen and have given them instructions as to what to do. Grand mal seizures are very dramatic and can be extremely scary for laypersons. However, our concerns proved unwarranted; in over thirty-five thousand sessions we have conducted over the years, we have seen only one grand mal epileptic seizure. It occurred in a participant who already had a history of this type of seizures. Following the episode, he was confused and fell asleep. After about two hours of sleep, he was absolutely fine and actually felt better than before the session.

Contraindications related to physical injuries and operations can easily be addressed using common sense. Participants who had recent physical traumas or operations either should not participate in the breathwork or should not receive bodywork in the afflicted areas. In individuals who are close to recovery, the physical work conducted with them has to be very careful, reflecting the seriousness and timing of the injury or surgery. This applies to bone fractures, herniated disks, dislocated shoulders or knees, incompletely healed surgical wounds, and similar afflictions. People with debilitating diseases might not have enough energy and stamina to carry on the breathing for an extended period of time. Persons who have had in the past detachment of the retina or are suffering from a type of glaucoma associated with elevated intraocular pressure should not engage in a form of bodywork that could increase the pressure in the eye. Faster breathing in and of itself does not have an adverse effect on this condition.

If the applicant for the workshop is suffering from a contagious disease, good judgment has to be used to determine whether it is safe for others to allow him or her to participate in the group. If it is a respiratory disease associated with coughing and sneezing, we apply the same criteria as we would in everyday situations—such an individual does not belong to a social milieu that involves close personal contact and should stay home. Different criteria apply to persons who are HIV positive or have AIDS. Here research has shown that the danger of contagion is minimal, with the exception of direct transmission of body fluids, particularly blood. Over the years, we have observed only a handful of situations where the breathwork triggered nosebleeds. Although these were rare cases, in view of the dangerous nature of the disease, we decided to have rubber gloves available in the workshops in case facilitators or sitters would have to deal with blood.

AIDS is a disease that triggers intense fear in many people. However irrational this might be, it has to be respected. If there are persons suffering from AIDS in the group (hopefully we would learn about this from the medical questionnaire), we feel strongly that their sitters should know about this fact. They then can decide whether or not they feel comfortable with their role as sitters under these circumstances. Holotropic Breathwork can involve a lot of close contact and it is important that it is offered unambiguously to make the breather feel accepted. For a person regressed to early childhood this could mean the difference between a deep corrective experience and a painful reinforcement of a sense of rejection. Our experience has been that there are always people in the group who have no problems sitting with individuals suffering from this disease. If there are two HIV/AIDS positive individuals in the groups, they might also decide to sit with each other.

Psychogenic asthma is a disorder that tends to respond favorably to Holotropic Breathwork combined with bodywork. We have seen in participants in our training and workshops many instances of significant alleviation or even lasting disappearance of asthmatic attacks. The general strategy of working with asthma is to release pent-up emotions and physical blockages responsible for the swelling, inflammation, and constriction of the bronchi and release them by sounds, body tremors, grimacing, gagging, and any other channels that become available. However, individuals who have suffered from chronic asthma for many years often develop serious cardiovascular problems. Once it happens, it is risky to expose them to the amount and degree of emotional and physical stress necessary for clearing the respiratory pathways. The decision whether or not to accept individuals suffering from asthma into a breathwork group requires careful evaluation of their physical condition. Whenever we work with asthmatic individuals, we always ask them to bring their inhalers into the session. If at any point their breathing becomes too difficult, they can use these devices and attain symptomatic relief.

Holotropic Breathwork has also very important emotional contraindications that have to be taken into consideration. While the physical contraindications are independent of the circumstances and apply whenever and wherever this method is used, what we consider emotional contraindications depends on the set and setting. If we are conducting a short-term workshop, the criteria for screening are much stricter than those we would use for work in a residential facility that has provisions for an overnight stay and a trained staff experienced in the work with holotropic states. If these conditions are not met, it would not be wise to conduct breathwork sessions with individuals who have a history of serious emotional problems that in the past required psychiatric hospitalization.

As we discussed earlier, healing in any work with holotropic states typically involves temporary activation of symptoms. In people with reasonably good emotional and social adjustment, this process leads to successful resolution of the surfacing unconscious material within several hours. Some individuals have had in their past spontaneous episodes of emotional disturbance of long duration, which they were not able to contain and which required hospitalization. For them, Holotropic Breathwork could bring to the surface a large amount of deep unconscious material that might require days to work through. This could produce serious technical problems if it occurs in a facility rented for a specific amount of time (e.g., Friday evening to Sunday noon).

From the perspective of a traditional psychiatrist, if a breathwork session releases large amounts of unconscious material that cannot be brought to a successful resolution within the context of the workshop, it has caused a "psychotic break." This would then create the reputation of Holotropic Breathwork as being a dangerous and risky procedure. Within the philosophical framework of holotropic therapy, this situation presents logistic problems because of the circumstances but, in and of itself, it constitutes a major therapeutic opportunity. It means that very important traumatic material from the deep unconscious has become available for conscious processing. With the right understanding, guidance, and management, this could be extremely beneficial and result in radical healing and positive personality transformation. The same principle applies if the opening of the unconscious was spontaneous, was triggered by a psychedelic session, started during rigorous meditation practice, or occurred in the context of some other powerful experiential method of psychotherapy.

The difference in interpretation of the same situation reflects the paradigm clash that we are currently experiencing in psychiatry and psychology in regard to the understanding of the nature and function of symptoms. As we discussed earlier, mainstream clinicians tend to see them as problems and use their intensity as a measure of the seriousness of the disorder. As a result, they focus much of their effort on finding ways of suppressing symptoms and consider their alleviation to be clinical improvement. For Holotropic Breathwork facilitators, symptoms are the expression of a healing impulse of the organism and represent its attempt to free itself from its traumatic past. Their intensity then indicates the depth, scope, and speed of the healing process.

However, to be therapeutic and transformative, this process has to be recognized as such and requires special conditions for its successful completion. It might require a twenty-four-hour residential facility and a staff trained to work with holotropic states. The lack of centers of this kind is the major problem in working with holotropic states of longer duration, whether these are spontaneous ("spiritual emergencies") or are triggered by psychedelics, sessions of experiential psychotherapy, spiritual practice, or near-death experiences. Centers that have existed in the past, such as John Perry's Diabasis in San Francisco and Chrysalis near San Diego or Barbara Findeisen's Pocket Ranch in Geyserville, California, inevitably ran into financial problems and sooner or later had to be closed.

Treatment in these centers was substantially cheaper than the treatment in mainstream psychiatric hospitals with their astronomical overhead. However, the clients were unable to receive compensation for their treatment by the insurance companies because the therapy offered in these alternative centers was not recognized and acknowledged as legitimate by the medical and legal authorities. Although occasional subsidies and donations to these centers somewhat eased this situation, clients had to cover a substantial portion of the costs from their own pockets and these alternative facilities generally were not able to survive for an extended period of time.

The major problem in dealing with prolonged reactions to Holotropic Breathwork (or any other experiential therapy) is thus the absence of twenty-four-hour residential centers, where the process could be brought to successful resolution and completion by competent, specially trained facilitators. When these conditions are not met, people needing around-the-clock care to complete their emotional process might have to seek help in a conventional psychiatric facility. Under the present circumstances, this would very likely mean the diagnosis of "acute psychotic reaction" and routine administration of suppressive psychopharmacological medication, which would interfere with positive resolution and successful closure of the episode.

Holotropic Breathwork can actually be used in the therapy of a wide range of emotional and psychosomatic disorders, including spiritual emergencies, if we have the appropriate facility and support system. However, until the theory and practice of psychiatry is revolutionized and centers based on the new paradigm readily available, a history of psychiatric treatment will represent a contraindication for participation in short Holotropic Breathwork workshops. Occasionally, we have made exceptions to this rule, if the nature of the episodes for which the applicants were hospitalized met our criteria for spiritual emergency rather than more serious conditions, such as paranoid schizophrenia or severe bipolar disorder.

5. Practical instructions for breathwork sessions

Unless Holotropic Breathwork is conducted on a one-to-one basis as a private session with a facilitator or under the guidance of a therapist, it involves working in pairs. In each session half of the participants breathe and the other half function as sitters. Choosing a partner is an important part of the preparation. We ourselves do not have any fixed rules for this process, but we do have a few suggestions. We warn participants, particularly those who have not yet experienced the breathwork, that automatically choosing as a partner a person they know well might not be the best choice. Working with a person with whom we have an emotional relationship has disadvantages as well as advantages. It could be more difficult to open up and show certain aspects of ourselves to an individual when we have a strong investment in the relationship. It might also be difficult to watch a close person go through experiences that are emotionally difficult and painful. Another potential problem is that the session might result in transference/countertransference issues that might carry over into everyday life and create problems.

Here is an example from one of our Canadian workshops. After we had explained the pitfalls of choosing close persons as partners, a couple with no previous experience with Holotropic Breathwork decided to work as a dyad, disregarding the warning. "We have a great relationship," they asserted, "there will be no problems." In the first session, the wife was a breather and her husband was her sitter. About an hour into the session, the husband started experiencing a strong reaction to the evocative situation in the room—the intense music, emotional outbursts of his wife, and the loud screams of the other breathers. In a short time, he was not able to function as a sitter and "went into process." He lay down and, instead of being a sitter, he became an experiencer; we had to take care of both him and his wife. This was a residential workshop and we had a room adjacent to theirs. The two of us had difficulties falling asleep that night; the couple was fighting and we could hear their loud verbal exchanges. Among others, we heard the wife's angry reproaches: "You are never there for me and this is just another one of those!"

Over the years, we have seen many instances where combinations—wives/husbands, girlfriends/boyfriends, parents/children, bosses/employees, and even therapists/clients—worked out well when they involved experienced breathworkers. However, for the aforementioned reasons, these types of dyads generally are not recommended for newcomers. If during the session problems arise between breathers and sitters, much can be done in the processing group to dissolve them and participants can learn from this situation important lessons. Even then, it is better when this occurs with people who are not part of each other's life, so that no residual interpersonal tensions are carried into the partners' everyday life.

We generally recommend that participants do not spend much time trying to find the "right partner." We have seen repeatedly extraordinary synchronicities, when people who chose each other randomly, or even ended up as partners without having a choice at all, found out that they were perfect for each other, because they shared important problems, represented exact opposites to each other, or found that their issues were complementary. This made their partnership an extremely valuable learning and healing experience. The process of choosing partners can run into unexpected difficulties when we work in countries with unfamiliar cultural norms. The section on culture-bound challenges for Holotropic Breathwork facilitators in chapter 6 of this book gives a few specific examples from our workshops in India, Japan, and Ireland.

When the group has an odd number of participants, we create a situation where one person sits for two breathers or, even better, two sitters for three breathers. In the latter situation, the sitters sit between the breathers with the extra breather in the middle; it is unlikely that both sitters would be busy at the time when the extra breather needs assistance. If possible, we choose for these special breathing arrangements people who had previously experienced Holotropic Breathwork. Facilitators need to pay special attention to the breathers who are not fully covered and be ready to step in as soon as the situation calls for assistance.

Once all the participants have found their partners, we give them the necessary instructions for the session. We describe in some detail what the session will look like and what they will be doing in their respective roles of breathers and sitters. We will discuss their respective functions in the section on conducting Holotropic Breathwork sessions (pages 66ff.). In large groups, we include one more step. We divide the participants into smaller groups. The number of participants in these groups depends on circumstances. If both breathwork sessions and the sharing for the entire group are conducted on the same day, the groups are smaller (approximately twelve participants). If the breathwork sessions and the following sharing are done with half of the group on separate days, as is the case in five-day workshops and in our training for facilitators, the number of participants in the small groups can be doubled.

After participants are divided into small groups, we introduce the certified facilitators and apprentices, who will be assisting them in the breathwork and lead their processing sessions. The small groups then spend about an hour with their facilitators to get to know each other and to give participants the chance to ask any questions they need to have answered before the session begins.

6. Preparation for the session and the relaxation exercise

Before the session begins, facilitators have the important task to make sure that the mattresses are evenly distributed in the room and that the floor space is used in the best possible way. Without guidance, participants often crowd certain areas in the room and leave others wide open. Another common problem is that the mattresses face in many possible directions; this is not a good use of the space, particularly if the number of participants is large and the size of the room barely adequate.

The best solution of the space problem is to place the mattresses parallel to each other in long lines, leaving a sufficient gap between them for participants to be able to walk in and out of the room if they need to and for facilitators to do their work. When people, particularly the breathers who are in a non-ordinary state of consciousness, have to step over bodies, pillows, and blankets on the way to the bathroom, they tend to disrupt the process of others. People in our training jokingly refer to such a situation as a "holotropic obstacle course."

Before the breathers choose a place where they want to work, it is important to warn them that the music in Holotropic Breathwork sessions can reach a fairly high volume, particularly during the culmination period. People who are sensitive to sound can thus choose places that are far from the speakers. On occasion, participants who are extremely sensitive to acoustic stimulation use foam earplugs or cotton balls to protect their delicate ears. If the room is large enough, the problem of uneven distribution of the volume can be mitigated by placing the speakers near the walls, several yards from the nearest breathers. It also helps if the speakers can be placed on high stands.

The last thing to do before we start the session is to check that all the breathers and sitters are in the room. If some people are temporarily out of the room, we wait until everybody has returned. When some of the breathers or sitters, who were expected to be in the session, have not turned up, we have to make arrangements for substitute sitting. As we mentioned before, a person with previous experience of Holotropic Breathwork can sit for two breathers or two such persons can sit for three breathers. These constellations require special attention of the facilitators, since they can lead to reinforcement of abandonment issues in unattended breathers or management problems with breathers who suddenly become active.

When the physical setting has been adequately prepared and everybody is in the room, the session can begin. The relaxation exercise initiating the session was developed by Christina in the early years of our work at the Esalen Institute, drawing from her many years of hatha yoga practice and various forms of meditation. The main function of this introduction is to help participants relax and open up as much as possible and aim toward a state that Zen Buddhism terms *beginner's mind*. This means letting go of any plans they might have for the session, suspending what they have read and heard about Holotropic Breathwork, and focusing fully on the present moment. The quality of attention that is ideal for Holotropic Breathwork is the same as the attitude toward inner experiences practiced in Vipassana Buddhist meditation: The basic principle is to give full and sustained attention or mindfulness (*sati*) to our body, feelings, content of consciousness, and actions and then letting go of the experience, so that we are always prepared for the next moment.

After the breathers assume a reclining position on their mattresses with their eyes closed or covered with eyeshades and the sitters find their place beside them, we begin talking to the group slowly and with a soft voice, leaving enough space between the various suggestions:

Lying on your back . . . feet comfortably apart . . . arms beside you . . . palms facing up. . . . This is a very open, very receptive pose. . . . Now, feeling the contact of your body with the mat . . . adjusting anything that needs to be adjusted, and sinking into the floor . . . and as much as possible, letting go of any programs you may have going into this session, any expectations, any ideas about accomplishing something, or about avoiding something that is unacceptable, too scary, or too challenging. . . . Opening the mind, allowing whatever experience that presents itself, trusting that it is brought by the part of you that is a healing force . . . the inner healer . . .

We will gradually go through the body from your toes to the top of your head . . . relaxing. . . . So now relaxing your toes . . . the soles . . . and the tops of your feet . . . your ankles. . . . Relaxing the calves, the backs of your lower legs . . . and the shins . . . relaxing. . . . Relaxing your knees, the backs of your knees . . . and now moving up to your thighs. . . . Relaxing your thighs . . . and the backs of the thighs. . . . Relaxing your buttocks . . . sinking more deeply into the mat. . . . Relaxing the area around your genitals, and your hips . . . relaxing the hips. . . . By now your whole pelvis is as relaxed as you can make it today . . .

Bringing your attention to your stomach. . . . Relaxing the abdominal muscles, the belly that you may try to hold in your everyday life . . . and all the inner organs in that area. . . . Relaxing. . . . Moving up the body, relaxing your spine . . . traveling from the base of your spine . . . to the middle of the spine, slowly, slowly to the base of your neck. . . . Relaxing your chest, upper back . . . relaxing. . . . Relaxing your shoulders . . . your upper arms, bicepses . . . elbows . . . relaxing your lower arms, wrists, hands . . . relaxing the hands and the fingers . . . down to your fingertips . . .

Moving to the back of your neck, relaxing your neck, up to the base of the skull, opening and relaxing your throat . . . your mouth . . . your tongue. . . . Shifting your attention to your jaws, an area where a lot of us carry tension . . . letting go of the tension in your jaw . . . allowing your mouth to fall open slightly . . . relaxing your chin and your cheeks. . . . Relaxing your eyes, your eyelids, relaxing your eyebrows, and your nose. . . . Relaxing your face, your forehead . . . maybe making a face, tensing the facial muscles, holding the tension for a second or two, and letting it go . . . suspending any expression on the face—any public image—so that the face is completely blank. . . . Relaxing the ears, the back of your head, your scalp, and finally, all the way to the very top of your head . . .

Now, your entire body is relaxed. . . . Loose . . . open. . . . If you survey your body, from the toes to the top of your head, your body is as relaxed as possible . . . and when you feel you have relaxed, relaxing even more deeply.

Now that your body is more relaxed, open, bringing your attention to your breath . . . feeling the normal, everyday rhythm of your breath . . . and as you continue to be aware of your breath, beginning to increase the rhythm of your breathing . . . so your breath becomes faster than usual . . . allowing the breath to travel all the way to your fingertips, all the way to your toes, as the breath fills the entire body . . . the breath is quite a lot deeper and faster than usual. . . . Now increasing the rhythm of the breath even more . . . so that it becomes faster than usual, and deeper . . . and deeper and faster . . .

At this point, if you have a source of inspiration in your life, you may try to connect with it asking for guidance . . .

So by now, the breath is quite a lot deeper and faster than usual. . . . As the music begins, allowing the music to support your breathing . . . finding your own rhythm . . . Opening yourself to the breath, to the music, and whatever experience that presents itself . . .

Christina's introduction continues to be used with some variations and modifications by most practitioners of Holotropic Breathwork. About thirty years ago, we started the tradition of retreats combining Holotropic Breathwork and Vipassana meditation in cooperation with our dear friend, psychologist and Buddhist teacher Jack Kornfield. Jack added to Christina's introduction *paired breathing*, used in certain Buddhist practices. This exercise helps establish a deep connection between people who practice it with each other. After the breathers finish the relaxation and begin to focus on their breath, we invite the sitters to join in:

. . . and now, sitters: synchronizing your breathing with that of the person you are working with and mark every exhalation with the sound "aaaah" . . . loud enough for others to hear . . . aaaah . . . breathers: tuning into the sounds your sitters are making, connecting with them through breath . . . aaaah . . . and if you wish, you can synchronize your breathing with other pairs in the room, so that the entire group is breathing as one organism . . . aaaah (continue paired breathing for a few minutes). . . . And now continuing the breathing in silence . . . sitters: maintaining this quality of attention throughout the session, so that you are present, really present for your partner . . . and breathers: beginning to increase the rate of your breathing . . .

At this point, we resume the introduction as described earlier asking breathers to accelerate their breathing and surrender to the music.

7. Conducting Holotropic Breathwork sessions

Once the session has started, the task of the breathers is to remain in the reclining position, with the eyes closed, and sustain a faster breathing rhythm using a pace they feel comfortable with. The quality of attention and the attitude toward the experience seems to be more important than the speed and intensity of the breathing. As a matter of fact, approaching the session with strong ambition and determination and exerting too much effort can become a major hindrance, since the purpose is ultimately to surrender control and to let go. And trying hard to let go is a contradiction in terms.

The ideal attitude of the breather to the experience is to focus his or her full attention on the process as it unfolds from one moment to another, rather than on any specific goal or outcome. The breathers ideally maintain the faster breathing rhythm irrespective of the form the experience takes—buildup of physical tensions, surfacing of intense emotions, emergence of specific memories, or progressive relaxation. As much as possible, breathers suspend intellectual judgment and give full expression to emotional and physical reactions that emerge spontaneously.

As long as the breathers do their inner work independently, the sitters watch them and occasionally send them the agreed upon signal if their breathing seems to have slowed down. They might hand their partners a Kleenex if they cry or if their nose is running, bring them a glass of water if they are thirsty, provide a blanket if they feel cold, or take them to and from the bathroom. The facilitators walk around, monitoring the situation in the room, looking for instances where some special assistance might be needed. They might be asked to step in and sit with a breather while the sitter visits the restroom. Occasionally, they also might offer emotional support to the sitter who responds to the situation with intense emotions.

When some breathers become active and threaten to move into other breathers' space or behave in a way that seems dangerous for them or others, the sitters and facilitators cooperate in making the situation safe for everybody involved. Additional reasons for intervention are situations when some of the breathers refuse to continue because they experience too much fear or unpleasant physical symptoms. Then the facilitators try to give them reassurance or offer relieving bodywork to make them more comfortable. Once these reluctant breathers are "in process," it is essential to keep them in the room and support them until they reach successful resolution of their sessions.

Much of the active work with trained facilitators is done in the termination period of the sessions with breathers whose experience has not reached an adequate closure and who are experiencing some residual symptoms. This is the time for releasing bodywork and subsequent soothing massage or nourishing physical contact. If the experience is significantly longer than usual and the room is needed for the next session, we use a breakout room in which the bodywork can continue and provide double-sitting for the breather who is now without a sitter.

Many of the breathers process the emerging material on their own and do not need any assistance from the sitters or facilitators. They are able to bring the experience to spontaneous resolution and end up in a deeply relaxed meditative state. After they return to everyday reality and talk briefly and quietly to one of the facilitators, they move to a special room to work on their mandalas. Depending on the circumstances and their own inclinations, the sitters decide to stay with the breathers or leave them alone.

8. The spectrum of holotropic experiences

The experiences in Holotropic Breathwork sessions are highly individual and cover a very wide range. They do not represent a stereotypical reaction to faster breathing ("the hyperventilation syndrome") as one reads in the handbooks of respiratory physiology, but reflect the psychosomatic history of the breather. In a group of people who have all had the same theoretical preparation, received the same instructions, and listened to the same music, each person will have his or her own highly specific and personally relevant experience. And, if the same person has an entire series of sessions, the content of the experiences changes from session to session and they constitute a continuous journey of self-discovery and self-healing.

Sometimes the experiences do not have any specific content and are limited to physical manifestations and expression of emotions. The entire session can, for example, consist of intensification of the tension and blockages the breather carries in his or her body (Wilhelm Reich's "character armor") and subsequent profound release. If, at the time, anger is the primary issue of the breather, intensification of the anger and subsequent major catharsis can be the predominant content of the session. The source of these physical feelings and emotions might not be immediately identified and the breather might have to wait for relevant insights in this regard until one of the future sessions.

On occasion, the Holotropic Breathwork session is also without specific content, but it takes a form that is in sharp contrast with those described in this chapter. Here faster breathing leads to progressive relaxation, dissolution of boundaries, and experiences of Oneness with other people, with the universe, and with God. The breather progressively enters a mystical state without having to face any emotionally or physically challenging material. This can be associated with visions of white or golden light. It is important to inform the breathers ahead of time that this might happen. It is common to dismiss a developing experience of this type and see the session as a failure, because "nothing is happening."

If the experience has a specific content, it can be drawn from the different levels of the unconscious charted in the extended cartography of the psyche discussed earlier (pages 12ff.). The breathers can relive various highly emotionally charged events from their infancy, childhood, or later life that involved a psychological or physical trauma or, conversely, moments of great happiness and satisfaction. Sometimes the regression does not lead directly to these memories, but takes the breathers first to an intermediate zone of symbolic sequences or fantasies that represent variations on the same theme.

Memories of various stages of the birth trauma—basic perinatal matrices or BPMs—belong to the most common experiences in Holotropic Breathwork sessions. They accurately portray various aspects of the birth process, often with photographic details, even in individuals who have no intellectual knowledge of the circumstances of their birth (Grof 2006a). This can be accompanied by various physical manifestations indicating that the memory of birth reaches to the cellular level. We have seen individuals reliving birth develop bruises in places where forceps were applied, without knowing that this was part of their early history; the accuracy of this fact was later confirmed by parents or birth records. We have also witnessed changes of skin color and *petechiae* (tiny purplish red spots caused by seeping of small amounts of capillary blood into the skin) appearing in people who were born with the umbilical cord twisted around their neck.

Age regression often continues further and takes breathers to fetal memories from various stages of prenatal existence. This often involves quite specific situations that the breathers can identify—blissful episodes of undisturbed intrauterine life or, conversely, experiences of various toxic influences, disturbances caused by concussions or loud noises, maternal diseases or stress, and chemical or mechanical attempts at abortion. And to make things even more remarkable, breathers can experience their own conception on a cellular level of consciousness.

The repertoire of transpersonal phenomena occurring in Holotropic Breathwork sessions is very rich and diverse. It includes experiences of identification with other people, entire groups of people, and various other life forms. Transcendence of linear time leads to experiences of ancestral, racial, collective, phylogenetic, and karmic memories. Encounters and identification with archetypal figures from various countries of the world, visits to various mythological realms and states of cosmic unity figure prominently in the accounts from Holotropic Breathwork sessions. All these experiences can bring important new information previously unknown to the breathers, which can later be verified by consulting the appropriate sources.

External manifestations and behavior during holotropic sessions also vary widely. Some people stay absolutely quiet and peaceful and appear to be sleeping, although they might have powerful inner experiences. Others show great psychomotor excitement—they flail around, move back and forth, get on their knees, shake violently, or move their pelvis forcefully up and down. We often see behaviors that are characteristic for various animal species, such as slithering, swimming, digging, clawing, or flying movements. There are breathers who do not make a single sound throughout the entire session, while others cry loudly, scream, make distinct animal sounds, talk in tongues and foreign languages they do not know, or utter incomprehensible gibberish.

However bizarre the sounds and external behavior might appear to an external observer, they are meaningful expressions of the breather's inner experience and they are ultimately healing, because they help to discharge withheld emotions and blocked physical energies. The reason people in the industrial civilization have difficulties understanding how the holotropic experiences described in this section could be healing is that they believe therapy has to be rational. Contrary to our cultural expectations, the methods used by shamans and other native healers and, for that matter, psychedelic therapy and Holotropic Breathwork, can achieve therapeutic success by mechanisms that transcend and bewilder reason.

The following are several examples of Holotropic Breathwork experiences that focus on different levels of the psyche, beginning with two accounts that point to events in postnatal biography. They show that severe physical traumas have also a strong psychotraumatic effect and can profoundly influence an individual's future life. The first of these reports is the description of an early breathwork session of Elizabeth, a thirty-seven–year-old freelance writer and editor, who later participated in our training and became a certified facilitator. In this session, she revisited and worked through a forgotten childhood accident.

At age thirty-seven, I felt ready to try Holotropic Breathwork. The birth of our first child five years before had precipitated an unexpected and prolonged period of postpartum depression. The ensuing challenges of parenting had brought up more unresolved psychological issues, and I had begun a regular course of psychotherapy. But I still felt very confused, powerless against the rage that erupted from deep inside of me in response to some trivial event, and scared that I was hurting my husband and small son. I thought that breathwork, an experiential form of psychotherapy, might help.

I signed up for a weekend workshop and drove eight hours from my home in the mountains of Vermont to the dunes of Cape Cod. Sand drifted across the highway like snow. The ocean was everywhere. Provincetown in October felt like a ghost town, stark and abandoned. The old, creaky hotel faced the bay at the site of the Pilgrims' first landing. In the emptiness of this place loomed an eerie presence of wind, sea, and Cape Cod folklore. It was Halloween weekend. That evening we listened to a lecture by psychiatrist Stanislav Grof; we heard about non-ordinary states of consciousness, the birth process, and the transpersonal realm. We saw slides that showed fantastic and beautiful drawings done by people who had experienced what we were to do the next day. During the break, we paired up with partners for the breathwork sessions.

The next morning, I lay on the floor with more than a hundred other people. My partner sat beside me as I embarked on a journey that was to change my life. Breathing more quickly and rapidly, listening to evocative music, I surrendered myself to the unexpected sensations that began to flow through me. My body immediately took on a life of its own. My arms moved in large, sweeping circles so powerful that I felt possessed by some superhuman strength. This dance continued for some time. The energy then became very concentrated in my left wrist, until I was experiencing precisely the pain I felt at age eleven when my wrist was broken. At that moment, I heard myself saying, "My father broke my wrist when I was eleven." Images and sensations from this long-forgotten accident came flooding back.

More than simply remembering this event, I felt myself a child, back in the front yard of the home that I had grown up in. The early fall day was warm. We were all at home, even my father, whose profession as a medical doctor kept him away much of the time. It must have been the weekend, then. His car, a white Saab, was parked in the driveway by the front entrance to our house. My father was getting into the car. He was about to back it down the hill and put it into the garage. I rushed up to him eagerly. "Can I sit on the car?" I asked. He agreed without hesitating and I perched myself on the hood, anticipating the thrill of riding in this unorthodox way. We started down the driveway. At first the ride was exhilarating, like sailing as we sometimes did together off the Maine coast. The pavement moved right underneath me, flecks of rock passing by like the sea.

But when we reached the bottom of the hill and my father began to move the car forward, the sensations shifted abruptly. My body had lost its balance. I groped frantically for some hold on smooth metal as I felt myself falling towards the pavement. Even as I groped I knew I would surely fall, fall onto hard pavement in front of this moving car. And just as certainly I knew that I would be crushed by the car unless I did something to get out from underneath it.

As soon as I hit the pavement, I wrenched my body into a roll that propelled me to the side of the driveway. Unsure how I had gotten there, I found myself sitting on soft green grass, shivering and shaking. My father was beside me, asking me how I felt. All my attention was on my left wrist. I knew it was broken, just as surely as I had known I would fall, had known I must roll to get out of the way of the car. I held up the wrist for him to see. The hand hung at an odd angle, reminding me of a flower whose stem had broken. "My wrist," I said, "something is wrong with my wrist. I think it's broken." My father examined it briefly. "No," he pronounced, with his air of medical authority, "it's all right. There's nothing wrong."

I believed him, or at least tried to. But the basic split between my trust in my father and the signals I was getting from my body was impossible to bridge. I retreated to my bedroom, not knowing where else to go, and lay in bed, suspended between the painful certainty of a broken bone and my father's definitive denial of it. My left arm, now useless, extended out on a pillow beside me.

I felt strangely detached from this arm, except when I felt the sharp pain of some small movement. The room was very dark. Strips of sunlight framed the edges of the drawn shades.

When the certainty of my condition prevailed, my mother took me to the hospital. There were X-rays and then a cast that I wore for six weeks. My friends wrote their names on it. My father said nothing. I hadn't thought much about this accident in the intervening years. It had been overshadowed by other events that had seemed more significant. But the breathwork session had taken me right back to a place in myself that needed attention. Although I had healed physically many years before, something inside was still broken.

By now the movement of my body—especially my arms—had progressed, and I felt an incredible healing power emanating from my right hand and being directed at my left wrist. Again I heard myself speak, this time saying in a surprised tone, "My right arm wants to heal my broken wrist." At this point I was drawn to a standing position by some invisible force, and I felt myself surrounded by supportive people in the room who encouraged me to continue until this incredible dance resolved in its own beautiful and mysterious way.

After the session I was flooded with gratitude to have found within myself the capacity for self-healing. In the following years, I was able to process this event with my family, including my parents, and establish a more honest relationship with them. I soon realized that the themes of this accident extended into other events of my childhood, and eventually recognized familial patterns spanning generations. Helped by ongoing breathwork and a supportive life partner, I began to face some of the pain in my life and reclaim major pieces from my past.

The second account describes one of the sessions of Katia, a forty-nine-year-old psychiatric nurse participating in our training. It revolves primarily around a traumatic experience in early childhood, although the resolution of this trauma has strong transpersonal features. In this session, the dissolution of the bioenergetic armoring caused by long immobilization in childhood was experienced as escaping from a turtle shell and enjoying the freedom of movement in a beautiful natural setting.

Intense breathing at the beginning of the session made me feel that my body was blocked and frozen in a supine position. I tried desperately to turn on my belly, but was not able to do it. I experienced myself as a helpless turtle turned on her back unable to escape her dangerous predicament. I began to cry for not being able to change my position, because it seemed that my life depended on it. I noticed that this turtle had on her belly the image of a child needing nourishment (see figure 10.b) and I felt that there was some connection between this experience and my own inner child. I kept crying for a long time without consolation.

Then something changed and I felt that this turtle's shell had on it the image of a beautiful landscape (see figure 10.c). Then my experience changed again and I became a small child, who could not change her position and needed help from someone else in order to do it. (I later asked my mother and she told me that when I was a year old, my pediatrician decided that I had to be put in a cast with my legs apart, because of an imperfect structure of my hip joints. I had to stay immobilized for forty days).

After some time and with great effort, I finally succeeded to turn on my belly and saw myself in a beautiful landscape—running on the beach and diving and swimming in crystal-clear water. I realized that the landscape in which I found myself was the same as the one that was depicted on the turtle's shell. I felt free and enjoyed the scent of the flowers, the rushing cascades, and the air filled with the fragrance of the pines. I felt old like the earth and young like the Eternal Puppy (a playful reference to the Jungian archetype of Puella Eterna). I saw a small pond and I went to drink; as I did, the sense of health and great well-being filled my body and my mind.

The night following the breathwork, I dreamt about being in Rome in front of a church and encountering a Buddhist nun. She shared with me the story of her initiatory journey and I told her about mine that involved a pilgrimage from Mount Everest (which, in my dream, I had in the north of Europe) to the Sahara Desert, with a stop in Assisi. The landscape, which I described to the Buddhist nun in the dream, was the same landscape that I had envisioned earlier in my breathwork session on the turtle's shell. (see figure 10.d)

The following account describes the Holotropic Breathwork session of Roy, a fifty-three-year-old psychiatrist and passionate mountain climber, which took him back to his birth and to traumatic experiences and emotional deprivation in the early postnatal period of his life. Having relived the memories of these events, he realized how deeply they had influenced his later life. He also gained some extraordinary insights into the connection between his favorite sport and his biological birth. Although the main focus of Roy's session was biographical and perinatal, much of its healing power came from the transpersonal dimension.

The weather on Tuesday, July 15 is brilliant—warm sun, cool breezes, deep clear blue sky—reminiscent of Yosemite Valley in the summer. I notice other feelings that are reminiscent of those before a big Yosemite climb: the same sense of apprehension, the same tentative determination in the face of foreboding challenge, even the same nervous diuresis [unusually large urine output]. Would I rise to this challenge or be pushed back? Would I emerge whole or injured? I do not know.

I begin to breathe deeply, more rapidly, deeper still. My hands begin to tingle, and my feet also. The music is pulsating, and all of a sudden I am climbing high on the face of El Capitan in Yosemite. I am cranking out the moves on a challenging vertical crack with ease and grace. The sun feels warm on my back, the breezes cool and gentle, and the view of the valley floor is spectacular. I am fully alive, rejoicing in the movement, the sun, the feel of the rock. I am climbing in the lead, so strongly that I do not need to stop to set protection. I feel a deep yearning to be free of the rope, to untie it and to—fly.

With this desire comes the sense that I am being held back, tied down—by what? My inner voice—my father's voice—is fearful: freedom would be too dangerous. I do not discern who my climbing partner is, but I sense that it is my father who is holding me back. I feel stuck in old beliefs, old ways of thinking. I need his approval for my identity. I continue to believe and act as if my identity, my value, my worth come from outside myself. The urge to break free, to soar, grows more intense. I begin to cry and to become angry.

How long am I going to continue to let myself be held back by Dad's (or my own) insecurities, his fears, his notions of right and wrong, his guilt, his lack of gusto? When am I ever going to be able to set myself free, to untie the rope and soar? I become angry at all that holds me back—and it seems to have a masculine face. In the midst of my tears and anger, I begin to untie the rope. I sense resistance and strong objection—whether from my climbing partner or from my inner voice. I do not know. This resistance seems to be rooted in fears and moral judgments.

I do not finish untying the knot, the image fades, and I collapse back onto the mat.

But my anger grows more intense and my tears become more bitter. I do not really know why I am so furious, but I feel that I have not received the guidance I need, I have not been taught what it means to be a man in middle age, or shown how to age gracefully. Dad is now frail, an old man towards whom anger is no longer permissible, and for whom the appropriate emotion is compassion, not anger. Thus, he has robbed me of my right to my anger. I am angry at some great omission, some great need that has gone unmet. Perhaps the need for his understanding and approval. Perhaps the desire for a father who is more engaged in life, who could have helped me become a whole man. My anger is therefore fueled by a vague sense of unmet need.

As the intensity of the music builds, I approach another great omission in my life: having been separated from my mother during the first few days of life. I was born with an *intestinal volvulus*, a twisted small intestine that would not allow nourishment to pass. On the fifth day of life, I underwent surgery. I was not expected to live. I remained in an incubator and was given back to my mother two weeks later. I become that infant again and am engulfed in waves of grief, sorrow, feelings of total isolation. After the difficult journey of birth, when I should have received comfort, I am in great pain, I am cut open, I am left all alone. My mother is unable to hold me. All I want is to be held. I cry bitterly, feeling the full weight of being left alone, without nurture, without being held. I feel, "the cost of being alive is too high, too high." I become angry at God. Why do I have to suffer like this? Why couldn't God have figured this out better? I weep bitterly. I am angry at the doctors, the medical system that keeps me isolated and alone.

I am now able to step back and to see myself, the newborn, lying there. I feel tremendous compassion for this baby boy, this self who suffers all alone. Can I not treat this boy with more compassion as he grows up? I lift him up and hold him close to me, offering him comfort. I then enter the consciousness of my mother and am overcome with her sense of desolation, loss, anger at God. How much she is suffering! How young and afraid and, in her own way, equally alone. What great loss she is experiencing! Her firstborn child is stripped away from her, and she is unable to hold him. I weep even more bitterly, seeing

that she is not consoled, that she feels as alone as I do. I cry
great tears of compassion for her.

I think it is at this point that Ashley and Linda, the
facilitators, lie down on either side of me and hold me as I weep.
I hold their hands. My anger begins to dissolve as I realize that
I am not totally alone. Nana was praying for me, and the whole
church with her. Dad was doing the best he could, as were the
doctors and the nurses. A priest had been called in to anoint
me with oil. I realize that the situation was nobody's fault. This
realization dispels the anger, but heightens the sense of human
tragedy. How terribly tragic! Was God himself in the suffering?
Was God also a victim?

After a very long time, I am able to be held by my mother.
I feel my skin against hers, feel finally comforted, spent but
relieved. Safe at last. I have flashes of a faint memory, of being
back inside the womb, floating. At some point I wonder or sense
that it is only God who can satisfy my yearnings for wholeness,
for completion. Only God can hold me safe, take me to my
higher Self. I sense that somehow, although I could not see or
feel it, God has held me all along. How I yearn to rest in God's
arms always, as I am doing at this very moment!

At this point, animated African music, with drumming
and choral chants, erupts joyfully. I, a newborn baby boy, am
transported to a dusty village in Mali. I am placed on a small
table, swaddled, in the middle of a gathering. The village residents
dance around me in a circle, singing and drumming, celebrating
my birth and welcoming me to the village. I am happy. I feel
that I am smiling; I notice that my head is moving from side to
side on the pillow in rhythm with the music. I am reminded of
ubuntu (a Bantu word describing self-assurance that comes from
knowing that one belongs in a greater whole)—I am made human
and whole as I am held in this community's warm welcome.

Again, the music shifts, and I return to a sense of being in
a struggle for my freedom. Suddenly, I am transported back to
the scene of an official dinner, where I had confronted those in
authority with an unpleasant truth. I became the lightning rod
for their anger for having spoken boldly when it was not polite
to do so, for their feeling blindsided by this issue, and for not
backing down. The event had left me deeply shaken, feeling for
weeks that the emotional cost of stepping into this role had been
too high. For me, the experience had opened up memories of
being between Dad and Mom during a fight, when Mom feared

for her physical safety. Once again, I had experienced confronting or challenging a powerful angry father, whose approval I desired. The energy that evening had been extremely intense.

As I return to this scene, I am fighting for my life. A very powerful man, whom I know, is attacking from the right; I enter the battle, blocking his punches and fighting back with karate. It seems as if my freedom, my very essence is threatened. This man symbolizes male authority, the disapproving father. He is seeking to destroy me and I am fighting for my freedom and my survival. I get my hands around his neck and begin to choke him. My grip tightens more and more. His face begins to turn red, then blue; his eyes are bulging. I scream at him, "Tell me what I need to know! Tell me the secret! Tell me why!" He remains silent, shaking his head to say "no" as I tighten my grip even more. I am choking him with all my might, demanding, screaming, "I need to know! Why? How am I to live? What is the purpose?" He does not, or cannot, answer.

I suddenly realize that I do not want to kill him. I am not choking him to kill him, or to destroy him, or to exert my supremacy, or to overthrow him. Rather, I seek his blessing—or an answer. I am reminded of the story of Jacob wrestling with the angel. I scream, "Why are things so screwed up? Why couldn't you old men—and Dad—and God—have done a better job at things? You incompetent old men—what is the answer? Why are you keeping me from untying the rope and really becoming free?" I squeeze the neck even harder. "Why did I have to be so all alone after I was born?"

I realize, as this struggle comes to a climax, that they do not have any answers. They don't answer me because they can't. They are just frail old men, without answers, with no real power, more worthy of compassion and pity than of fear and obedience. They had never had the answers, and they cannot give me answers now. I can no longer rely on them to define my worth, my identity, my salvation. Their approval will not buy my freedom. I scream even louder. Finally exhausted, I release my grasp and they fall backwards, shaken, while I collapse back on the mat. I seem to drift into sleep for a few moments.

The music shifts again, and I am again a newborn baby, being held (Linda and Ashley are still on either side of me), and also have feelings of being back in the womb. I experience oneness with God—God the feminine. My mother is saying: "It's OK now, everything is going to be OK." I begin to weep bitterly.

Is that really possible? Is it too good to believe? Can I put any weight on this faith? I have been through so much hopelessness and depression and despair and darkness and tragedy—dare I believe that it's going to be OK?"

I see a blue light, repeatedly, that moves across my field of vision. In the background is a coarse woven pattern, with the color and texture of the inside surface of blue jeans. I feel comforted and happy. I am now being held, as a newborn, and I realize that the twenty-some years of my marriage, when I never felt completely held, recapitulated my first twenty days of life. While being held now, I see the trials ahead in my life, like Jesus in the Garden of Gethsemane.

I do not want to die. I do not want this now-comforted old self to die. I do not want to pass through the tribulation. I remember Stan's words that submission to ego annihilation is necessary for the final passage to new birth. I say to God, "I am going to continue to struggle towards the light—to climb onward—to fight for my life, even the life of this old self. But if you want my life, if you want this old self to die, well, into Thy hands I commend my spirit. In the meantime, don't expect me to give up. I am going to keep searching for, and struggling towards, the light."

The music softens and I hear birds singing and a soothing waterfall. I emerge into the sunlight and feel gratitude. If the price for being alive is having to do battle and to be alone at times, I accept the price. I still do not know "why," do not have the answers, but the blessings of life, the unconditional love that I am experiencing from these two women—standing in for my mother and the feminine God—is sustenance enough.

I vaguely sense that I am back in Yosemite. I have reached the summit of El Capitan. I feel strong. I open my eyes to see Stan looking at me with his typical compassion, interest, care, and curiosity. I begin to wake up, slowly, to emerge from this amazing journey. Stan mentions the concept of a "key log"—the one log in a logjam that, if removed, allows all the other logs to shift free and begin to float down the river. He suggests that this experience may prove to have been a "key log" experience for me.

Two months after his Holotropic Breathwork session, which was his first and—as of now—the only one, Roy sent us a letter describing some of the changes he had observed as a result of his experience. Here we include excerpts from this letter:

In the first several days that followed the breathwork, I recognized two major components to my session: 1) an experience of the feminine, which allowed me to comfort and nurture and hold the little baby (myself) who had felt so abandoned after birth; and 2) a masculine component, in which there was an intense struggle for power, truth, and survival with male authority figures in my life (including my father and my boss). Initially, I felt a sense of closure and healing with the first, but not the second, of these.

The feminine aspect of the breathwork session deepened earlier conversations with my mother about her own feelings of abandonment and fear fifty-three years ago when I was taken from her and she was not allowed to hold me, really, for two weeks. I do not fully understand it, but the breathwork enabled me to release the negative power of that experience in my subconscious. Again, I do not have words for this, except to say that I sense that healing has taken place. In that space, the baby is now being held.

I initially felt that the masculine component to the session was still raw and unprocessed, and that although I had received some new insights, the healing was incomplete. Now I recognize significantly more healing and inner opening. This involves my relationship with my father, whose health has been faltering in recent months, as well as my still-emerging-and-new relationship with "the esoteric."

First, my father's illness has created a new opportunity for dialogue on deeper core issues of being human. As an adult, my strategy for dealing with his rather authoritarian form of religion and his authoritarian pronouncements on life has been to share less and less of who I am with him. In part this is based in fear. The breathwork session helped me realize that by not sharing who I am with him, I deprive both of us. I am committed to more frequent contact and more transparent and authentic representation of myself with my father, in a spirit of love.

Second, and more difficult to explain, is the healing that is taking place around my relationship to the esoteric. I have experienced this trend with some wariness, because of several reasons: 1) I have always eschewed the esoteric as something incompatible with my scientific training; 2) I am unfamiliar with esoteric teachings and my Baptist upbringing did not provide much space for even considering them (except as "of the devil"); and 3) if there were a secret agenda, it could lead to manipulation.

I learned from you all that esoteric teachings (like those of mainstream religion) can be instruments of light and love or—if manipulated through the abuse of power and ego—of darkness. I have learned to trust my intuition in this area, and in doing so, have been able to open myself to new exploration.

So, for me, the effect of breathwork has been to open me emotionally, intellectually, and spiritually. It has brought healing. I am sure, as I continue to live with and reflect on the experience, it will continue to bring even more healing. Even as I write, I sense that other areas of my life are opening to the insights from the Holotropic Breathwork. Your notion that the experience was like a "key log" for me is accurate.

Following is an excerpt from of one of the sessions that Janet, a forty-five-year-old psychologist, experienced during her Holotropic Breathwork training. In her sessions, she relived various traumatic episodes from her difficult childhood, including torturous physical and sexual abuse. These sessions often focused on her father, who was Janet's abuser and had also played a very unusual role in her birth as her mother's midwife for a home delivery. During this procedure, he was guided by telephonic instructions of a medical doctor.

Janet had some of the most powerful and colorful experiences we have seen during all the years of our practice of Holotropic Breathwork. She had an unusually easy access to the transpersonal domain and even her biographical and perinatal sessions were often interspersed with rich archetypal symbolism. They often featured figures and themes from shamanic, Tantric, and Greco-Roman mythology—encounters with various deities, challenging ordeals, dismemberment, and psychospiritual death and rebirth. During the training, she became deeply immersed in astrology and was fascinated by the correlations between the content of her sessions and the archetypes associated with her planetary transits.

The first experience in this session was running through a meadow, similar to the countryside where I spent my summers as a child, but running now as an adult, feeling as if I am running towards someone. I have a vague sense of a group of women dancing with Dionysus, it is very sexual and quickly becomes violent. I have the impression that the dance is turning into dismemberment. My consciousness expands outward as if I can see a sequence of epochs, first the one in which the feminine dismember the masculine and then when the masculine dismember the feminine, as if the same myth is being enacted in mythological-historical reality with the roles reversing between the genders.

I see a black stallion; he is running and sweating, I run towards him and climb on his back, feeling like I am riding primal instinctual masculine energy. I feel my sense of self both merged with the stallion and separate as a human female. He runs towards a cave and drops me off. I descend into the cave and have the sense that it is the threshold to Hades. Just as I sense this, a massive, dark, masculine figure appears to be trailing me. He is an elusive figure, anthropomorphic in shape but not human and has a dark intense numinosity to him. His presence feels life-threatening. As I realize this, I know he is Hades, the Greek god of Death. I run for my life downward into the cave, trying to escape from him into the earth.

I have the strange sense that I am simultaneously running away from him and running towards the earth mother as Persephone. I keep running. Every time I think I am escaping, he suddenly and unexpectedly appears in front of me and sadistically laughs at my attempts to evade him. After a series of this pattern of action—running away to escape him and his sudden reappearance—repeats multiple times, Hades ominously says: "You can not escape Death." I have the sensation of being captured just at that moment and being abducted by Hades as Death into the underworld. . . .

The scene shifts and now I am a child, running simultaneously through both houses I grew up in. It is a familiar feeling, but the experience of the feeling sensation is more intense. I keep breathing and feel myself shrink to the size of middle childhood, seven or eight years old. I fall forward and land face down on the floor. I cry and continue to crawl to try to escape my father, who grabs me by the ankles and tells me "there is no escaping him." I cry out. There is no one else in the house. It is the house on Main Street, my first childhood home. I feel my body being dragged along the wooden floor towards his large, threatening, looming dark presence. He has an erection and I begin to feel the sensation of him raping me. I feel this not as a single episode but as multiple episodes condensed into one experience.

I feel my body being raped in multiple ways, from sodomy, to being tied up and vaginally raped, to oral penetration. I start to feel extremely nauseous and gag on my mat. I try to escape, but begin to feel numb; I ask my sitter to hold my ankles to see if I can feel into the sensation again. The whole scene goes blank and my body now feels complete loss of sensation. I return to the breath, but feel nothing. I use the bathroom and return and ask Tav to help me. I know I can't go there alone and that I have lost the capacity to feel.

Tav guides me through the process; I lie back on the mat and the feeling of pain arises in my chest and throat. It then turns into a black shadow and hides invisibly inside my heart. I lose the sensation again. Tav encourages me to continue breathing. Now I have a memory of the intense pain after one of the most torturous episodes of sexual assault and abuse by my father when I was older, around eleven years of age. I feel sharp pain in my genital area from being brutally raped and also the intense emotional pain of being alone. It seems like the pain is going to kill me and I sense a strong desire to die to escape the intense pain and my father.

I am aware that this sensation of desire to die in order to escape the intense pain is a familiar COEX system; it is associated with my self-destructive tendencies that in the past led to a series of suicidal attempts. Tav is with me and I keep breathing into the pain. As it moves into my throat, the scene shifts and I am the small child again. It is the first scene where my father is dragging me by the ankles, thrusts his erect penis into my throat and I cannot breathe. He purposefully keeps it in my throat and sadistically laughs.

I tell Tav that I am choking and cannot breathe; he keeps encouraging me to stay with it. I move my hand to my throat and he tells me to squeeze his hand instead. As I hold his hand, pressing it against my throat, the sensation of choking and not being able to breathe intensifies. It ramps up almost to the point where I feel like I would die. I cannot sustain my ability to experience it, because my mental focus shifts to being able to experience my father's intense wanting me to die. I keep breathing into the feeling and I experience his death wish for me as the suicidal COEX it later became. I am leaving my body's field of consciousness, overwhelmed by the experience, and cry on Tav's shoulder. At first I can hold him and then I go completely limp.

He tells me again to stay with it, that I am doing great and to keep breathing. I lie down again and feel my father's intense hatred for me. I experience it simultaneously in the specific episode and throughout my life. He wanted my mother to have an abortion and he hated me the entire time I knew him, up until a later attempt on my life at eighteen years old. I feel myself as the small child looking at him and having this intense feeling sensation of not being able to understand why he hates me. Again, as I feel this sensation, I am simultaneously aware of the COEX of not understanding why I can't have loving relationships with the men I am in love with. I can see this is the seed experience of my problem with men and cry "why, why, why" and say "I don't understand" repeatedly.

I tell Tav that I cannot go all the way through the choking. He keeps encouraging me to breathe and reassuring me that I am doing fine. I take a few breaths and sit up; my head starts to spin and I feel an extreme dizziness and eventually complete disorientation. I know Tav is there, but I cannot tell where the ground is. I spin around on the mat not knowing which way is up. (Later as I recounted the story to my sitter, I realized I must have passed out when my father was choking me to death and this sensation of dizziness and disorientation must have been what it was like when I came to taking my first breaths again.)

As I fell to the mat I felt this incredible wash of an oceanic wave; I was completely immersed in a Neptunian intoxicated oceanic state. Then the sensation became love as a drug, and I experienced making love with all my boyfriends throughout my life simultaneously—all the years of sex and drugs. I re-experienced the progression from using drugs and having sex to being able to have sex without drugs after PTSD therapy for the sexual abuse and then back to using drugs and sex again. Finally, I connected with the most recent experience of making love with John and preferring not to use drugs. The feeling of love and the erotic energy was more intense and beautiful and divine when we did not use drugs.

I took a break and thanked Tav, who was still sitting with me. I knew that after floating in the intoxicating Neptunian-Venusian state through my entire sexual history of intimate relationships, I was done with the hard work for the day. I drank some water, lay back down, and returned to my breath. I had the experience of dancing with Pluto in the field surrounded by trees, he was a dark non-anthropomorphized figure. I had the awareness that he was Dionysian and greater than Dionysus, but also simultaneously the god. Our dance became intensely, powerfully sensuous and erotic. He laid me down on the ground as he made love to me; we merged into the ground, into the earth. I had the awareness of the earth as being both Dionysus and the Divine Feminine in a state of fecund sexual union. I no longer had sensation of myself as a human, nor of Pluto as a god, we were now the earth. I could feel the Sunlight penetrating my earthly soil and felt this intense sensation of creative power.

Suddenly and unexpectedly I felt myself as the earth giving birth to a field of flowers and a female voice saying this is Persephone as spring. The series of births continued. A vast sequoia grew rapidly out of my center, then a deer, then a mountain spring gushed out of the ground and down the mountain side. It flowed into the ocean and I felt myself as the mother ocean penetrated by the sunlight giving birth to dolphins. This time I also simultaneously felt the dolphins giving birth and felt them rushing all along my body as I lay on the mat. I felt the Neptunian-Venusian ocean giving birth, the dolphins, and their presence against my body.

The last example is a session of Katia, a forty-nine-year-old psychiatric nurse, whose resolution of a traumatic childhood experience we described earlier (see pages 72f). Katia had in the past experienced a spiritual emergency related to Kundalini awakening and has an easy access to the transpersonal domain. Her account features a rich array of spiritual experiences and contains no material from postnatal biography or the perinatal period.

On the day when we did this session of Holotropic Breathwork, it was very windy; the windows were not completely closed and at times strong gusts entered the room. My sitter, a beautiful Argentinean woman, was concerned that I might catch a cold and tried hard to keep me covered. The two days preceding the breathing session, the discussion in the group revolved around the theme of death and rebirth, a subject very close and dear to me. In the past, I had experienced a spiritual emergency that took the form of psychospiritual death and rebirth: its full completion and integration lasted a few years.

I love the wind, like any other natural phenomenon, but that day I felt a great need for peace and all that whirling somewhat troubled and irritated me. I surrendered and accepted that the wind was blowing outside, as well as inside me, but at the beginning of the session I did not feel the need to breathe very deeply; it seemed that all that windy activity outdoors in a sense breathed for me. I let the music carry me, I let my mind follow the musical sequences, and I started to feel that my body was being molded to different shapes, as if I were a soft piece of clay shaped by the hands of a skillful sculptor.

I assumed the form of flowers, trees, rocks, shining cascades of water, and various animals. As if kneaded by a protean wave of impermanence, I started to turn into a squirrel, a deer running in a forest, and a large turtle immersed in a deep blue sea. In the bushes appeared an archer and I saw with amazement that this archer looked just like me. He looked at me, tensed without delay his bow, struck my heart with his arrow, and disappeared. The arrow did not harm me; it made me feel that the space of my heart became an eternal tunnel through which my consciousness began to travel at supersonic speed.

The mercurial game continued and I became a shiny mountain lion, a big green grasshopper sitting without motion on a flower, then a small hummingbird, a horse beginning to gallop, and a mountain covered with dense forests. This shape-shifting gave my body great pleasure. Then the sequences started to accelerate and the quality of the experience became more and more like the incessant and perpetual motion of waves. I was pervaded by a sense of eternal mutability and the music (I did not know if it was coming from the outside or from within me) accompanied and supported this perpetual dance of continuous transformation.

I became an ocean full of fish and aquatic plant forms, a starry sky, the sun and the moon chasing each other in the sky ever more quickly, day and night alternating at high-speed, clouds flying in the air carried by the wind. My entire being vibrated, the volume of my body expanded, the light particles that shaped me gravitated in luminous ether. The space between them was greatly expanded, yet the gravitational center, centripetal and centrifugal, maintained cohesion in perfect synchrony.

My Self, witness of the experience, kept whispering: "Do not get attached, let it happen, have confidence, let go!" The great speed at which I was transforming made me feel dizzy. I entered into a vortex and suddenly found myself in a very, very quiet and relaxed state, in complete weightlessness, opposite to my previous experience. I observed a large bright green lawn, strewn with flowers of many colors, and two nude bodies, one male and one female, lying on the grass side by side, connected in a loving embrace. The light in this dimension was emitted from the bodies and from various objects; it did not come from the outside.

Those clear and shiny bodies emitted a pleasant velvety light. Watching the tender, loving, and intimate dance, I was overwhelmed by great emotion. As I was observing this scene, I felt that behind my back materialized a great Being. I said "I felt," because I was looking in the direction of these two beings making love, but I actually saw and felt in every direction of space. I recognized that the great Being, who materialized from the waist up, was a blessing figure of Christ.

It radiated such a strong attraction and great love that I was completely absorbed. I became a cell of his body but had not lost my identity; I was simply conscious of being a cell of his body and simultaneously being whatever I focused on. I had a feeling of great peace and completeness, was inundated with love, and sensed that I was finally home (see figure 10.a). I remained in this experience of unity until the end of this session, immensely grateful and touched in the depth of my soul.

We asked Katia how her experiences in the Holotropic Breathwork training influenced her emotional condition, personal life, and professional work. This is a brief summary we received from her:

In the spring of 1997, when I read your book *The Stormy Search for the Self* and decided to start the Holotropic Breathwork training, I was reordering my inner world after a spiritual emergency activated by a long fast and shamanic practices, which had lasted since the year 1992. What I had experienced would be by mainstream psychiatry considered pathological—a psychotic break with auditory and visual illusions, hallucinations, and psychosomatic disturbances. Fortunately, because of my professional background, I had sufficient experience and knowledge to be able to face this crisis of transformation without going crazy.

During my spiritual emergency, I experienced a deep inner transformation that was extraordinary and of apocalyptic proportions, but it left me frightened and isolated, a stranger in this world. I was shaken and afraid to communicate about it with other people. In my breathwork sessions, I was able to complete, accept, and integrate many non-ordinary experiences from my spiritual crisis that had not yet been completed and settled and to achieve more self-assurance and self-reliance. Being able to participate in the Holotropic Breathwork training and to have the opportunity to share my experiences with others who could understand them, reassured me and allowed me to accept them without reservation and with feelings of gratitude. My Apocalypse was transformed into Revelation.

I am now at peace, reconciled, emotionally stable, whole, and complete. I have achieved greater professional self-confidence in my counseling work. Before the training—as Joseph Campbell says in his book *Hero with a Thousand Faces*—I did not want to return from my inner journey. Since my training, I have returned completely to this world; I have been able to bring love, patience, and tolerance into my relationships with other human beings.

Katia

9. The role of the facilitators

The number of external interventions required in the first two hours of Holotropic Breathwork varies. Most of the work the facilitators need to do falls into the final period of the sessions. Between the second and third hour of the session, we briefly check with the breathers who are still in the room. Some of them might be finished with their process and be simply resting or meditating. Others might be experiencing residual symptoms or even an impasse—be "stuck" in an uncomfortable emotional or physical state. If that is the case, we offer them bodywork and whatever else is necessary to bring the experience to a good completion.

The timing of this offer is important. The willingness of the breathers to cooperate tends to decrease with the amount of time that has elapsed in the session. They might notice that many people have already left, feel that they have taken too much time, or realize that it is lunchtime or dinnertime. Once the faster breathing is discontinued, the unresolved unconscious material also tends to become increasingly less available for processing. When the breather accepts the offer, the facilitator's task is to find ways to help the breather release and express the pent-up emotions and blocked physical energy that the breathing brought closer to the surface.

External observers who are not familiar with Holotropic Breathwork see the facilitators perform a wide range of interventions. This leads them to the conjecture that the facilitators use a wide range of specific techniques that they learned during their training. Nothing could be farther from the truth. Everything that the facilitators are doing has one common denominator and is guided by one basic principle. They take clues from the breathers and cooperate with their inner healing intelligence. They simply find the best way to intensify what is already happening. This reflects the understanding of the nature of emotional and psychosomatic symptoms and of the therapeutic strategy that has emerged from the study of holotropic states of consciousness.

Mainstream psychiatrists tend to focus on symptoms as the main target of their interest and of their interventions. This goes often so far that the presence of symptoms is seen as the disorder itself. The intensity of symptoms is used as a measure of the seriousness of the problem and great effort is exerted to find effective ways of alleviating or suppressing them. Although it is clear that this approach does not resolve the underlying causes, this "allopathic" strategy is often referred to as "therapy."

Psychiatry shares the use of symptomatic treatment with somatic medicine. However, in the treatment of physical diseases it would be considered bad practice to limit one's approach to suppressing symptoms. Symptomatic therapy is used primarily to make the patient more comfortable and is indicated in two situations: 1) as a complement to therapy that addresses the cause of the illness, and 2) in incurable diseases where causal therapy is not available. From this perspective, limiting psychiatric therapy to suppression of symptoms amounts to treating them as incurable.

The difference between symptomatic and causal treatment can be illustrated by the following thought experiment. Imagine that we are driving a car. We do not know much about the mechanics of the car, but we know that the appearance of red light on the dashboard means trouble. Suddenly a red light appears in front of us; unbeknown to us, it indicates that we are running out of oil. We take the car to a garage to consult a mechanic. The mechanic looks at the dashboard and says: "Red light? No problem!" He rips out the wire leading to the electric bulb; the red light disappears and he sends us back on the road.

The person who "solves" the problem in this manner would not be the expert whose help we would want to seek. We need somebody who intervenes in such a way that there is no reason for the warning signal to appear, not one who makes it impossible for it to appear without addressing the underlying problem. The parallel between this situation and limiting the therapy of emotional and psychosomatic disorders to pharmacological suppression of symptoms is obvious. And yet, much of routine psychiatric treatment does exactly that.

Research of holotropic states of consciousness has revealed an important alternative. It has shown that symptoms are more than just a major inconvenience in the patient's life. They represent the manifestation of a self-healing impulse of the organism that is trying to free itself from traumatic memories and other disturbing material from the biographical, perinatal, and transpersonal domains of the unconscious. Once we realize that, it becomes clear that symptoms should be encouraged to emerge and brought to full expression rather than suppressed. This understanding of the function of symptoms and the associated therapeutic strategy characterize an alternative system of medicine called *homeopathy*. It was developed in the first half of the nineteenth century by a German doctor, Samuel Hahnemann (Vithoulkas 1980).

Homeopathy has a rich armamentarium of remedies of mineral, plant, and animal origin, whose effects have been tested in healthy individuals in a process called "proofing." When a homeopathic therapist sees a client, he or she chooses a remedy whose effects best match the client's symptoms. Healing then happens through temporary intensification of the symptoms. The holotropic state of consciousness functions as a universal homeopathic remedy. It tends to intensify all preexisting symptoms (which are functional or psychogenic and not organic in origin), rather than intensifying a specific cluster of symptoms like the traditional homeopathic remedies. It also brings into manifestation previously latent symptoms and makes them available for processing.

An aspect of homeopathy that makes it particularly questionable and suspect in the eyes of traditional physicians is the fact that homeopaths subject their remedies to a series of dilutions associated with vigorous shaking before they administer them to their clients. This process is continued so far that no molecules of the active substance are left in the final solution. Homeopaths claim that it is the energetic imprint of the substance and not the substance as such that has the therapeutic effect. The work with holotropic states uses homeopathic understanding of symptoms, but does not present any great theoretical challenge, because it does not involve any chemical substances.

A psychogenic symptom indicates that, because of local weakening of the psychological defense mechanisms, important unconscious material has emerged so far that it can be consciously experienced, but not far enough to be energetically discharged and resolved. The large array of the interventions Holotropic Breathwork facilitators are using thus has one common denominator; it is the effort to intensify the existing symptoms and bring the material underlying them to full expression.

The facilitator asks the participant to focus his or her awareness on the area where there is a problem and do whatever is needed to intensify the experience of it. Then the facilitator uses an external intervention that further intensifies the physical sensations and emotional feelings involved. The next step is to encourage the breather to give single-pointed attention to the intensified sensations and feelings in the problem area and find out what is the natural response of his or her body to this situation. Once the nature of the spontaneous reaction becomes clear, it is important to encourage full expression of all the physical movements, sounds, and emotions that constitute this response, without censoring anything, without judgment, and without efforts to hold back or change the spontaneous reaction. This process then continues until the facilitator and the breather reach an agreement that the problem has been adequately resolved.

Once the joint effort of the facilitator and the breather brings the session to a successful closure, it is possible to help the integration of the experience by more subtle means. When the experience involved deep age regression to early infancy or to the perinatal period, nourishing and comforting physical contact can be very important and meaningful. After intense physical bodywork, good massage can prove to be a useful complement, whether its purpose is refined clearing of residual tensions or just generally soothing effect. This part of the work can be relegated to the sitters, who can do a very good job in spite of the fact that they have not had any specific training and, in many instances, have not done anything of this kind in the past. The breather and sitter reach a mutual agreement as to when it is time for the breather to leave the room and—depending on how long the session was—go to the mandala room or to the dining room to have lunch or dinner.

Witnessing intense emotional expressions and behavior of the breathers and exposure to powerful evocative music can have profound impact on the sitters. Part of the role of the facilitators is to keep an eye not only on what is happening with the breathers, but also on the reactions of the sitters, and offering them support if necessary. It is not uncommon that the effect of the atmosphere in the room is so strong that in some sitters it triggers their own process and they are unable to support their breathers. Facilitators then have to arrange a situation that provides adequate support to both the breather and the former sitter. With this in mind, it is important to have sufficient number of facilitators and apprenticing students to cover such unexpected events.

As we said before, all the interventions of the facilitators can be traced back to a single principle: to help the breathers intensify the feelings they are already having and to facilitate expression of the underlying blocked emotions and physical energies. However, there is a group of situations and problems regularly occurring in the sessions, where certain strategies for intensifying symptoms have proved particularly useful. Dealing with these situations requires special training and it might be too technical for readers without previous experience in Holotropic Breathwork to discuss them in this context. We have relegated the discussion of these strategies to appendix 1 of this book.

10. Mandala drawing and the processing groups

When the breathers complete their sessions and return to an ordinary state of consciousness, their sitters accompany them to the mandala room. This room is equipped with a variety of art supplies, such as pastels, magic markers, and watercolors, as well as large drawing pads. On the sheets of paper are light pencil drawings of circles about the size of a dinner plate. These barely visible circles are there to help the breathers focus on their experience and express it in a concise way. However, we stress that they may completely ignore the circle and stretch their drawings to the very edges of the page if they desire.

The instructions for the breathers are to sit down, meditate on their experience, and then find a way of expressing what happened to them during the session. The mandalas are later used in the processing group as a visual ("right-brain") complement to the verbal accounts of the participants describing their experiences in the breathwork sessions. There are no specific guidelines for mandala drawing. Some people prefer formless color combinations capturing the general atmosphere or emotional tone of their sessions, others construct geometrical mandalas or make figurative drawings and paintings. The latter might portray specific visions that emerged during the session or be assembled into complex travelogues depicting various sequences and stages of the inner journey. Some breathers decide to document a single session with several mandalas representing its different segments or aspects. In rare instances, the breather has no idea what he or she is going to draw and produces an automatic drawing.

Facing a blank sheet of paper, sometimes for the first time in years, some participants may panic. As children they might have had traumatic experiences with their art teachers or feel artistically inadequate for some other reasons. We address this common problem during the preparation for the session and reassure the group that in the mandala work there is no right and wrong, nor is it a painting competition or an art class. It is the psychological content that is important, not the artistic skill with which it is conveyed. Often the quality of the mandala surprises not only the group members, but also the person who created it. It is as if the emotional power of the unconscious material drives the artistic process, uses the breather as a channel, and finds its own expression. On occasion, we have seen instances where the experience in the breathwork actually revealed and liberated a genuine artistic talent, which had been dormant in the person's unconscious or was actively suppressed by some traumatic experiences in childhood.

About twenty years ago, we saw an extreme example of such a sudden artistic awakening in Alice, who participated in a residential workshop that we held in a center near Brisbane, Australia.

During her Holotropic Breathwork session, Alice relived a series of episodes from her childhood, in which the adults laughed at her fledgling artistic creations. While they were amused, because they found her drawings very funny, Alice perceived their reaction as ridicule and felt very ashamed and hurt. In later years, she was very shy, inhibited, and miserable in school-required art classes. While she was reliving these childhood memories in her breathwork session, she experienced a rich array of emotions ranging from shame and feelings of hurt to intense anger and was able to give them full expression. After a long struggle, Alice reached a sense of resolution of her traumatic memories and to her surprise painted two powerful and artistically beautiful mandalas. Next morning, when we walked into the breathwork room, we found her sitting in the middle of it, surrounded by a large number of astonishing mandalas covering every bit of floor space. It turned out that she had not slept that night and continued to paint with feverish passion and at a hectic pace until dawn. In the following years, painting became an important part of her life.

A therapist trained in Freudian analysis would expect that it should be possible to understand the mandalas using the same approach that psychoanalysts employ to decipher the symbolism of dreams or neurotic symptoms. They would try to relate their content to the events in the breathers' life—his or her infancy, childhood, and later life. This approach reflected Freud's belief that the processes in the psyche show strict linear determinism and are products of the individual's postnatal history. While this is certainly often true to some extent, we have frequently seen instances when the mandala could not be fully understood as a product of the individual's past.

It has happened frequently that the mandalas did not portray occurrences in the sessions, but actually anticipated themes of future sessions. This is in agreement with C. G. Jung's idea that the products of the psyche cannot necessarily be fully explained from preceding historical events. In many instances, they have not only a *retrospective*, but also a *prospective* or *predictive* aspect. The Self—as Jung called a higher autonomous aspect of the human psyche connected with the collective unconscious—has a certain plan for the individual involved and provides guidance toward a goal that remains hidden until it is attained. Jung called this movement in the psyche *the individuation process*. Consequently, the explanation for certain aspects of the mandalas lies in the future. The mandalas are not just historically determined, but are also products of a process that can be referred to as *teleological* or *finalistic*. This principle seems to resemble what in chaos theory is called *strange attractor*.

This is one of the reasons we ask participants to save their mandalas, even if they do not feel satisfied with them or do not understand them. Very often various forms of future introspective approaches, such as analysis of dreams from the following nights, additional Holotropic Breathwork sessions, Jungian sandplay, meditation, or Gestalt practice, can bring important insights into the mandalas that were not available at the time when these were created. At the end of our month-long workshops at the Esalen Institute and of our Holotropic Breathwork training, we have provided time for each participant to display his or her mandalas and share with the group the process they had gone through during our time together. It is extraordinary how a series of mandalas from consecutive breathwork sessions shown in chronological order can often provide a clear and instant picture of the process of inner transformation that the person underwent. By comparison, it takes a very long time to describe it in words.

Many sitters decide to stay with the people with whom they worked, even after these have returned to ordinary state of consciousness. Some of these sitters do not just watch the breathers paint the mandalas, but decide to join in and create mandalas of their own, related to the experiences they themselves had while assisting their partners. It is quite remarkable how often these mandalas parallel the breathers' experiences or offer extraordinary insights into the breathers' process.

An interesting alternative to the mandala drawing just described is the process developed, practiced, and taught by the French painter Michelle Cassoux. Michelle first developed this approach in Paris in her work with children and later used it as a way of coping with her own difficult and stormy experiences of Kundalini awakening. After moving to California, she named her process the Painting Experience and started teaching it with her then-husband Stewart Cubley in classes and workshops. They described this work in their joint book *Life, Paint, and Passion: Reclaiming the Magic of Spontaneous Expression* (Cassoux and Cubley 1995).

Michelle uses large sheets of paper stretched on vertical panels and encourages her students to paint not only with brushes, but also with their fingers and hands. She teaches them how to tap into the deeper energies of creation and use painting as a tool for self-discovery and for exploring the spiritual dimensions of the creative process. Ideally, the painting is absolutely spontaneous, without any preconceived ideas about the form or content. For this reason, Michelle's Painting Experience is a perfect complement to Holotropic Breathwork, which uses the same principles of self-explora-tion—being in the moment with the "beginner's mind" and allowing the unconscious material to emerge without censoring or changing anything. In several instances, we combined our Holotropic Breathwork training module with a following weekend workshop with Michelle and experienced the compatibility of these two approaches.

Another interesting alternative to mandala drawing is the method of Soul Collage developed by Seena B. Frost (Frost 2001). Many participants in holotropic workshops, training, and therapy, experience psychological blocks when they are confronted with the task to draw or paint. As we mentioned earlier, this usually has its roots in some traumatic experiences that they had as children with their parents or teachers and peers in art classes; sometimes it is their generally low self-esteem that makes them doubt their abilities. Soul Collage helps these people overcome their emotional blocks and resistances; it is a creative process that anyone can do since it uses already existing paintings or photographs.

Instead of drawing and painting utensils, participants receive a rich selection of illustrated magazines, catalogues, calendars, greeting cards, and postcards. They can also bring their personal photographs from the family album or pictures of people, animals, and landscapes they have themselves taken. Using scissors, they cut out parts of these pictures that seem appropriate in portraying their experience; they fit them together and glue them on a thick, precut piece of paper. If they participate in ongoing groups, they end up eventually with a set of cards, which have deep personal meaning for them. They can take these cards to a friend's house, to sessions of individual therapy or support groups, or use them as decorations in their home.

Another interesting alternative or complement to mandala drawing is sculpting with clay or with various plastic modeling materials. We introduced this method when we had in our group participants who were blind and unable to draw mandalas. It was interesting to see that some of the other participants actually preferred to use this medium when it was available, or combined in a creative way mandala drawing with sculpting or with various material objects (pieces of fabric, feathers, wool, fragments of wood, leaves, seashells, etc.).

Later during the day, usually after a tea break or dinner break, breathers bring their mandalas, collages, and sculptures to a processing session, where they talk about their experiences. The facilitators leading the group encourage maximum openness and honesty in the sharing of the experiences, after everyone in the group agrees that any personal disclosures will be strictly confidential and will stay within the circle. Willingness of participants to reveal the content of their sessions, including various intimate details, is conducive to bonding and development of trust in the group. It deepens, intensifies, and expedites the therapeutic process.

By contrast to the practice of most therapeutic schools, facilitators abstain from interpreting the participants' experiences. The reason for this is the lack of agreement concerning the dynamics of the psyche among the existing approaches. We discussed earlier that under these circumstance any interpretations are questionable and arbitrary. Another reason for staying away from interpretations is the fact that psychological contents are often overdetermined and meaningfully related to several levels of the psyche. Giving a supposedly definitive explanation or interpretation carries the danger of freezing the process and interfering with therapeutic progress.

A more productive alternative is to ask questions that help draw out additional information from the perspective of the group member who, being the experiencer, is the ultimate expert as far as his or her experience is concerned. When we are patient and resist the temptation to share our own impressions and insights, participants very often find that their own explanations best reflect their experiences. On occasion, it can be very helpful to share our observations from the past concerning similar experiences or point out connections with experiences of other members of the group. When the experiences contain archetypal material, using C. G. Jung's method of *amplification*—pointing out parallels between a particular experience and similar mythological motifs from various cultures—or consulting a good dictionary of symbols might be very useful. However, facilitators emphasize that any comments or amplifications they offer are tentative suggestions. Participants are invited to take what they find helpful and leave the rest.

The processing in the group does not necessarily have to be limited to verbal accounts and descriptions of the mandalas; it can be very effectively complemented by various experiential approaches. On occasion, breathers can be encouraged to express in a psychodramatic way various elements from their sessions or their mandalas. When it seems appropriate, we can suggest that they assume the identity of various protagonists in their experiences—a person from a past life memory, real animals or power animals, and archetypal figures—and embody them in an expressive dance, pantomime, or impersonation. During their performance, the group might support them by using drums, rattles, and improvised vocalization.

Other times, the group can provide a profound corrective experience to breathers, who in their sessions have relived memories that have brought to a sharp relief feelings of estrangement, ostracism, loneliness, and not belonging. Breathers often encounter episodes of rejection and emotional abuse by their parents, schoolmates, and society at large. The feelings of not belonging also tend to occur in persons who grew up in interracial marriages or were brought up by parents with different church affiliation who were rigidly committed to their respective creeds. Deep roots of feelings of social isolation and abandonment can often be traced to lack of human contact in the early postnatal period.

A loving, supportive, and nourishing attitude of the peers expressed in words, touch, and hugs can go very far in providing a corrective experience for breathers who are wide open as a result of their breathwork sessions. In rare instances, we have used a very effective way of healing such old and present emotional wounds. We asked the breather to lie down on the floor in the middle of the room face up. The rest of the group surrounded the individual and lifted him or her using their forearms and palms of their hands. The group then gently rocked the individual back and forth, accompanying it by soothing sounds. Over the years, a collectively produced OM sound, carried for an extended period of time seemed to be the favorite choice; it often emerged spontaneously from the group without any programming or prompting. The healing power of this exercise has to be witnessed or personally experienced to be believed.

In some instances, breathers are still in process when the sharing group starts. It is important to have enough facilitators, so that someone can stay with such persons until they complete the process. Other breathers might be finished, but not ready to participate in the sharing group. We have found it useful to bring such participants into the group and provide for them a mattress outside of the sharing circle. This way they are included in the group, but can choose the degree to which they are able or willing to participate in the sharing. If some people decide not to talk in the group, it is essential for a facilitator to speak to them briefly after the processing session to find out what their condition is and if they need any help.

The list of guidelines that we have described here applies in its entirety when we conduct Holotropic Breathwork in introductory workshops. When the format involves repeated sessions, as is the case in ongoing groups meeting regularly at specific intervals, in the training for Holotropic Breathwork facilitators, or in month-long seminars, the screening of participants, the theoretical preparation, and the practical instructions are naturally done only at the beginning. In open groups, the necessary information is given to newcomers in private individual sessions.

An alternative is to provide the necessary theoretical information and practical instructions in the form of videotapes and to schedule a subsequent session in which we answer any questions that the tapes have elicited. Recordings covering this material are available from Grof Transpersonal Training (holotropic.com). The theoretical preparation for Holotropic Breathwork is the subject of a DVD entitled *Healing Potential of Non-Ordinary States of Consciousness: A Conversation with Stanislav Grof*. Practical aspects of conducting Holotropic Breathwork sessions are explored in the DVD called *Holotropic Breathwork: A Conversation with Christina and Stanislav Grof*.

At this point, we would once again like to extend a word of caution: These videotapes are designed to give newcomers basic information about Holotropic Breathwork before they participate in sessions supervised by trained facilitators. They do not represent adequate preparation for self-experimentation with the breathwork, let alone for conducting sessions with others. Work with holotropic states is very powerful and can open up deep levels of the unconscious psyche. The management of the ensuing experiences requires adequate experience and therapeutic skill. A necessary prerequisite for conducting this work with minimal risk and maximal benefits is intensive training that combines theoretical study with repeated personal sessions under expert guidance. Information about such training can also be found on the GTT website (holotropic.com).

When Holotropic Breathwork sessions are conducted on an individual basis, some of the information contained in this chapter is not applicable or needs to be modified. Theoretical and practical preparation, as well as the processing of the experiences, are done in private sessions. The setting for the breathwork is an office or a private room and the person conducting the sessions combines the role of a trained facilitator with that of a sitter and basic caregiver. Ideally, a second person—a colleague or apprentice—assists in the process. This is strongly recommended if we use supportive physical contact in these private sessions. While this approach does not present problems in group situations where external witnesses function as important safeguards, we do not recommend practicing it behind closed doors on a one-to-one basis.

We would like to close this chapter by referring readers to a series of books by Kylea Taylor that represent very useful complements to the present volume. The first of them, *The Breathwork Experience: Exploration and Healing in Non-Ordinary States of Consciousness* (Taylor 1994), is a very concise, informative book on Holotropic Breathwork. The second, entitled *Ethics of Caring: Honoring the Web of Life in Our Professional Healing Relationships*, with a foreword by Jack Kornfield (Taylor 1995), is an exploration of ethical issues concerning sex, power, money, and spirituality that therapists encounter in their work with clients. Kylea's third book, *The Holotropic Breathwork Workshop: A Manual for Trained Facilitators* (Taylor 1991), is a treasure trove of practical information for facilitators who have completed their GTT training and are planning to conduct their own workshops. And finally, *Exploring Holotropic Breathwork: Selected Articles from a Decade of the Inner Door* (Taylor 2004), is a large selection of articles that appeared in *The Inner Door*, a newsletter for the breathwork community. They cover a wide variety of personal and professional topics that emerge from the Holotropic Breathwork process.

CHAPTER FIVE

Integration of the Breathwork Experience and Follow-Up Work

Holotropic Breathwork sessions can open up the psyche on a very deep level and radically change the relationship between the conscious and unconscious dynamics. The final outcome of the session does not depend on how much traumatic material was brought into consciousness and processed, but how well the experience was completed and integrated. Facilitators therefore need to stay with the breathers as long as necessary to help them reach a successful closure. In this chapter, we will focus on what can be done before, during, and following the session to make Holotropic Breathwork safe, productive, and rewarding. We will discuss how to create conditions for optimal integration and how to help participants in their transition from the workshops to everyday life. In the following section, we will briefly review various other approaches to self-exploration that are compatible with Holotropic Breathwork and have been used occasionally by some practitioners as its complement.

1. Creating conditions for optimal integration

The first steps toward successful integration are made during the preparation period before the experiential work begins. It is important to inform the breathers that a necessary condition for a successful session is to keep their attention on the inner process, surrender fully to the experience, and express without judgment the emotions and physical energies that emerge in the session. We also stress that, as much as possible, participants suspend rational analysis and trust their inner healing intelligence and guidance more than their intellect.

During the sessions, facilitators can help breathers who show reluctance to continue and want to terminate the session by reassuring them and encouraging them to stay in the reclining position, keep their eyes closed or covered with eyeshades, and continue to breathe at a faster pace. If necessary, the facilitators might stay with the reluctant breathers for a while and hold their hand or offer some other form of support. At all cost, we try to avoid termination of the session at a time when the breather is still facing difficult experiences, because this leads to poor resolution of the unconscious material and unpleasant post-session periods.

The emotional and physical condition of the breathers is usually critically determined by how they feel when they complete the session. The facilitators need to talk briefly with all breathers before they leave the room and find out how they are feeling. Ideally, after their sessions the breathers are without pain and without any other form of physical distress, relaxed, and in an emotionally comfortable state. If that is not the case, facilitators must offer them bodywork and stay with them until the experience is satisfactorily completed.

2. Easing the transition to everyday life

Participation in a group in Holotropic Breathwork, even if it is only a short stay in an introductory weekend workshop, tends to create an extraordinary emotional and intellectual climate that tends to separate participants from the culture at large, not unlike the rites of passage in native cultures. However, in rites of passage this separation is temporary and, at the end, the non-ordinary experiences of the initiates validate the spiritually informed worldview of their culture and create a closer bond between the initiates and the rest of the tribe.

However, this is not the case in workshops of Holotropic Breathwork conducted in technological societies; as a matter of fact, the situation is exactly the opposite. Here participants are introduced to an understanding of the psyche and of the universe that is radically different from the worldview created by materialistic science, which dominates the industrial civilization. The new perspective that emerges from the work with holotropic states of consciousness is alien to both atheistic Westerners and to followers of many organized religions. In Holotropic Breathwork groups, this new vision of reality is not only imparted intellectually, but also validated by the profound personal experiences of participants.

The idea of a God who lies outside of creation and can be reached only through the mediation of the church hierarchy, is replaced with the concept of cosmic intelligence that has created the universe and permeates all its parts. It is the "Beyond Within," the divine that can be found within each of us, because we are ultimately identical with it. The world of separate objects and beings is an illusion; underlying it is a unified field, a cosmic matrix, which connects everything there is. Each human being represents a microcosm that contains the information about the macrocosm and, in a sense, is commensurate and identical with it ("as without so within," "as above so below" of esoteric spiritual systems).

The material world accessible to our senses and their various extensions is not the only reality. There exist domains of existence that are hidden from us as long as we are in the ordinary state of consciousness. They harbor archetypal beings and realms, which form and inform the world of matter. The possibility or even plausibility of reincarnation, karma, and survival of consciousness after death is not a matter of belief, but a conclusion based on the existence of very intense and convincing personal experiences of past life memories encountered in holotropic states.

Self-exploration using holotropic states thus tends to create a distinct subculture that accepts or even takes for granted certain realities that an average person in our culture would find weird or even crazy. This is particularly true if a group has shared holotropic experiences for an extended period of time, for example, in a month-long workshop, in our training for facilitators, or in an ongoing group, which meets at regular intervals over a number of months.

This newly discovered worldview is not irrational, bizarre, or idiosyncratic for individual breathers. It is transrational in the sense that it includes and transcends reason. Its essential tenets are discovered independently by most individuals involved in this form of self-exploration. In its totality, this perspective on existence shows great similarity to the ideas found in the great Eastern spiritual philosophies and in the mystical traditions of the world—Aldous Huxley's "perennial philosophy" (Huxley 1945). Holotropic experiences also often illumine and validate certain beliefs held by shamanic traditions and native cultures in general.

Many of us who have discovered the understanding of the psyche and of the universe described here find it very interesting and encouraging that this perspective, while incompatible with the seventeenth-century Newtonian-Cartesian thinking of monistic materialistic science, is sustained and validated by various avenues of the new emerging paradigm, such as quantum-relativistic physics, optical holography and holonomic thinking, new biology, systems theory, and other fields (Capra 1975; Pribram 1971; Bohm 1980; Sheldrake 1981; Laszlo 1993 and 2004).

Our experience has been that some people returning from Holotropic Breathwork workshops tend to be overenthusiastic about what they have experienced and seen and they might feel the need to indiscriminately share it with other people. They talk about having relived their birth, experienced memories from their previous lifetimes, encountered archetypal beings, or communicated with their dead relatives. All such experiences represent everyday occurrences in the breathwork sessions of ordinary people, but would very likely appear impossible or crazy to people on the street.

It is, therefore, important to discuss this issue with participants before they leave the workshop. We ask them to take enough time to let the experience settle down before they talk about it with others and, even then, carefully choose people with whom they may share the experience and the metaphors they will use. We recommend that after a powerful session they do not immediately throw themselves into busy social situations and that they refrain for several days from sharing the experience with others. If their circumstances allow, it is useful to take long baths, walk in nature, get a good massage, meditate, paint, or listen to music.

Typically people do not get in trouble because of the experiences they had, but because of what they do with them. This is true whether these experiences are induced by various psychotherapeutic techniques and psychedelic substances, or occur spontaneously in the middle of everyday life. The Spiritual Emergency Network (SEN) is an organization that Christina started in 1980 to support people undergoing crises of spiritual opening. In its early stage, the SEN Newsletter published a cartoon that represented a graphic illustration of this fact.

Stan, who drew the cartoon, got the idea for it when he was in India and saw a group of yogis meditating while suspended from trees by their feet. The cartoon showed a bearded yogi with a loincloth, hanging upside down from a tree. Sitting under the tree was a man in a straitjacket; a dialogue cloud above his head asked the yogi: "Why do they call you a mystic and me a psychotic?" The yogi's balloon read: "A mystic knows whom not to talk to."

3. Conducting follow-up interviews

Ideally, Holotropic Breathwork sessions would be combined with follow-up interviews on a one-to-one basis. This is mandatory when this method is used in the treatment of emotional and psychosomatic disorders. When the emotional condition of the client allows it, the Holotropic Breathwork sessions, as well as the follow-up interviews, can be conducted on an out-patient basis. If we work with severely disturbed clients, the entire treatment—the breathwork sessions and the processing interviews—requires an in-patient facility, a twenty-four-hour residential center.

In our training for Holotropic Breathwork facilitators, which consists of a series of six-day modules scheduled in pairs, we have the possibility of combining group sharing with individual interviews. The situation was also similar in our month-long seminars that we conducted when we lived at the Esalen Institute. However, over the years, we have conducted a large number of weekend and five-day workshops, where the discussion about the experiences was limited to the processing groups. People often came to these workshops from great distances and had to leave shortly after the workshops ended.

This situation requires more careful screening of participants for history of emotional disorders. Whenever possible, we provide participants the addresses of trained facilitators, preferably in their area, whom they can contact if they have questions or need any assistance. This is becoming easier as the number of trained facilitators is growing. As of now, over one thousand people in different parts of the world have completed our training. This has made it possible for us to conduct public workshops in places where trained facilitators can provide such back-up.

Individual post-session intervals have several functions. They provide an opportunity for attaining a deeper and more refined understanding of the experience in the session using the material that has emerged since the breathwork session in dreams or during meditation, drawing of additional mandalas, writing of session reports, or journaling. Breathwork sessions regularly bring specific archetypal images or material related to shamanism, Tantra, alchemy, or other esoteric teachings. It can be very useful to direct the attention of the breathers to specific literature that may help clarify such experiences and can be used to guide them in further explorations.

If the session took place in an ongoing group and some specific problems occurred in its course, the post-session interview can also be used to chart the strategy for the next session, should the same issues emerge again. An example of such a situation is fear of losing control, which requires reassuring the breather that such fears are unwarranted and explaining why. Another common hurdle is the experience of hopelessness associated with reliving of the onset of birth (BPM II). Here we have the task of convincing the breather that the fastest way out of such a situation is to go deeper into the experience of hopelessness until it reaches the intensity it had during the actual birth process. When that happens, the feeling of hopelessness disappears and the process automatically moves to the next stage. Fears of death, insanity, and not coming back from the experience are among other important problems that need to be discussed.

Many breathers with a history of anaclitic deprivation have, for a variety of reasons, great difficulties in accepting supportive physical contact. If this resistance persists, we need to discuss its causes and try to develop the breather's trust, so that this problem can be solved. Additional examples are various programs from childhood that prevent the breather from fully expressing emotions, such as "children should be seen, but not heard," "boys don't cry; if you cry, you are a sissy," or "good girls don't show anger." Here facilitators try to convince the breathers that their behaviors, reflecting injunctions and prohibitions that were imparted on them in childhood by parental authorities, are no longer relevant and actually work against them by interfering with their healing process.

The most important function of the follow-up interviews is to assess the condition of the breather and suggest specific complementary approaches if indicated. We will discuss these in the following section.

4. Using various methods complementing holotropic breathwork

On the days following an intense session that involved a major emotional breakthrough or opening, a wide variety of complementary approaches can facilitate integration. Among them are discussions about the session with an experienced facilitator, meditation, writing down a detailed account of the experience, drawing more mandalas, and working with Soul Collage. Jogging, swimming, expressive dancing, and other forms of aerobic physical exercise can be very useful, if the holotropic experience has freed excess of previously pent-up physical energy. Conversely, good bodywork with a practitioner who allows emotional expression or an acupuncture session can help to release various residual blockages of energy. While Holotropic Breathwork stands on its own as an integral approach to self-exploration and therapy, it is compatible and can be combined with a broad spectrum of other uncovering methods, of psychotherapy.

Gestalt practice can help the integration of powerful Holotropic Breathwork sessions and provide refined insights into the unconscious material that has emerged. This method was developed in South Africa and at the Esalen Institute in Big Sur, California, by Fritz Perls (1893–1970), a German psychiatrist and psychoanalyst trained in Berlin and Austria. Gestalt practice emerged in the middle of the twentieth century as a school of humanistic psychotherapy and became very popular in the 1960s and 1970s. Among the influences that shaped this original method of therapy and self-exploration were Eastern religions, existential phenomenology, physics, Gestalt psychology, psychoanalysis, theatrical performance, and systems and field theory (Perls, Hefferline, Goodman 1951; Perls 1973, 1976).

Gestalt practice represents a radical shift from the Freudian emphasis on the exploration of the client's history to the present psychodynamics between the client, the therapist, and the group. The emphasis is on what is happening in the "here and now"—what is being done, thought, and felt at the moment rather than on what was, might be, could be, or should be. The objective of Gestalt therapy, in addition to helping the clients overcome symptoms, is to enable them to become more fully alive, creative, and to be free from emotional and physical blocks and unfinished issues ("incomplete gestalts"). This enhances the quality of their lives and increases satisfaction, fulfillment, personal growth, self-acceptance, and the ability to experience more in the present without excessive interference from the baggage of the past.

Sandplay is a unique method of nonverbal psychotherapy developed by the Swiss Jungian analyst Dora Kalff after C. G. Jung encouraged her to use this approach in her work with children. The basic tools of the sandplay are a box of prescribed dimensions partially filled with sand and a large collection of small objects—figurines of people from different cultures and ages, animals, archetypal beings, miniature buildings and trees, and a variety of natural objects, such as shells and stones of interesting shapes and colors. Using these objects, clients create their individual compositions that reflect their internal states. The essential assumption underlying this technique is Jung's hypothesis that there is a fundamental drive toward healing in the human psyche, which he referred to as the *individuation process*. Dora Kalff recognized that the images created by children and adults correspond to the inner psychic processes of individuation (Kalff 2003).

Psychodrama is another experiential method that can occasionally be used in certain specific situations as a useful complement to Holotropic Breathwork. This technique was developed by Jacob Levy Moreno, a Romanian psychiatrist, social scientist, and foremost pioneer of group psychotherapy. While still a medical student, Moreno rejected Freudian theory and began experimenting with methods of role-playing in group settings, at first in the form of street theater with volunteer passersby and later in professional contexts. Psychodrama has strong elements of theater and is often performed on a stage with the use of various props. Various intrapsychic and interpersonal conflicts can be worked through by asking the peers in the group to assume the roles of the protagonists, identify with them, and act out their attitudes, emotions, and behaviors (Moreno 1973, 1976).

Another useful approach is Francine Shapiro's eye movement desensitization and reprocessing (EMDR). This method is based on the observation that the emergence of unconscious material is typically associated with rapid eye movements (REM) and, conversely, rapid eye movements can facilitate the emergence of unconscious material. During therapeutic work with this method, clients are instructed to focus on a previously identified target, such as vivid visual images related to a memory, a negative self-image, or specific emotions and physical sensations. Clients then follow for a period of twenty to thirty seconds the movements of the therapist's fingers across their visual field. Acoustic stimulation by tapping or prerecorded tones can be used in lieu of moving fingers. The therapist encourages the client to notice thoughts, feelings, or sensations that come to mind. This process is repeated many times during each session (Shapiro 2001, 2002).

Some facilitators occasionally complement Holotropic Breathwork sessions with a method called Family Constellation or Systemic Constellation. This controversial technique was developed by Bert Hellinger, a German Roman Catholic priest who used as his main inspiration Zulu rituals and native group dynamics that he had observed during his missionary stay in Africa (Hellinger 2003). Under the guidance of the facilitator, individuals working on some personal issues or problems involving the dynamics of their family choose group participants who would represent them and various family members. They arrange these representatives into a constellation according to what they feel are the right positions for them and distances between them at the moment. Then they sit down and observe what is happening.

Unlike in psychodrama, representatives do not act or role-play. The objective is to tap into the Knowing Field—as German psychiatrist Albrecht Mahr calls it—and let the intuition of the representatives guide the group dynamics and the changes in the constellation (Mahr 1999). The basic assumption underlying this method is that the Knowing Field makes it possible for the representatives to sense and articulate the feelings of the real family members. Dissatisfaction and discomfort concerning placement is seen as an indication of "systemic entanglement" between the family members. This happens when the family is afflicted by an unresolved trauma, such as suicide, murder, or early death of a family member, death of mother in childbirth, abuse, war, or natural disaster. A healing resolution is achieved when all the participants in the constellation feel that they are in the right places and other representatives agree.

While Bert Hellinger's family constellation has achieved great popularity internationally, Hellinger himself has become a highly controversial figure and has been subjected to severe criticisms, particularly in Germany. His critics point out his rigid patriarchal and autocratic attitude, erratic judgment, extreme unsubstantiated claims, obscure mysticism, siding with perpetrators, and condoning of incest, war criminals, and dictators, including Hitler. However, these attitudes and behaviors are symptomatic of Hellinger's personality and not integral parts of the technique itself. Many of Hellinger's followers—such as Albrecht Mahr—seem to be able to practice the family constellation method without the extremes and distortions reflecting Hellinger's personal bias and find this method very interesting and rewarding.

Voice Dialogue is a therapeutic technique and personality theory developed by American psychologists and authors Hal Stone and Sidra Stone (Stone and Stone 1989). Like C. G. Jung and Roberto Assagioli before them, the authors suggest that each of us consists of many separate selves, subpersonalities, or energy patterns of our psyche. Their technique allows us to dialogue with our inner selves and to discover how they operate within us, how they feel, what is their hierarchy of values, how they make us feel, what they want from us, and so on. By bringing awareness into different facets of ourselves, we can reach the state of the Aware Ego—experience our selves as separate from us and "unhook from being identified with a particular self."

Since Holotropic Breathwork—as we currently see it—is as much an approach facilitating spiritual opening as it is a strategy for self-exploration and a healing method, it is perfectly compatible with various forms of spiritual practice—Buddhist and Taoist meditation, hatha yoga and other yogic exercises, movement meditation, Tai Chi Chuan, qi gong, Sufi dancing and chanting, Kabbalah, Christian prayer, Native American spirituality, and many others. This is an ideal combination that over time can result not only in emotional and psychosomatic healing, but also in permanent positive personality transformation.

CHAPTER SIX

Trials and Tribulations of Holotropic Breathwork Facilitators

Over the years, we have conducted Holotropic Breathwork workshops in different countries of the world and in cultures with different social structures, political systems, customs, and religious beliefs. On occasion, people in these environments showed an adverse reaction to various aspects of this new method of self-exploration and therapy—the use of loud music, unusual choice of pieces that were played, non-ordinary state of consciousness of the participants, intense vocal expression of emotions, strange physical manifestations, and close physical contact between the breathers, sitters, and facilitators. In many instances, the physical setting for the sessions and the quality or reliability of the musical equipment were far from ideal. The following stories illustrate some of the challenges that facilitators can encounter while practicing Holotropic Breathwork.

1. Encounter with the military junta in Buenos Aires

Our Argentinean adventure started in our five-day workshop at the Esalen Institute in connection with one of the most remarkable and puzzling instances of healing we have witnessed over the thirty years we have been practicing Holotropic Breathwork. Gladys, a young woman participating in this workshop, told the group during our first meeting that she had suffered for about four years from serious chronic depression accompanied with intense anxiety. She expressed hope that breathwork would give her some insights into this debilitating problem.

In her two breathwork sessions, Gladys relived several important traumatic memories from her childhood and infancy and experienced a series of intense sequences related to her biological birth. She felt that the unconscious material that had emerged in these sessions was the source of her depression. The second session involved the activation and release of large amounts of pent-up energy. This is usually an important step in the therapeutic work with depression, which is a condition characterized by major blockages of emotional and physical energy. However, in spite of intense bodywork in the termination period, the session did not result in a satisfactory resolution and relief.

The morning following Gladys' second session, her depression appeared, but was considerably more pronounced than usual. It also took a different form than it had had before. Instead of the familiar inhibition, lack of initiative, and apathy, Gladys was agitated. We had originally planned the morning session to be an open forum—a group discussion during which participants could ask any questions about their experiences and about the theory and practice of Holotropic Breathwork. However, seeing Gladys' condition, we decided to change our program and do experiential work with her without delay.

We asked her to lie down in the middle of the group, do some deep breathing, surrender to the flow of the music Christina was playing, and accept any experiences that might emerge under these circumstances. For about fifty minutes, Gladys experienced violent tremors, choked and coughed, made loud noises, and seemed to fight some invisible enemies. Retrospectively, she reported that this part of her experience involved reliving of her difficult birth, but this time much deeper than before.

Later in the session, her screams became more articulate and started resembling a language. We encouraged her to allow the sounds to come out in whatever form they took, without censoring or judging them, even if they made no sense to her. Gradually, her movements became stylized and emphatic and her words clear but in a language that we did not recognize. At one point, she sat up and began chanting a haunting repetitive sequence that sounded like a prayer. This went on for quite some time.

The impact of this event on the group was profound. Without understanding the words or knowing what Gladys was experiencing internally, most participants felt deeply moved and started to cry. Some assumed a meditative posture and joined their hands as if in prayer. When Gladys completed her chant, she quieted down and resumed a horizontal position on her back. She moved into a state of bliss and ecstatic rapture for more than an hour, entirely motionless. Later, when Gladys was giving a retrospective account of her experience, she described that she had felt an irresistible urge to do what she did. She did not understand what had happened and indicated that she had absolutely no idea what language she was using in her chant.

Carlos, an Argentinean Freudian psychoanalyst from Buenos Aires and a member in the workshop, recognized that Gladys had chanted perfectly in the Sephardic language, which he happened to know. This language, also called Ladino, is a Judeo-Spaniolic hybrid, a combination of medieval Spanish and Hebrew. By strange coincidence Carlos, who was Jewish, had studied the Sephardic language for many years as his personal hobby. Gladys was not Jewish and knew neither Hebrew nor Spanish; she had never heard of Ladino and did not know that it existed. Carlos translated the words of Gladys' repetitive chant, which had such a powerful effect on the group: "I am suffering and I will always suffer. I am crying and I will always cry. I am praying and I will always pray."

During this dramatic finale of her experience in the group, when she chanted the Sephardic prayer, Gladys broke through the depression and her condition stabilized in a psychologically very positive place. Carlos was deeply impressed by what he just had witnessed. His own Freudian framework with which he had come to the workshop was already seriously undermined by his own profound experience of birth and a very convincing and meaningful past life memory, none of which were part of his scientific worldview, as well as by similar experiences of other group participants.

Gladys' experience was the turning point in Carlos' deep conceptual conversion toward transpersonal psychology. He was eager to continue this approach to self-exploration and asked us to come to Buenos Aires as soon as possible to conduct a Holotropic Breathwork workshop. We already had a very busy schedule for the rest of the year, including a forthcoming long trip to Europe. Carlos insisted that we make a detour and stop in Argentina on the way from Europe to California. He offered to pay the extra airplane fare and added a very tempting honorarium that was hard to resist.

The two of us arrived in Buenos Aires after a long flight from Frankfurt. We knew that Argentina had a military regime, but were rather naïve in regard to the malicious nature of this regime, which was not fully revealed until much later. Our arrival coincided with the beginning of the right-wing dictatorship of the Argentinean military junta that had seized power during the March 1976 coup amid violent conflicts between far-left and far-right supporters of the recently deceased President Juan Domingo Peron. The junta practiced what was called the Dirty War—state-sponsored disappearance, torture, and murder of thousands of suspected political dissidents and leftists, as well as their family members.

On our way from the airport, we passed areas surrounded by barbed wire fences and saw numerous armored cars and tanks. In some areas, the number of soldiers seemed to exceed that of civilians. Carlos arranged our accommodation in the Bauen Hotel on one of Buenos Aires' spacious avenues and reserved a space for the workshop in the same hotel. As we were entering the hotel, we noticed that the entrance was guarded by two young soldiers holding submachine guns. Somewhat intimidated by our first impressions of Buenos Aires, we asked Carlos if he was sure that it was really all right to do the breathwork workshop under these circumstances. "No problem," he assured us pointing to a bulletin board in the lobby with the inscription: INVESTIGATIONES CIENTIFICAS PSICOLOGICAS. "I told the manager and the personnel of the hotel," he said, "that we would be conducting an important scientific experiment."

The workshop took place in a large conference room ordinarily used for meetings of various business companies. At Carlos' request, the furniture was removed and replaced by mattresses. Participants, clearly not well informed about the nature of the workshop, arrived in business attire—men wearing jackets and ties; women skirts, stockings, and high-heeled shoes. After we prepared them for the breathwork, many took off their shoes and removed all extraneous accessories.

Following the introductory relaxation, the breathwork started and we were playing music at a high volume. It did not take long before loud screams resounded in the room. This alarmed the two soldiers guarding the entrance of the hotel; in the tense political situation in Argentina, loud screaming was suspect as a possible indication of dissent and revolt. In the midst of the session, the soldiers dashed up the stairs, kicked the door open, and stormed the breathing room with the submachine guns ready. Dumbfounded by the scene they encountered, they froze, aiming their weapons into the room and trying to figure out what was going on.

It took Carlos and our translator more than ten minutes to assure the soldiers that the situation was harmless and that there was no reason for military intervention. Carlos kept reminding the soldiers of the large inscription in the lobby, describing what we were doing as an important scientific experiment conducted by two famous American psychologists. After the soldiers somewhat reluctantly left the unusual scene, the session continued for some time without interruption.

Then, about an hour later, the door flew open again. This time, two young men in waiters' uniform entered the room carrying trays with full cups of coffee and mid-afternoon snacks, as they were used to doing during break-time of business meetings. They were so taken aback by what they saw that they almost dropped their trays. By this time, people were lying on the mattresses, some dressed in slips and boxer shorts, and many of them in close physical contact; it was not the scene the waiters were used to seeing in the business meetings.

While the sitters naturally witnessed both intrusions and experienced various degrees of fear and concern during the first interruption and amusement during the second, we found in the sharing group following the breathwork session that the breathers were so deeply immersed in their process that none of them noticed that anything unusual was going on.

2. Competing with the exhibition of Doberman pinschers

By 1988, we had certified enough facilitators that we could consider offering Holotropic Breathwork to larger groups. The International Transpersonal Conference that we organized in Santa Rosa, California, seemed to offer an ideal opportunity to explore what a large-scale Holotropic Breathwork session would look like. Since many people who were coming to the conference had previously experienced Holotropic Breathwork in our workshops and training, we decided to offer as part of the program a preconference Holotropic Breathwork reunion for experienced breathers. We were aware that this workshop would attract a large number of people and reserved for it the Grand Ballroom, the most spacious meeting room in the Santa Rosa Flamingo Hotel.

Two weeks before the beginning of the conference, we discovered that two alarming problems had emerged in the preparation for our two-day preconference workshop. A volunteer, who had stepped in for the person handling the registrations, was not adequately informed and accepted into the workshop a large number of participants who did not have previous breathwork experience. In addition, the staff member in charge of reservations at the hotel somehow missed the fact that we had reserved the Grand Ballroom and gave it to another group for an exhibition of Doberman pinschers. When we discovered what was happening and stopped the registration, the number of accepted participants already amounted to 360 and we were facing the seemingly impossible task of accommodating them in a much smaller hall.

In the morning before the workshop began, we were wakened from a deep sleep by loudspeakers blasting "The Star-Spangled Banner." Half asleep, Christina went to the window and peeked out through a slit between the curtains; she began to giggle and called Stan. When we looked out of the window of our room, we saw a scene that was surreal: Around the swimming pool marched a long line of Doberman pinschers dressed in tuxedo collars and bowties. The handlers marched proudly next to their dogs holding taut red leashes; following them came helpers carrying long-handled dustpans and trowels. They were the "pooper-scoopers" in charge of keeping everything neat and clean. The next couple of days, on the way to and from the workshop, we had to walk carefully and watch for places that the "pooper-scoopers" had missed. This scene by the swimming pool was a humorous and harsh reminder of the challenge we were facing: the Doberman pinschers had usurped the Grand Ballroom that we had reserved and we had to conduct the breathwork session with 360 participants in the relatively small Rainbow Hall.

When the mattresses were distributed in the room, the spaces between them barely allowed the facilitators to walk around and the participants to get to the bathroom. Two unexpected developments saved the day and turned a nearly impossible situation into a success. Among the participants was a group of fifty-five individuals from Japan, who preferred to breathe in close physical contact with only inches between them. In addition, the arms and legs of all the active breathers moved in perfect non-choreographed coordination, dancing through the air without touching. It seemed as if the entire group was one organism; this perfect integration of the movements was reminiscent of what we have seen in giant flocks of birds or schools of fish. Thanks to these two fortunate developments, the first large Holotropic Breathwork experience that seemed to be heading for disaster and potential fiasco ended up as a thundering success.

3. Culture-bound challenges for Holotropic Breathwork facilitators

Accepting invitations from individuals and groups to conduct breathwork workshops in different countries of the world, we encountered occasionally specific problems related to the history, culture, and customs of the regions we visited. None of them were as serious as to make conducting the workshops impossible, but they occasionally came as a great surprise to us and required special effort or adjustment.

In 1984, we visited India as guests of the Indian American Friendship Council to give lectures and conduct workshops in Mumbai (Bombay), Dilli (New Delhi), Kolkata (Calcutta), and Chenai (Madras). A significant number of participants were Indian professionals, psychiatrists, and psychologists. To our surprise, they initially seemed to show an even stronger critical attitude and greater resistance toward transpersonal psychology and the new paradigm than an average Western academician.

They were very deeply influenced by the materialistic philosophy of Western science and considered behaviorism and Freudian analysis to be superior, scientifically validated approaches to the understanding of the human psyche. At the same time, they tended to dismiss—at least in professional discussions with their colleagues—their own spiritual traditions as primitive, unscientific products of superstition and magical thinking. However, when we shared with them the scientific evidence from modern consciousness research supporting the transpersonal perspective, they seemed to be greatly relieved. It was a revelation for them that there were members of the Western academic community who asserted that it was possible to be scientific and spiritual at the same time. It was obvious that they had not been able to reject Indian spiritual philosophies and their own cultural tradition without deep inner conflict.

The only problem that we encountered in experiential work with this population emerged before the breathwork started. As Westernized as they seemed to be, it was difficult for Indian participants to accept the idea that people of different gender could partner up for the breathing sessions—men sitting for women and vice versa. In spiritual gatherings in the Indian ashrams, it is customary for men and women to sit separately in different parts of the meditation hall. However, after some initial resistance, many of them were able to adjust to this unusual situation. Neither of us remembered ever having encountered this difficulty with people of Indian origin who had occasionally participated in our workshops in the United States or other parts of the world.

Our workshop in Bombay presented an unusual challenge for Christina that had long-lasting consequences for her everyday life. A very effective way of helping breathers release general body tension is to ask them to intensify this tension and flex their arms; the facilitator then stands astride them, grasps their wrists, and lifts their body in the air. This position is maintained for as long as the breather is able to hang on (see pages 187f). This maneuver usually results in a major release of blocked physical energy and pent-up emotions. When Christina encountered a situation that required this type of intervention with one of the male participants, she felt strongly that it might be culturally inappropriate in India for a woman to straddle a man. After some deliberation, she decided to lift the breather in an awkward and mechanically untoward way—standing with both feet on his right side. As a result, she hurt her back; this incident undoubtedly contributed to her back problems in the years to come.

Our first breathwork in India brought a surprise of a different kind. One of Christina's favorite pieces for the termination period of Holotropic Breathwork sessions was the Indian devotional hymn "Raghupati Raghava Raja Ram." Participants in our workshops usually found this piece of music to be very meditative, soothing, and relaxing. Since we were in India, Christina thought that it would be very appropriate to play it in the later part of the session. No sooner did the participants hear the melody than the previously peaceful and quiet breathers became animated and agitated and the entire room was filled with loud weeping and wailing sounds.

This intense reaction was not limited to the breathers; many of the sitters seemed deeply moved and were crying, some of them quietly, others loudly. This sweet and innocent chant had a more powerful effect on the group than the previously played intense evocative music. More than half an hour later, the room quieted down and participants seemed to have reached completion of their emotional outburst. We did not understand what caused this seemingly paradoxical reaction involving the entire group until later when we found out from the participants that "Raghupati Raghava Raja Ram" was the favorite chant of Mahatma Gandhi; it was played in India non-stop for three days after his assassination and at the time of his funeral. It was clear that many Indians had not completed their mourning process and still carried powerful unresolved emotions about the death of their legendary spiritual leader.

During our first Holotropic Breathwork in Japan, we encountered an unexpected situation of a different kind. Before our first workshop, which took place in Tokyo, we expected that Japanese participants might have difficulties letting go and surrendering to the experiences that may surface. During our previous visits when we had come as tourists, the Japanese seemed to us to be generally more emotionally inhibited and restrained than Westerners. However, our anticipation proved to be incorrect. The breathwork sessions in Japan were very powerful and the participants did not seem to have any more problems letting go than we had seen in Western countries.

As a matter of fact, they seemed to be unusually willing to follow all our suggestions. We were told by our Japanese host that this might have something to do with the fact that—as published authors and originators of the Holotropic Breathwork—we fell into the category referred to as "sensei," or venerated teacher. This title is used in Japan for individuals who have achieved a certain level of mastery in some unique skill or art form. Professionals, such as lawyers and doctors, spiritual teachers, artists, and other figures of authority are addressed in this way; it is deeply ingrained in the Japanese psyche to show respect to such figures and follow their instructions.

However, there was one situation that even the magic of the title "sensei" could not overcome, something that we had not previously seen in our groups: the process of choosing a partner. In our first Japanese workshop, we explained to participants that they would be working in pairs and asked them to look around and choose a partner to work with. To our surprise, they suddenly appeared puzzled and completely lost. They looked around and at each other, seemingly confused. It was clear that the process of choosing a partner hit an unexpected impasse.

Fortunately, our host came to our rescue. "They cannot choose partners because they do not want to offend anyone," he said. "It would be impossible for them to justify why they chose one person over another." He then offered the group an alternative that turned out to be perfectly acceptable for everybody. He left the room and returned with a large gong and a mallet. "Close your eyes, mill around, and turn in circles. When you hear the gong, stop and open your eyes; whoever is in front of you will be your partner." The group responded without the slightest hesitation and the selection process was solved within seconds. Participants, who were earlier unable to make a personal decision, had no problems accepting a solution involving an impersonal process. We realized how different this was from the dynamics in our Western groups in which it was very important for participants to have the right of individual choice and where random assignment of partners would be met with resistance.

In a workshop that we conducted for the staff of a psychiatric hospital in Ireland, we encountered a hierarchical structure that was stronger than we expected. The doctors initially refused not only to partner up with nurses in the breathwork sessions, where hierarchical concerns were more understandable, but also wanted to sit separately from them during the theoretical preparation. Fortunately, these kinds of problems usually occur only in the initial stages of holotropic workshops. The barriers tend to dissolve very fast once we start the experiential process.

4. Technological ordeals in Holotropic Breathwork sessions

As we have discussed earlier, music is an essential element in Holotropic Breathwork. Wherever we go, we are very conscious of this fact and always try to do anything we can to have an excellent musical system capable of delivering stereophonic music of high quality and sufficient volume. Unfortunately, the ideas of the workshop hosts as to what represents a good music system can vary widely. One of our earliest breathwork workshops was held in Finland, in a center located several hundred miles north of Helsinki, in the middle of nowhere and far from the nearest town. When we arrived, we were very pleasantly surprised by the quality of this facility, particularly by its beautiful sauna with an adjacent ice-cold pond and a supply of fresh birch branches for stimulating the circulation of blood.

An unpleasant surprise came when the organizers of the workshop showed us the music system they procured for the breathwork sessions. It was a cassette player about a foot long with built-in speakers. The workshop was about to start and there was absolutely no hope of finding a better alternative. We did the best thing we could do under the circumstances: we placed the cassette player in the middle of the room and asked the twenty-some participants to form a circle and lie down on the floor with their heads toward the center of the room. Since the breathwork, in and of itself, can induce holotropic states of consciousness, most people in the group had significant experiences. Fortunately, none of the participants had previously experienced Holotropic Breathwork; not knowing how much better it could be under the right circumstances, they were quite impressed and satisfied.

Even if we have a music system that meets our specifications, there are other potential problems that are not under our control, such as unexpected malfunctioning of the music system and loss of electrical power. It would therefore be ideal to always have back-up music equipment and a generator ready to provide an alternate source of electricity. However, these conditions are seldom met. When we lived at the Esalen Institute, we had the luxury of an alternate music system and a reliable electric generator ready to kick in whenever we lost electricity. The latter was a necessity in Big Sur, where the rough natural conditions—fires, rainstorms, windstorms, and landslides—caused frequent blackouts. Unfortunately, the situation was often different when we conducted workshops in other parts of the world. This was the case in a Holotropic Breathwork workshop with more than 130 participants that Stan conducted jointly with Tav Sparks in New York City.

About half an hour into the session, when many participants were already in the process, the music system started overheating and the quality of the music was getting progressively worse. This was a very precarious situation, since there was no back-up system and the music was getting so bad that it threatened the continuation of the workshop. A large fan slowed down the overheating, but the distortion of the sound reached a level where what was coming out of the speakers had little resemblance to the original recording.

The system did not completely break down and managed to produce an awful cacophony till the end of the session. Tav and Stan expected harsh and fully justified criticism from the group, but none of it came. Most of the participants had not had previous experience with Holotropic Breathwork and very likely thought that what they had heard was special sound technology used with this method. Even more surprisingly, most of the breathers had very powerful experiences that did not seem to be particularly different from what we had seen in other groups. However, this experience should not serve as indication and reassurance that the quality and condition of the music system makes no difference in Holotropic Breathwork sessions.

On the rare occasions when we lost music and had no backup, we used to encourage the breathers to continue breathing in silence, since—as we already said—faster breathing, in and of itself, can cause profound changes of consciousness. Then in a weeklong retreat at the Omega Center in Rhinebeck, New York, with over 150 participants, during a blackout and a simultaneous failure of the back-up generator, Christina found a very effective solution. She took a metal trash basket from the corner of the room and started beating it with her hand in a regular rhythm. A couple of facilitators and a few sitters joined her by clapping and stomping their feet. Two people found some drums and others brought chimes, bells, and a tambourine. Before long, this improvised musical performance was complemented by humming and wordless chanting. Soon an organic feedback system developed between the breathers and the noisemakers, as the two groups were responding to each other's energy. This created a scene resembling aboriginal tribal ceremonies. During the processing group, we discovered to our surprise that many participants found this situation equally powerful as the music or even more so.

Even if the sound system functions perfectly, external circumstances can disturb the acoustic experience of the participants. Although we always warn the hotels where we conduct our workshops, as well as other hosting institutions, that we will be playing music at high volume and that there will likely be loud sounds coming from the breathers, it has happened on a number of occasions that the management tried to intervene and terminate our sessions because they found the noise level too disturbing. Because of the nature of Holotropic Breathwork, premature termination of the session naturally was not possible nor negotiable, but we were on occasion forced to turn down the volume of the music far below the optimal level.

In 1987, in the course of our very first certification intensive held in Breckenridge, a ski resort in the Colorado Rocky Mountains, we experienced a different type of acoustic intrusion. In the middle of one breathwork session, the penetrating shrill sound of a siren filled the room; it was persistent and much louder than the music. We ran into the hallway where hotel staff members told us that lightning hit the building and triggered a fire alarm. The building's top floor had a small fire and the elevators were stopped. We looked out the window and saw fire personnel running toward the outside doors. This was the last thing we wanted to happen to our trainees who were at the time absorbed in a deep emotional process. Some facilitators and the two of us stood on chairs holding pillows over the hotel speakers to muffle the obnoxious sound.

Two fire inspectors stormed the room and insisted that we evacuate the building immediately. This was a task that was not only technically difficult, considering that we were dealing with a large number of people (thirty-five breathers) experiencing non-ordinary states of consciousness, but also potentially dangerous, since a brutal interruption of a deep experience could have serious emotional consequences. We explained to the inspectors the precariousness of the situation and told them that they would have to assume full medical and legal responsibility if they insisted on evacuation. Hearing that and admitting that it was after all a very small fire, they very reluctantly agreed that we could stay and continue. Most breathers had had extensive previous exposure to the breathwork and were familiar with one of the basic tenets of this method: Try to incorporate all external sounds into one's experience. Others were less successful and experienced the siren as a serious disturbance. However, they were able to use the remaining time in the session and bring their experiences to successful completion and integration.

5. The pisspot, oinking piglets, and smoldering Kleenexes

In the early eighties, we were invited by a German group to do a Holotropic Breathwork workshop. It took place in Austria near Vienna and
the Slovak border, at a farm the group had bought as a place to conduct
various forms of experiential work. The complex consisted of a residential
building, a courtyard, and a large two-story barn. Soon after our arrival,
we discovered that the space designated for experiential work was on the
second floor of the barn and could be reached only by climbing a vertical
ladder. It was dusty and dirty, as one could have expected considering it
was an agricultural structure.

In addition, the only bathroom in the complex was in the residential
building and to reach it from the breathwork space meant to climb down
the ladder and walk across the courtyard into the main building. This was
a feat too challenging and dangerous for individuals in non-ordinary states
of consciousness. Since the Holotropic Breathwork was not the first experiential workshop that was conducted on the farm, we were curious how this
problem had been handled in the past. We found out that the group used a
large container (referred to as the "pisspot"), located in one corner of the
experiential area; privacy of the people relieving themselves was provided
by a vertical sheet suspended on a line.

People in the group assured us that they had done so much intense
inner work together and were so closely knit that this situation did not
present any problems. Since there was no alternative available, we had to
accept these conditions and go ahead with the workshop. The farm was
located in an isolated rural area and there was not much to do there. Our
thirteen-year-old daughter Sarah who traveled with us volunteered to assist
in the sessions; although she had seen our work at Esalen, she had never
participated in one of our workshops before. She ended up helping the
breathers to get to the "pisspot" and return to the mattresses.

The breathwork sessions of the participants were long and very intense,
as it often was the case in German workshops at that time. Although most
of these people had been born after the Second World War, they seemed to
carry the emotional burden of this ominous time of their national history.
We worked hard and had the feeling that we deserved every pfennig we
earned. In spite of the less than favorable circumstances, the sessions were
generally very productive and satisfactorily integrated. However, the closing
ceremony was a complete flop.

At the time, we used to conduct at the end of our breathwork workshops
a little ritual; it involved a fire purification ceremony that we had learned at
Esalen from visiting shamans. We made a fire and participants approached it
paired up with the partners with whom they had worked in the breathwork.

They then moved the warm air from the fire with the palms of their hands toward their faces and bodies, imagining that the fire element was burning any leftover negative energies from the session. Each of them also burnt a handful of Kleenexes used in the course of the sessions.

Unfortunately, the weather was very wet and we had problems making and maintaining a good fire. In addition, the group did not provide any Kleenexes and people were using in the sessions a peculiar kind of very tough pink toilet paper; its surface was undulated and stretched when pulled apart. More importantly, it did not catch fire, but was smoldering and producing ugly dark smoke. Considering the heavy, gloomy, and foul-smelling cloud hanging over our heads, it was difficult to feel very festive.

Moreover, the air was filled with painful high-pitched oinking of piglets coming from the neighboring farm. We remembered seeing on the way to the farm a large inscription that read: FERKEL-VERSTEIGERUNG ("Auction of Piglets"). The auction was running parallel to our closing ceremony and the unfortunate animals squealed loudly, probably in anticipation of their forthcoming destiny. It seemed as though the ceremony would never end, but finally it was over. We were leaving the farm with a firm determination that in the future we would carefully scrutinize ahead of time the conditions in which our workshops would take place.

6. Supreme ordeal Down Under

One of the greatest challenges we have encountered in all the years of doing Holotropic Breathwork was our workshop in a center located in the Australian outback about four hours' drive north of Sydney. The first surprises came as soon as we entered; the rooms were dirty, crammed with junk, and poorly maintained. The venue previously had been an old Boy Scout camp with triple-decker beds. Our hostess took us to our room, which was dark and grim; on the floor were two bare mattresses with straw protruding through several holes. "You'll have to make your own bed," she said and added: "I hope you brought your own towels; this place does not have any. Oh, and I hope you brought your own bedding." It was a strange expectation, considering we came all the way from California.

Our next stop was the kitchen and the pantry. Our hostess pointed to a large bag of potatoes, glass jars with rice, several loaves of bread on the shelves, and a couple of baskets filled with several kinds of vegetables. "The group will have to take care of the food," our hostess told us, "I am planning to take the workshop and will not have time to cook." Even participants used to tough conditions of the Australian outback were surprised and found this situation strange and unacceptable. After a day of culinary chaos, Christina became so angry at the situation that she finally ended up in the role of the chef, preparing for the group a large pot of hearty vegetable soup and sandwiches.

But the more than Spartan conditions at the center were not the most difficult challenge we faced during this workshop; it was the behavior of our hostess. We found out that her specialty and passion was "brushing of auras," which she practiced and taught at the center. And she was determined to demonstrate her skills on participants of our group. No sooner did the breathwork session start than she began tiptoeing around the breather for whom she was sitting, making magical passes in the air to clear what she felt were impurities in her partner's "auric field."

In spite of the explicit instructions we had given to the sitters—not to intervene in the process and to allow the breathers to use their own inner healing intelligence—she then proceeded actually touching and poking various parts of her partner's body. When she completed the intervention to her satisfaction, she left her partner and started to pace around the room intently observing other breathers and occasionally stepping in to brush their "auric fields." After each intervention, she walked to the sink, filled a glass with water and gargled loudly, spitting into the sink, flapping and fluttering her arms, and shaking her entire body.

During this procedure, evidently meant to be a purification ritual aimed at discharging all the negative energy collected from the afflicted "auric fields" of the participants, she looked in our direction to find out whether we had seen and appreciated her healing skills. Needless to say, considering the emotional investment she had in her activities, it was not easy to dissuade her from continuing what she was doing. When the weekend ended, our parting was rather cold and reserved and we felt greatly relieved when we left the center behind and were driving back to Sydney.

7. Conducting Holotropic Breathwork in adversarial settings

In 1985, French Socialist Party politician Alain Vivien wrote at the request of the French Prime Minister Pierre Mauroy a report on the danger of cults, which was published under the title "Cults in France: Expression of Moral Freedom or Factors of Manipulation." This report did not attract much attention and was of little relevance until the 1990s, when a series of group suicides and/or mass murders committed by the members of such groups as the Solar Cult in Switzerland, the Aoum Sect in Tokyo, and the Heaven's Gate UFO religious group in Santa Cruz, California, ignited a national hysteria. In 1995, a parliamentary commission of the National Assembly of France on Cults produced a report that included a list of purported cults compiled by the general information division of the French National Police in association with cult-watching groups.

This report included a long list of what the authors considered to be cults; for reasons that remained obscure to us until this day, both movements that we had initiated—Holotropic Breathwork and Spiritual Emergency Network (SEN)—appeared on this list. This blacklisting happened out of the blue and without any forewarning; nobody had contacted us, no interviews had been conducted with any members of these two groups, and no explanation was given for this blacklisting. This witch hunt, reminiscent of Nazi or Communist practices, came as a sudden and stunning surprise, considering that France is a country with a long democratic tradition. In the national hysteria following the 1995 report on cults, practitioners trained by us, who were conducting Holotropic Breathwork, became concerned about their professional reputation and the French president of the Spiritual Emergency Network decided to resign.

It was in this atmosphere that we arrived in France at the invitation of our French friends to conduct a large Holotropic Breathwork workshop to which we had committed ourselves long before the list of cults was published. The workshop took place in a large hangar-like structure with a roof made of undulated metal sheets that had no insulation. The sky was without a single cloud and it turned out to be a very hot day. As the morning proceeded, the temperature in the hall was rapidly rising forcing us to open all the doors. This exposed the neighbors to the loud volume of somewhat unusual music and made them wonder what we were doing. It did not take long before somebody called the police.

Fortunately, after one of the neighbors had appeared at the door and complained about the volume of the music, we closed all the entrances to the building and turned the music down. Responding to the call, two police cars arrived and the policemen walked around for a while, carefully listening and observing from the outside, without entering the complex. They clearly did not find the circumstances sufficiently suspect and potentially dangerous to break in. In the meantime, the new situation seriously compromised the breathwork. The volume of the music was way below the level that we consider optimal for the breathwork and the temperature in the hall was rising exponentially.

Finally we were forced to open the window to let in some cooler air, keeping the music at a very low volume. A few of the facilitators alternated in standing outside, assessing whether the music was reaching a level where it would disturb the neighbors. They also represented a safeguard against an unexpected return of the police. The problem was not just the volume of the music, but also the unusual activities associated with Holotropic Breathwork sessions that the police would have seen through the open doors or windows. This was something we did not want to risk, considering the cult hysteria.

In the course of the day, we developed a system that offered the least disturbance of the participants' experience. Whenever the temperature in the hall sank to a reasonable level, we closed the doors and increased the volume of the music. This situation lasted until the temperature and humidity became a more prominent problem than the inadequate music volume. We repeated this cycle until the afternoon session reached the termination period when the music becomes quiet and meditative.

Over the years, there have been many less dramatic situations during which we had to close the windows, such as the already mentioned experience in Switzerland, where the nearby farmers thought we were doing "the work of the devil" when they heard some of the ritual and spiritual music from other countries, such as Tibet, Africa, or Bali. More frequently, it was just the volume of the music we played that forced us to close the windows or turn down the music.

CHAPTER SEVEN

Therapeutic Potential of Holotropic Breathwork

The beneficial effects of Holotropic Breathwork conducted by trained facilitators cover a wide range. The most obvious positive results that we have observed over the years were related to various emotional disorders and to conditions traditionally seen as psychosomatic, such as psychogenic asthma, migraine headaches, and pains in different parts of the body that do not have an organic basis. However, on occasion, major improvements have occurred in individuals suffering from conditions that are usually seen as purely medical problems, such as Raynaud's disease and various chronic infections. Positive effects of repeated sessions of Holotropic Breathwork typically go beyond the amelioration of the emotional and physical condition; they may include distinct changes in the breather's personality, worldview, life strategy, and hierarchy of values. We have also anecdotal evidence that this approach can be used very effectively in healing of cultural wounds in native societies, such as Native Americans and Australian Aborigines.

1. Healing of emotional and psychosomatic disorders

We have developed and practiced Holotropic Breathwork outside of the professional settings—in our month-long seminars and shorter workshops at the Esalen Institute, in various breathwork workshops in many other parts of the world, and in our training program for facilitators. The focus in all these situations has been on self-exploration and personal growth rather than therapy. We have not had the opportunity to test the therapeutic efficacy of this method in clinical populations in the same way it was possible in Stan's psychedelic research program at the Maryland Psychiatric Research Center in Baltimore. This project was well funded and involved controlled clinical studies with psychological pre- and post-testing and systematic, professionally conducted follow-up at six, twelve, and eighteen months. This format would be an ideal model for future studies of Holotropic Breathwork.

Although the focus of our work has not been clinical, many participants in our workshops and training suffered from a variety of emotional and psychosomatic disorders. The results of Holotropic Breathwork in these people have often been so impressive and meaningfully connected with specific experiences in the sessions that there is little doubt that Holotropic Breathwork is a viable form of therapy. Over the years, individual researchers conducted studies of the effects of Holotropic Breathwork and reported encouraging results in their papers and dissertations. The papers of Russian researchers, who have studied various aspects of Holotropic Breathwork and its therapeutic effects, have been presented at many professional meetings and assembled in two special monographs (Bubeev and Kozlov 2001a and 2001b). Clearly, much more controlled research is needed to legitimize Holotropic Breathwork as a clinical tool.

Over the years, we have seen on numerous occasions that participants in the workshops and in the training were able to break out of depression that had lasted for many months or years, overcome various phobias and anxiety states, free themselves from consuming irrational feelings of guilt, and radically improve their self-confidence and self-esteem. In many instances, we have also witnessed the disappearance of severe psychosomatic pains, including migraine headaches, and radical and lasting improvements or even complete clearing of psychogenic asthma. On many occasions, participants in the training or workshops favorably compared their progress, achieved in several holotropic sessions, to years of verbal therapy.

When we talk about evaluating the efficacy of powerful forms of experiential psychotherapy, such as the work with Holotropic Breathwork or with other methods using holotropic states of consciousness, it is important to emphasize certain fundamental differences between these approaches and verbal forms of therapy. Verbal psychotherapy often extends over a period of years and major exciting breakthroughs are rare exceptions rather than commonplace events. Changes of symptoms occur on a broad time scale and it is difficult to prove their causal connection with specific events in therapy or the therapeutic process in general. By comparison, in a psychedelic or Holotropic Breathwork session, powerful changes can occur in the course of a few hours and they can be convincingly linked to specific experiences.

The basic principles and strategies that we use in Holotropic Breathwork are also effective with people undergoing spontaneous psychospiritual crises ("spiritual emergencies"). Here it is usually not necessary to use accelerated breathing, since the unconscious material is readily available for processing and the individuals involved actually struggle to prevent it from surfacing. Under these circumstances, all we have to do is to create a supportive environment, validate the process, offer encouragement, and work with the emerging material. Faster breathing becomes indicated if psychological work with people in spiritual crises encounters a psychological block and runs into an impasse.

2. Favorable Effect on Physical Diseases

The changes observed in connection with holotropic therapy are not limited to conditions traditionally considered emotional or psychosomatic. In many cases, Holotropic Breathwork sessions lead to significant improvement of physical conditions that are described as organic diseases in medical handbooks. On a number of occasions, individuals suffering from chronic infections, such as sinusitis, pharyngitis, bronchitis, and cystitis, discovered in their breathwork sessions that the corresponding areas of their bodies were severely bioenergetically blocked. When the combination of breathwork and bodywork removed the bioenergetic blocks, these infections significantly improved or even completely cleared.

These observations show that the cause of these chronic infections is not the presence of bacteria, but the inability of the tissue to protect itself against them and hold them in check. In most instances, the microorganisms that cause the inflammation are not vicious and virulent strains, but normal inhabitants of these regions, such as *Streptococcus pneumoniae* (*Pneumococcus*) or *Escherichia coli*. If the organs are not bioenergetically blocked, adequate blood circulation with an abundance of leucocytes, lymphocytes, and antibodies prevents them from multiplying to such an extent that they would cause problems.

We have also seen restitution of full peripheral circulation in people suffering from Raynaud's disease, a disorder that involves coldness of hands and feet accompanied by degenerative changes of the skin caused by defective nourishment (dystrophy). In some instances, Holotropic Breathwork also led to striking improvement of arthritis in the shoulders and in the temporomandibular joint (TMJ syndrome). In all these cases, the critical factor conducive to healing seemed to be release of bioenergetic blockage in the afflicted parts of the body followed by opening of the arteries (vasodilation).

This observation shows that the structural damage in some forms of arthritis is preceded by years of bioenergetic blockage in the adjacent area. Chronic contraction of the muscles causes compression of the capillaries and compromises the circulation of blood in the afflicted region. This leads to a reduced oxygen supply and undernourishment, as well as inadequate removal of toxic metabolic products with eventual accumulation of minerals. In the early stages, when the problem is still energetic, it can be fully reversed by experiential therapy. However, when these changes are allowed to persist a long time, they eventually result in the structural damage of the joints, which makes this condition permanent and irreversible.

The most remarkable observation related to blood circulation that we have seen in our work with Holotropic Breathwork was a striking improvement of advanced symptoms of Takayasu arteritis, an inflammatory disease of unknown etiology that afflicts the aorta and its branches. Its most characteristic symptom is gradually advancing blockage (occlusion) of arteries in the upper part of the body. Takayasu arteritis is a condition that is progressive, difficult to treat, and often fatal. A young woman suffering from this disease came to our training at a time when she had no pulse left in the arteries of her arm and was not able to lift her arms above a horizontal line. At the time of her graduation from the training, her pulse was restored and she had free mobility of her arms. Within the course of the training, she had a series of very intense perinatal and past life experiences that released a massive bioenergetic blockage in the upper part of her body and in her hands and arms. Equally surprising was solidification of bones in a woman with osteoporosis that occurred in the course of her Holotropic Breathwork training; we have not been able to find an explanation for this extraordinary observation.

As we mentioned earlier, the therapeutic potential of Holotropic Breathwork has been confirmed by clinical studies conducted by certified practitioners trained by us, who independently use this method in their work. The Russian studies were conducted by clinicians, who learned the Holotropic Breathwork from our Russian trainees, particularly Vladimir Maykov, president of the Russian Transpersonal Association and Director of the Russian section of Grof Transpersonal Training (GTT). The list of papers and dissertations exploring various aspects of Holotropic Breathwork forms a separate section of the bibliography of this book.

On many occasions, we have also had the opportunity to receive informal follow-up reports from people years after their emotional, psycho-somatic, and physical symptoms improved or disappeared as a result of their Holotropic Breathwork sessions in our training or in our various workshops. This has shown us that the improvements achieved in holotropic sessions are often lasting. We hope that the efficacy of this promising method of self-exploration and therapy will be further confirmed by future well-designed clinical research.

1. Four paintings depicting Holotropic Breathwork experiences in an Esalen monthlong seminar (a–d).

a. Psychospiritual death and rebirth featuring a swan, a powerful spirit bird that plays an important role in Siberian shamanism.

b. The Great Mother Goddess, personification of divine feminine energy that is source of all creation.

c. Shiva Nataraja, Lord of the Cosmic Dance.

d. Oneness with the ocean and the setting sun on the spectacular Big Sur Coast experienced toward the end of a session.

2. A group of paintings from Holotropic Breathwork sessions depicting transcendental experiences (a–g).

a. "Wisdom Eye." An experience from the end of a breathwork session. The artist said: "Wholeness has been restored. The life power, (Kundalini/chi), is content and is resting in peace above the 'Eye of Wisdom.' Heaven and Earth and Masculine and Feminine are in balance" (Anne Høivik).

b. Snake Energy (Kundalini) rising from the most physical root chakra (*muladhara*) to the most ethereal crown chakra (*sahasrara*) and triggering a cosmic experience (Jan Vanatta).

c. "The Universal Heart." The little individual heart finding its way back to the big Universal Heart (Anne Høivik).

"Første visjon: Jeg så en hvit hest som red over himmelen. På hesten satt "Mor Ayahuasca" med meg i armene sine. Vi red inn i evigheten.
Amazonas, 17. juli 2002.

d. "Riding through the Air." Experience following a major breakthrough—"feeling like a baby in the arms of The Great Mother of the Void, completely safe and loved for who I am, and riding with her through the air into eternity" (Anne Høivik).

e. "Roundtrip Journey to the Cosmos." The lower picture portrays the astonishment of the artist by the order and harmony, totality, and completeness of the universe. The upper picture is related to feelings of extreme cold and tremors forcing her to leave this cosmic frontier and return. Toward the end, she experienced herself as a pentagon, which helped her with the grounding and integration of the session. (Katia Solani).

f. Vision of the Transformed Being of Light inside the body of a Female Christ (Anne Høivik).

g. "Mother Kundalini." Identification with a small child resting in a papoose on the back of a woman with a fiery garment, wrapped in a star mantle. The artist wrote: "I was both the mother and the child; I loved this Great Mother deeply, I loved my mother, I loved every creature, every sentient being" (Katia Solani).

3. Perinatal motifs in Holotropic Breathwork sessions (a–k).

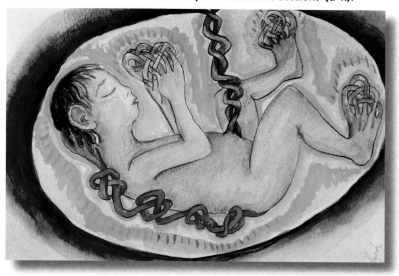

a. Undisturbed intrauterine life (BPM I). The entanglement and intercon-nectedness of the fingers and toes represent the experience of the fetal body image that is different than that of an adult.

b. Vision from a session governed by BPM II. Giant tarantula, an archetypal image of the Devouring Feminine, attacking the artist and threatening her life. The image of the tightly swaddled mummy reflects the confinement and constriction experienced during uterine contractions. (Jarina Moss).

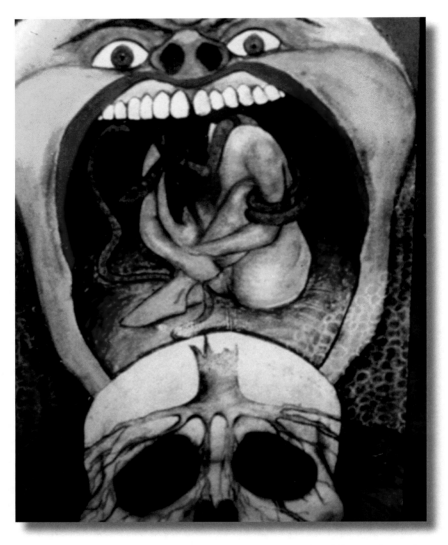

c. The onset of the process of psychospiritual death and rebirth experienced as engulfment by a grotesque archetypal figure. The skull represents the imminence of death, the root system and the snake, the placental circulatory system (Peg Holms).

4. "Journey into and through Mother Fear." Three drawings from a breathwork session in which the artist relived her birth (d–f). (Jan Vannatta).

d. The wounded inner child, who initially faced the ordeal of birth alone, is joined by the older, wiser adult self; together they enter the mouth of the Mother Dragon.

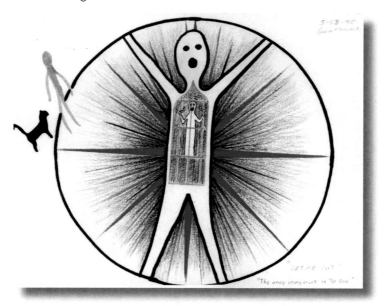

e. "Trapped Inside the Bad Womb." The experience of being caught and squeezed in a black, tight womb of the Mother Dragon. "There is no way out, the only way out is to die." (Jan Vannatta).

f. The inner child and the adult self travel through the tunnel of the birth canal. After they fully face the fear, the dragon's head dissolves into mist, allowing passage.

g. "Out of the Darkness." The combined experience of being born and giving birth. Sequences of this kind typically result in a sense of giving birth to a new self and can be very transformative and healing. (Jean Perkins).

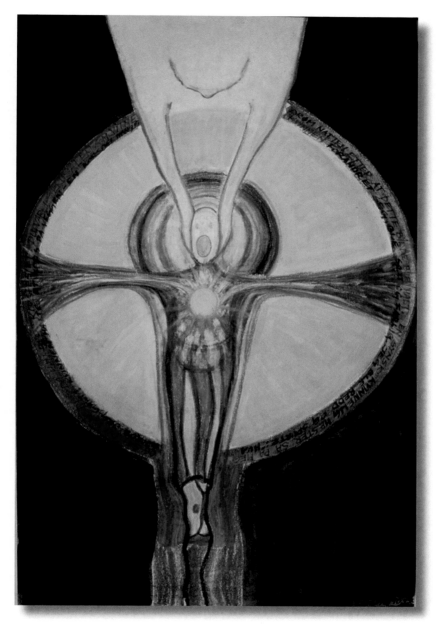

h. Vision of crucifixion in the final stage of the birth process. The artist said: "This experience showed me clearly how many levels of reality can be woven together and that God or The Great Spirit is behind it all." (Anne Høivik).

i. Experience of psychospiritual death and rebirth. The old personality structure has fallen apart; out of it emerges a new self (or Self), connected to the spiritual domain. The inscription at the bottom of the picture reads: LIBERATION. Dismemberment is a frequent motif in the initiatory experiences of novice shamans. (Jarina Moss).

j. Psychospiritual death and rebirth in which the vision of the peacock tail (like the famous *cauda pavonis* of the alchemical process) appears as a symbol of transformation and transfiguration (Anne Høivik).

k. Death and rebirth followed by the experience of *hieros gamos,* sacred union of the Feminine and Masculine. (Anne Hoivik).

5. A series of paintings from breathwork sessions featuring the snake, a very frequent motif in holotropic states (a–d).

a. "Activation of Kundalini." The artist felt that snake energy larger than herself was energizing her with untold powers to see, protect, and heal a young girl (left) and a fetus in the "womb-tomb" (right) (Jan Vannatta).

b. "Empowerment." Lightning energy converts to Snake Energy, then enters the artist's body. After the snake leaves her body, she accepts it, merges, and becomes one with it, as a wolf sitting at her feet witnesses this process. (Jan Vannatta).

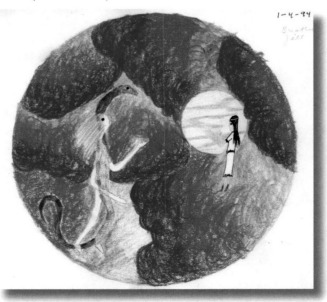

c. "Snake Energy and White Buffalo Woman." In the middle of chaos in the form of rising Snake Energy and clouds of raging, swirling colors appears White Buffalo Woman. She comes to teach the artist to channel this energy and transmute it into her own power, enabling her to pass through the dimensional doorway to a place of light, peace, and self-knowledge (Jan Vannatta).

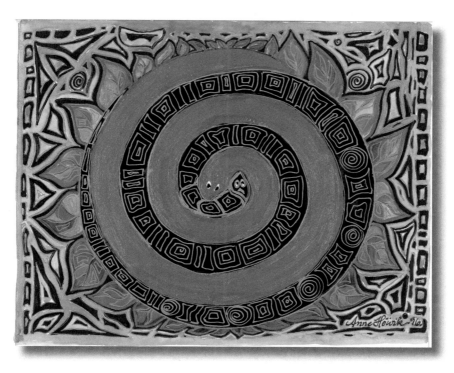

d. "Union of Heaven and Earth." A black snake (Earth Power) and a golden snake (Sky Power) mating on a bed of green leaves in the jungle. The experience was accompanied by feelings of great contentment and peace. (Anne Høivik).

6. Five paintings from Holotropic Breathwork sessions depicting experiences of intense emotions (a-e).

a. "Imprisoned aggression." Suppressed anger trying to find release and expression (Albrecht Mahr).

b. "Rage." Outburst of violent fury experienced in identification with an archetypal feline predator (Albrecht Mahr).

c. "Greed." Personification of insatiable greed, a powerful driving force of human life and history. (Anne Høivik).

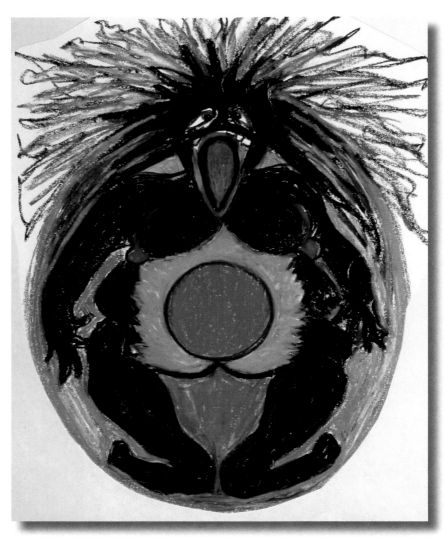

d. "Primal scream." Powerful release of deep emotions in a session in which the author experienced rebirth. (Anne Høivik).

e. "The Dragon Mother." The artist's traumatic childhood memory reflecting her mother's intolerance of strong emotions. The Dragon Mother shakes and frightens the infant to make her stop crying. Her message is: "If you cry, you die." (Jan Vannatta).

7. A series of paintings from Holotropic Breathwork sessions depicting experiences with shamanic motifs (a-d by Tai Hazard and e by Katia Soliani).

a. The Great Bear tears open his own chest with claws dressed with silver and turquoise and gives his blood to the shaman.

b. The shaman's heart is pierced by a walrus tusk and his spirit travels to the wolf, to the moon, to the sun, and to another shaman.

c. Overcoming the fear of darkness and the unknown and following a guide deeper and deeper into the underworld.

d. Resting deep in the womb of the earth and listening to the wolf chanting stories.

e. The experience of dismemberment, a universal archetypal motif appearing in the initiatory crises of novice shamans as an important part of the process of psycho-spiritual death and rebirth.

8. "Shamanic initiation." Four paintings from a Holotropic Breathwork session depicting a shamanic journey of descent in the context of Kundalini awakening (a–d) (Jan Vannatta).

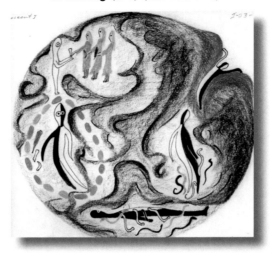

a. The Grandmothers paint white circles around the artist's eyes and present her with three talismans—a feather, a bone, and a claw for her journey down into the darkness. As she descends, the Grandmothers paint her body black and white. Reaching the bottom, most of the snake energy is released and she fights her way back up, out of the darkness, struggling to be reborn.

b. The artist's body becomes black and white and intricate designs appear all over her. Her entire being becomes transformed into a sacred geometric composition; she is enclosed in darkness and encircled by the Grandmothers and the Snake.

c. Surrounded by the Grandmothers, the Snake and the artist become one. They encircle the talismans which are integrated into a balanced center.

d. Fully integrated and transformed, the voyager sits in the center of the picture. She is surrounded and supported by darkness, the three talismans, the Grandmothers, the Snake, and the diamond-shaped shamanic reality. The experience is complex but orderly.

**9. Two paintings from the sessions in
Holotropic Breathwork training (a–b) (Peg Holms).**

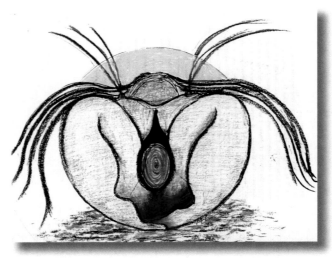

a. "Through the Gates of Hell into the Prison of Maya," the dual experience of being born and giving birth. According to the author, the depth of her feelings was so great that "crying, raging, wailing, and flailing around would only touch the tip of the submerged terror and anguish."

b. The artist sitting naked on a powerful Harley-Davidson motorcycle, triumphantly managing and controlling the powerful machine. She reclaims her feminine power and commands it without fear or guilt.

**10. Four paintings from Katia Solani's
Holotropic Breathwork sessions described in this book.**

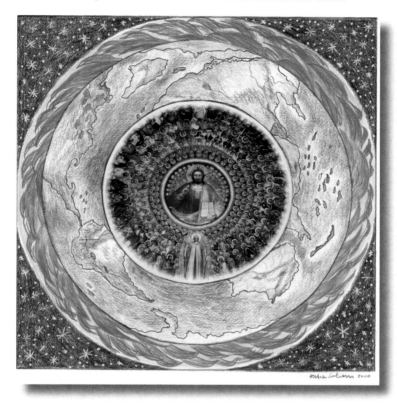

a. Corpus Christi. Painting from a Holotropic Breathwork session depicting an experience of becoming a cell in the body of Cosmic Christ, while at the same time possessing the ability to experientially identify with any part of creation (Katia Solani).

b. Identification with a turtle carrying on her belly the image of a child needing nourishment.

c. The image of a beautiful landscape decorating the back of the turtle's shell.

d. Picture of the same landscape as it appeared in a dream on the night following the session.

11. Three paintings by Marianne Wobcke, illustrating her experiences in Holotropic Breathwork training (a–c).

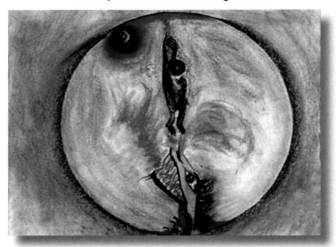

a. Marianne as a fetus attacked by a fire-breathing dragon coming through the cervix of the uterus and burning her legs. This experience was related to her mother's attempted abortion and on a deeper level also to her Aboriginal great grandmother's experience of having her legs doused in gasoline and set alight by a police tracker.

b. "Alienation." Dreaming Ancestor standing as a skeleton in a devastated landscape, representing the apocalypse of the Australian Aborigenes resulting from the separation from family, country, culture, and *"kanyini"* experienced by the "Stolen Generation." *Kanyini* is the principle of connectedness through caring and responsibility underpinning Aboriginal life.

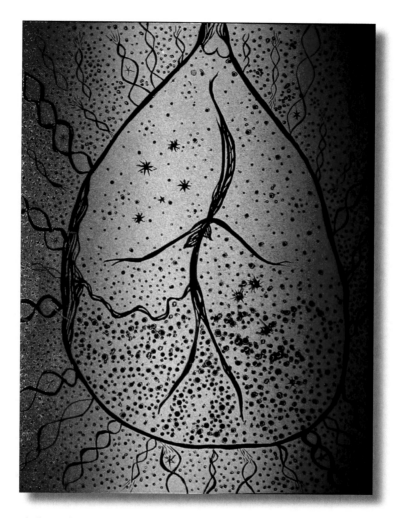

c. A linocut representing the profound connection between Marianne and her Aboriginal ancestors. It portrays a Mimi Spirit dancing against the starry sky. According to Aboriginal lore, Mimi Spirits are tall and slender beings, who in the Alcheringa (Dreamtime) taught Aboriginal people skills in hunting, cooking, and painting.

12. Two complex mandalas from Holotropic Breathwork sessions (John Ablett).

a. A mandala entitled "*Om Nama Shivaya.*" Amid the blood and choking of a difficult birth, a colossal skeletal figure of Death rampages through the world, crushing the false king of the ego beneath his foot. The skull bone is experienced as a doorway to transcendence, connecting with layers of cultural and ancestral history.

b. The fetus in the womb identifies with the processes of destruction on a personal and global scale threatening to annihilate his entire world in anger. He travels a spiral path through the birth canal into the light—first as a thirsty wasp emerging from a cocoon, then as a roaring tiger, and finally as a flower in full bloom.

THERAPEUTIC POTENTIAL OF HOLOTROPIC BREATHWORK 129

3. Effect on personality, worldview, life strategy, and hierarchy of values

Besides the emotional, psychosomatic, and physical healing, over the years we have also seen profound positive personality changes in many people involved in serious, systematic self-exploration using Holotropic Breathwork. Some of them happened in connection with the reliving of various postnatal emotional and physical traumas and as a result of corrective experiences in interpersonal relations. However, the most radical changes seemed to be linked to perinatal and transpersonal experiences.

In the process of systematic self-exploration using holotropic states of consciousness, sooner or later we come to the recognition that our deepest needs are not of material, but of spiritual nature. Pursuit of worldly goals cannot, in and of itself, bring us fulfillment, peace of mind, and happiness once we have reached the satisfaction of basic biological needs (food, shelter, sex, and security). When the process of self-discovery focuses on the biographical level, many people attain the insight that their life has been inauthentic in certain areas, because of various traumatic experiences they suffered in their family of origin and later in life.

For example, problems with parental authority can lead to similar difficulties in relationships with teachers, employers, policemen, officers in the army, and political or scientific authorities. Similarly, our behavior in sexual relationships reflects how our parents related to each other as models of the masculine and feminine roles and how they emotionally related to us and our siblings. Abusive, rejecting, or overprotective parents or parents who violate their children's sexual boundaries have a devastating effect on the adult life of their offspring. They play an important role in the development of repetitive dysfunctional patterns their sons and daughters have in their sexual relationships. In a similar way, the problems of sibling rivalry, jealousy, and competition for attention tend to reappear in later life in the relationships with schoolmates, coworkers, and members of other peer groups.

When the process of experiential self-exploration reaches the perinatal level, we typically discover that our life has been inauthentic not only in some specific areas, but also in its totality. We discover to our surprise that our entire life strategy has been erroneous and misguided and thus incapable of bringing us genuine satisfaction. We realize that many of our activities have been motivated by fear of death and other elemental unconscious forces associated with biological birth. We survived this apocalyptic event at the very beginning of our life, but we have not emotionally processed and integrated it. We still carry deep in our unconscious the sense of being trapped, victimized, and threatened. We have completed the formidable process of birth anatomically but not emotionally. It is as if a significant part of us is still imprisoned in the birth canal, struggling to free itself from its clutches.

When our field of consciousness is strongly influenced by the underlying memory of the entrapment and struggle that we experienced at birth, it causes a feeling of discomfort and dissatisfaction with our present situation. This discontent can focus on a large spectrum of issues—the unsatisfactory physical appearance, inadequate resources and material possessions, insufficient amount of power and fame, low social status and radius of influence, and many others. Like the fetus stuck in the birth canal, we feel a strong drive to get to a more satisfying situation that lies somewhere in the future.

Whatever is the reality of our present circumstances, we do not find them satisfactory. Our fantasy continues to create images of future situations that appear more fulfilling than the present one. It seems that until we reach these goals, life will be only preparation for a better future, not yet "the real thing." This results in a life pattern that participants in our workshops and training have described as a "rat-race" type of existence or "treadmill" strategy of life. The former term brings to mind the image of a rat running with great determination inside a rotating wheel without getting anywhere. The existentialists talk about "auto-projecting" into the future, a strategy that is a basic fallacy of human life. It is essentially a loser strategy, since it is in principle unable to bring the fulfillment and satisfaction that is expected from it. From this perspective, it does not make much difference whether or not it succeeds in achieving material goals. In Joseph Campbell's words, it means "getting to the top of the ladder and finding that it stands against the wrong wall."

When the goal is not reached, the continuing dissatisfaction is attributed to the fact that we have failed to reach the corrective measure that would have dispelled it. However, if we succeed in reaching the goal of our aspiration, it typically does not have much influence on our basic life feelings. These are more powerfully influenced by the situation in our unconscious psyche than by our achievements in the external world. The continuing dissatisfaction is blamed either on the fact that the choice of the goal was not correct or that it was not ambitious enough. The usual reaction to this situation is either augmentation of the old goal or its substitution with a different one.

In any case, the failure is not correctly diagnosed as being an inevitable result of a fundamentally wrong life strategy, which is in principle incapable of providing satisfaction. This fallacious pattern applied on a large scale leads to reckless irrational pursuit of various grandiose goals, which is responsible for many serious and dangerous problems in the world and causes much human suffering. It can be played out on any level of importance and affluence, since it never brings true satisfaction. The only strategy that can significantly reduce this irrational drive is conscious reliving and integration of the trauma of birth and establishing an experiential connection to the transpersonal level of the psyche by systematic inner work.

Responsible and focused deep self-exploration can help us come to terms with the trauma of birth and make a deep spiritual connection. This moves us in the direction of what Taoist spiritual teachers call *wu wei*, or "creative quietude," which is not action involving ambitious determined effort, but "doing by being." This is also sometimes referred to as the Watercourse Way, because it imitates the ways water operates in nature. Instead of focusing on a predetermined fixed goal, we try to sense which way things are moving and how we best fit into that movement. This is the strategy used in martial arts and in surfing. It involves focus on the process, rather than on he goal or the outcome. When we are able to approach life in this manner, we ultimately achieve more and with less effort. In addition, our activities are not egocentric, exclusive, and competitive, as they are during the pursuit of personal goals, but inclusive and synergistic. The outcome not only brings satisfaction to us as individuals but also serves the community at large.

We have repeatedly observed that people who operate in this Taoist framework tend to experience extraordinary beneficial coincidences and synchronicities that support their projects and help them in their work. They "accidentally" come across the information they need, the right people appear at the right time, and the necessary funds suddenly become available. The unexpected fortuitous occurrence of such situations is often so pervasive and convincing that we learnt to trust it and use it as a compass for our activities—as an important criterion that we "are on the right track."

Experiences in holotropic states of consciousness can bring even more fundamental insights concerning the roots of our dissatisfaction and the way to assuage it. We can discover that the deepest source of our discontent and our striving for being more than we are and for having more then we have lies even beyond the perinatal domain. This insatiable craving that drives human life is ultimately transpersonal in nature. In Dante Alighieri's words, "The desire for perfection is that desire which always makes every pleasure appear incomplete, for there is no joy or pleasure so great in this life that it can quench the thirst in our soul" (Dante 1990).

In the most general sense, the deepest transpersonal roots of human unhappiness and insatiable greed can be described in terms of what Ken Wilber called the Atman project (Wilber 1980). In the last analysis, we are identical and commensurate with the cosmic creative principle—God, Brahman, the Tao, Buddha, Cosmic Christ, Allah, or Great Spirit. Although the process of creation separates and alienates us from this deep source and our true identity, the awareness of who we really are is never completely lost.

The deepest motivating force in the psyche on all the levels of consciousness evolution is the desire to return to the experience of our own divinity.

However, the fact of our incarnation as separate beings makes the achievement of this task extremely difficult and challenging. It requires obliteration of our separate self, the death of the ego. Because of the fear of annihilation leading to grasping onto the ego, we have to settle for substitutes or surrogates—"Atman projects"—which are specific for each particular age. For the fetus and the newborn, this means the satisfaction experienced in the good womb or on the good breast. For the infant, it is the satisfaction of age-specific biological and anaclitic needs and the need for security. For the adult, the range of possible substitute projects is enormous; besides food and sex it includes money, fame, power, appearance, knowledge, specific skills, and many others.

Because of our deep sense that our true identity is the totality of cosmic creation and the creative principle itself, substitutes of any degree and scope—Atman projects—will always remain unsatisfactory. The Persian mystic and poet Rumi made it very clear: "All the hopes, desires, loves, and affections that people have for different things—fathers, mothers, friends, heavens, the earth, palaces, sciences, works, food, drink—the saint knows that these are desires for God and all those things are veils. When men leave this world and see the King without these veils, then they will know that all were veils and coverings, that the object of their desire was in reality that One Thing" (Hines 1996). Only the experience of our own divinity in a holotropic state of consciousness can ever fulfill our deepest needs. This makes systematic spiritual quest a high priority in human life.

Individuals who have chosen responsible systematic self-exploration with holotropic states as their spiritual path experience in the process profound personality changes. As the content of the perinatal level of the unconscious emerges into consciousness and is integrated, it results in a considerable decrease of aggressive tendencies and leads to greater inner peace, self-acceptance, and tolerance of others. The experience of psychospiritual death and rebirth and conscious connection with positive postnatal or prenatal memories tends to reduce irrational drives and ambitions. It causes a shift of focus and emphasis from the ruminations about the past and fantasies about the future to fuller experience of the present. This leads to enhanced zest, *élan vital*, and *joi de vivre*—a greater ability to enjoy life and draw satisfaction from simple circumstances of life, such as everyday activities, creative work, food, lovemaking, nature, and music.

Another important result of this process is the emergence of a spirituality of universal and mystical nature that—unlike faith in the dogmas of mainstream religions—is authentic and convincing, since it is based on a deep personal experience. It is universal, all-inclusive, and non-denominational. The process of spiritual opening and transformation typically deepens further as a result of transpersonal experiences, such as identification with other people, entire human groups, animals, plants, and even inorganic materials and processes in nature. Other types of transpersonal experiences provide conscious access to events occurring in other countries, cultures, and historical periods and even to the mythological realms and archetypal beings of the collective unconscious. Experiences of cosmic unity and one's own divinity lead to an increasing identification with all of creation and bring the sense of wonder, love, compassion, and inner peace.

What began as psychological probing of the unconscious psyche, conducted for personal growth or therapeutic purposes, automatically becomes a philosophical quest for the meaning of life and a journey of spiritual discovery. People who gain an experiential access to the transpersonal domain of their psyches typically develop a new appreciation of existence and reverence for all life. One of the most striking consequences of various forms of transpersonal experiences is the spontaneous emergence and development of deep humanitarian tendencies and a strong need to become involved in service for some larger purpose. This is based on a cellular awareness that all boundaries in the universe are arbitrary and that on a deeper level all of creation represents a unified cosmic web.

Such transpersonal experiences also lead to deep ecological sensitivity and the awareness that we cannot do anything destructive to nature without simultaneously damaging ourselves. Differences between people appear to be interesting and enriching rather than threatening, whether they are related to sex, race, color, language, political conviction, or religious belief. Explorers of the inner space—like many American astronauts who have seen the earth from outer space—develop a deep sense of being planetary citizens rather than citizens of a particular country or members of a particular racial, social, ideological, political, or religious group. These observations have larger sociopolitical implications; they suggest that a transformation mediated by holotropic states of consciousness would increase humanity's chance for survival if it could occur on a sufficiently large scale.

4. Potential for healing of cultural wounds and historical conflict resolution

Many—if not most—of the workshops we have conducted in the last thirty-four years have been multicultural. Esalen, where we developed Holotropic Breathwork, is a world-famous place; it is a "mecca of the human potential movement" that attracts people from all over the world. The modules of our training for facilitators also typically have participants who come from many different countries. The preconference workshops that we offered before eleven of the International Transpersonal Conferences held in the United States and abroad are in a special category in terms of the large numbers of participants and of the countries represented.

We have mentioned earlier Victor Turner's observation that sharing ritual events in a tribal context creates deep bonds between participants—a sense of community (*communitas*) (p. 49f). The multinational and multicultural nature of our workshops gave us the opportunity to ascertain that the same applies to groups composed of individuals from different nations. The largest ones among these, such as the preconference workshops in Santa Rosa and in Prague, had over three hundred participants each and over thirty trained facilitators assisting in the process. We have observed repeatedly that experiencing Holotropic Breathwork in a collective setting, witnessing the holotropic sessions of others, and sharing the experiences in groups rapidly dissolves language barriers and cultural, political, and religious differences. Our experiences from these groups made it clear that workshops of this kind could be invaluable in international meetings aimed at reaching mutual understanding and developing friendship.

We had an unexpected chance to test this potential of Holotropic Breathwork under very unique circumstances. In the 1980s, Michael Murphy, the cofounder of the Esalen Institute, and Dulce Murphy launched Esalen's Soviet-American Friendship Project, which served as a unique form of citizen-to-citizen "grass-root diplomacy." This program brought to Esalen many prominent Soviet politicians, scientists, and other cultural figures. In 1987 Michael held an invitational meeting in the Esalen Big House, a beautiful mansion perched on a cypress-covered cliff overlooking the Pacific Ocean on the Big Sur coastline. This small working conference involved four prominent Soviet scientists and the representatives of foremost American academic and research institutions, including John Mack, Candace Pert, Dean Ornish, and Robert Gale.

The Murphys invited Stan to join the group and give a talk on modern consciousness research and the conceptual challenges it presents for the current scientific worldview. During his talk, Stan mentioned the work we were doing with Holotropic Breathwork. This generated great interest among participants and they all wanted to have a personal experience of this method. The group decided to preempt the afternoon program of the meeting on the next day and have the two of us conduct a breathwork session instead. Holotropic Breathwork was very popular at Esalen and it was easy to find enough volunteers to function as sitters for this special group. Bringing a powerful experiential element into the meeting completely changed the nature of this international encounter, which up to that point had been strictly intellectual. By the end of the afternoon, the Russians were in close emotional and even physical contact with their American sitters, and we all felt an atmosphere of genuine friendship.

The processing group was very powerful and moving. The experiences involved regression into childhood and infancy, birth experiences, and even transpersonal and spiritual elements. One of the Russians had a profound experience of union with God and, to the surprise of everyone present, was willing to talk about it. "Of course, I remain a Communist," he stated firmly during his sharing, "but I understand now what people mean when they say God." Dr. Aaron Belkin, the leader of the group, was so moved by the experience that he later arranged for us an official invitation from the Soviet Ministry of Health, proposing that we come to Moscow and give lectures and Holotropic Breathwork workshops.

In addition, we discovered that the potential of Holotropic Breathwork for cultural healing had been subjected—unbeknown to us—to large-scale testing. In 1995, we were invited by Jim Garrison, president of the Gorbachev Foundation, to participate in the State of the World Forum in San Francisco. At this meeting, we were approached by Phil Lane Jr., Dakota-Chickasaw pipe carrier and sweat lodge keeper and cofounder and international coordinator of the Four Worlds family of organizations, who was invited to the forum to represent his people. Phil told us that Holotropic Breathwork was being used in a Native American intertribal healing experiment. He and one of his friends had attended a Holotropic Breathwork workshop conducted by one of our trained facilitators and were deeply impressed by its healing power. They decided to introduce this method to people of the Native Nation as a way to heal deep psychotraumas that they had suffered during their stormy history, including the brutal physical and sexual abuse that occurred in many American and Canadian Indian residential schools.

Phil then described the great popularity and success that Holotropic Breathwork groups achieved among Native people, although they were conducted by leaders without adequate training, only on the basis of the experience from one workshop that Phil and his friend shared with them. Respectful of the opinion of the elders, Phil decided to consult with them as to their opinion about this new approach to healing. When the elders became acquainted with Holotropic Breathwork, they gave Phil their permission and support to pursue his efforts. According to him, they concluded that the philosophy and practice of this approach was compatible with their tribal cosmology and cultural tradition. While we are very pleased with the new perspectives Phil's initiative has opened, we hope that in the future this work will continue under the guidance of properly trained facilitators.

We received more feedback about these groups when we connected with Duncan Campbell, an accomplished interviewer, whose radio program Living Dialogues in Boulder, Colorado, features pioneers in new paradigm thinking in a broad variety of fields. Through him we have gotten to know his wife, Edna Brillon Da Laa Skil Gaa (Rain Flower), who is deeply connected with her Native American heritage and had taken part in Phil Lane's groups. She confirmed for us the profound impact that these sessions had on everybody involved. Later she and Duncan participated in our weekend workshop in Boulder. Edna gave us the permission to include in our book the following account of her remarkable Holotropic Breathwork sessions.

Connecting with the maternal lineage: The story of Edna

I started deliberately working on healing myself in 1990 when I was thirty-six years old. As a mixed blood Native American and being an empathic child, I was surrounded by other people's pain and was extremely aware of it. My family and all the families I was related to were in a lot of pain, resentments, and traumas. My parents are both mixed bloods, or "half-breeds" as was the term back then. They both had very difficult childhoods. My mother without her father, my father without his mother, and that was not their only problem. My search for understanding and answers started young; I seemed to know that my parents were misunderstanding each other over events in the past.

When we moved from our tribal territory when I was six and a half, I told myself I would come back when I was old enough to help my people. I was acutely aware of their pain, even though it was often denied; I could feel it viscerally. My mother is Haida and Welsh and my father is Cree and French; their traumas run deep like those of all Natives, especially of that era. I began to find methods to help our healing process—a combination of psychotherapy, non-denominational spirituality, group work, psychodrama, shamanism, and constellation work.

One of the most powerful methods was breathwork. There I had some of my deepest insights and breakthroughs, although I always resisted it for some unknown reason. The first time I did it was with a large group in a Vancouver hotel with Phil Lane. There were about one hundred and fifty people in attendance; they paired everyone up and did some drumming and smudging, while one of each pair at a time did their breathing.

My Haida grandmother, Edna, whom I was named after, had been raised in a Residential School from five years old till eighteen. She had been in the extended care unit of the hospital for ten years with Alzheimer's at the time of this experience. As we began breathing to the drumbeat, the native people were in altered states very quickly, as they do. I like to be in control of my altered states, so it took a lot of breathing for me compared to the others. I began to weep, and understood viscerally the purpose of the *"wailers"* (criers) that were part of our culture in the grieving process. It was the belief that crying too hard by a close loved one held the spirits on the earth plane rather than allowing them to go all the way to the light.

Then I had a succession of all my deceased relatives that I knew; they came right before me, one after another, not necessarily in the order of their deaths. Uncle John, my dear and famous Auntie Blanche, who both died too young from cancer. Uncle David, my mom's brother, who also died young leaving ten children. My beautiful-souled Cousin Tommy, who died at twenty-two, Cousin Randy, Grandma Eliza, and another cousin . . . who? Who are you? I did not know, but I knew that I recognized her spirit. They greeted me and we loved one another, just like when we finally have a dream of a beloved relative after they passed over and you know their spirit visited you.

Last but not least, the face of my grandmother Edna came to me. I got confused, since all the others had passed on, but my Nuni (grandmother) is still alive and in the hospital with Alzheimer's. Then the realization came clear as day that she was already on the other side; her body was in the hospital but her spirit was able to be on the other side if she wanted to be, outside herself. She knew who loved her. She also knew who didn't and would act up when they showed up. One of my last visits with her, she kept saying in a catatonic state over and over: "Love one another, love your brothers and sisters." She was giving us a message, even though she was not in there. Our family was split and separated—brothers/sisters, mothers/fathers not talking to each other. She wanted us to heal it. She was telling me to tell the others to love one another.

I have no doubt now that people with Alzheimer's can go to the other side and do quite often. And they can come back in too, as my Nuni did. That little cousin, whom I could not remember, made contact with me in the breathwork session and kept making contact with me after that. It took me a few years to understand and remember, but I finally did during another healing session. I remembered being four and a half and going to a funeral of my little cousin Minnow, who was my exact same age; I did not know her very well. She had a new chiffon-type dress on at the beach near the fire and it caught; she burnt and everyone was in shock and horror. I remember her mother at the funeral wailing so loud I got very frightened. I looked at my mother sitting there so dignified and quiet and thought: "I wonder if mom would cry if I died." I had never seen her cry once, but I could feel her crying all the time.

With that thought, in my pain, I rose out of my body and joined my little cousin Minnow. Many years later, I realized I had helped her cross over to the light and then she became a guide—even though it took me a few years to get it. I remember that it was after this funeral when I started to leave my body frequently and so did my brother; we would go together too when things got too rough. We never said a word about that to anyone, not even each other, we just knew, no need to talk about it.

I finally saw my mother cry forty years later at her older brother's funeral. Just last year, I did another Holotropic Breathwork session at Naropa University in Boulder, Colorado, with Stan Grof. By then I understood that "we are our own ancestors," the same DNA. I went through the experience of how my emotions were when I carried my daughter Erin. Oh, my girl, no wonder you are so strong. What a terrible time we had. I also felt the emotions of my mother when she was carrying me in her womb, how heartbroken she was while carrying me, even though I was the one they planned. My father was philandering the whole time, even the days right after my birth. Then I could feel the full emotions of how my Nuni felt when she was carrying my mom. It was as though I was the one carrying the child and simultaneously the baby in the womb. It was not as traumatic as the two generations before her but still not good.

This was not just imagining; my spirit moved through time and space and I was in the wombs of my own ancestors going back to my great-great-grandmother. She was the dark-skinned one that was abused terribly by the mean-spirited Frenchman who treated her like a workhorse. She carried her little Haida-French children whose father she hated; that one felt the worst of all. What absolute compassion I felt for those four generations of Indian women whose lives were so very hard and full of suffering, shock, and trauma!

I discerned that it was my great-great-grandmother Jeanie who had the most intense suffering that we inherited. In one lifetime, she observed the severe contrast of before and after white contact. She was the one who had traveled in canoes up and down the Pacific Coast from Alaska to California and saw the complete devastation of all the Indians from the most food-rich and culturally abundant tribes on the continent. After so many died of smallpox, there were so few left that my grandmother's brother paddled all the way to Tacoma, Washington, from just under Alaska to pick up his sister, knowing she was being mistreated by that Frenchman and our tribes were becoming too small.

Our people know that we come back as our own ancestors, I believe that my sister was my great-great-grandmother and I was my great grandmother; sometimes you can tell by the corresponding wounds and other complex things that happened. I had been praying for a deeper understanding and healing of my grandmother's pain that we seemed to have inherited; the breathwork did the healing and the understanding, literally showing me that what our people knew before colonization was true and right. I wanted to write a book called "No Wonder I'm Crabby." Maybe I still will.

If you ever wonder why Indians are mad, or drink too much, or don't seem to care about life, believe me there are thousands of reasons. As chief Dan George said: "We paid, and we paid, and we paid." The white man ended up with our inheritance and we got left with the trauma that has been passed down for generations. Thank you, Stan and Christina, for sharing with us your work that is sorely needed, at this time more than ever. It brings us awareness about ourselves and the recognition how essential it is to introduce indigenous wisdom and methods like breathwork to mainstream culture.

I got to believe in our own ways once again as being a very sophisticated healing system. Due to colonization, government, and the Church's assimilation plan, we were forced to doubt our cultures and ourselves to have any value at all. The breathwork made me see that just by feeling it and having compassionate understanding, I was able to begin to let it release, but not in one fell swoop. I did go back to my Haida land and helped with the healing work; in fact, I went to many reservations in British Columbia, Ottawa, and Alaska, honoring my six-year-old's promise. "I'll come back when I'm old enough to help."

At the Sixteenth International Transpersonal Conference held in June 2004 in Palm Springs, California, Marianne Wobcke, an Australian midwife, presented a paper describing her experiences from our Holotropic Breathwork training, which in many ways resemble those of Edna. In her sessions, Marianne relived traumatic events from the life of her mother and great-grandmother that she was later able to verify. In this case, her ancestors were Australian Aborigines, people whose tragic history parallels that of Native Americans. Marianne, who has since completed our training and become a certified Holotropic Breathwork practitioner in Australia, gave us the permission to include her story in our book.

Retrieving memories of the stolen generations: The story of Marianne

I was told on my thirteenth birthday by my parents that I was adopted. However, when I shared this information at school, I was teased and shamed so I never mentioned this fact again. This issue seemed to hold no relevance to my life, although I was puzzled by the dreams, nightmares, and later experiences with magic mushrooms and LSD in my teens and early twenties that all featured Aborigines.

It wasn't until I was thirty and had just commenced my midwifery training at Toowoomba Base Hospital that I had a reason to reflect again upon my adoptive status. In April 1991, on my first day in the Birthing Unit, the first birth I attended was a traditional Aboriginal woman from a regional town in South-East Queensland who had been raped by a prominent local person's son resulting in this pregnancy. No charges had been laid and in the handover report, it was insinuated it was unlikely to have been rape, relieving the staff of any responsibility for providing appropriately sensitive care in this situation.

I was a student midwife, full of enthusiasm and eager to support this woman, but without any cultural education or awareness to equip me for this experience. In my determination to prove my authority and value to my client, I repeatedly invaded her space. Ignorant of traditional cultural practices, I persistently tried to make eye contact with her and communicate that she was required to submit to a relentless tirade of diagnostic procedures to determine if there was any incident of maternal or fetal distress. To protect herself, the woman crouched with her back to me, exuding mistrust and covering her nose and face with her hands as she edged away. I later learnt from another staff member that she was nauseated by my smell, which to her reeked of soap and perfume. Desperate and confused, following fruitless attempts to engage support and guidance from the experienced staff, I eventually responded intuitively to the situation. I stepped back, squatted a respectful distance from the birthing woman, and surrendered my authority; in doing so, I allowed her the privilege of birthing silently, without my interference.

This Indigenous woman's birthing experience, culminating in her abandoning the baby, had a profound and life-changing impact on me. The baby stayed in the nursery for three weeks while Family Services searched for the mother, who had effectively disappeared. I was deeply moved and strangely infatuated with the baby. I rationalized this by assuming that my reaction was connected to my maternal instincts, triggered by witnessing the birth. Nevertheless, I was shocked by the intensity of my emotional response. By coincidence, I was on duty in the nursery three weeks later, on the day three Elders/Grandmothers from the Aboriginal woman's community arrived at the ward to claim the infant girl. I relinquished the baby to them personally. This triggered an intense grief process that heralded my personal journey into my ancestral heritage.

It was this experience as a new midwife that resulted in my curiosity about my adoptive status. My parents had never alluded to it again so I felt reluctant to approach them with my concerns. Instead I wrote to Family Services to answer the emerging questions concerning my identity. It was still a shock when I received in the mail a brief outline confirming my adoptive status. A birth certificate revealed my mother's name and age at the time of birth and the names she had called me. There was also a book called "*No More Secrets.*" But there were still plenty of secrets, and the following decade there were times when I almost gave up on ever unraveling the mystery of my past. There were so many disappointments, so many trips up dry gullies.

My quest received new impetus when I met Mary Madden, a therapist who had trained with Doctor Stanislav Grof and Christina Grof in the United States and was a certified Holotropic Breathwork practitioner. Mary and later Tav Sparks (the Director of the Grof Transpersonal Training) became central facilitators for my Holotropic Breathwork sessions and training, both becoming close friends. With their support, I embarked on the challenging journey of self-exploration during which I had many difficult experiences in both holotropic sessions, in dreams, and in the course of my everyday life.

I had memories emerge of repeated sexual abuse as a child and being violently raped by a man who spoke only Italian, no English. I was concerned I couldn't connect these experiences to specific events in my earlier life. I started having migraines that seemed somehow related to my traumatic birth, involving forceps. At different times, bruises would appear spontaneously on my forehead and body, reflecting the marks I had seen forceps leave on babies during the numerous assisted births I had witnessed. I was desperately trying to remember if these experiences had actually happened and I had repressed them from consciousness.

At this difficult stage in my self-exploration, I withdrew from my partner, family and friends. I was confused and disorientated. Temporarily, I seemed to lose all points of reference and the will to live. Retrospectively, I appreciated the consistent loving support from Mary Madden and Tav Sparks, along with the Holotropic Breathwork community and family that made it possible to survive this crisis. I am convinced without it I would have taken my life.

Although I had very limited connection with the Indigenous community up to this point, many of my inner experiences involved Aboriginal people and themes. Some emerged during breathwork sessions and others occurred spontaneously in dreams and my everyday life. I imagined with extraordinary clarity and intensity Aboriginal Elders/Grandmothers coming to me, sharing their knowledge with me and showing me practices that powerfully enhanced my abilities as a midwife. This inspired me to collaboratively establish through *Blue Care* Queensland's first partially state-funded, independent midwifery program.

Throughout this time, however, I had no luck in my search for my birth mother. I continued to carefully document my experiences in my journals and by drawing prolifically the scenes that haunted me. This resulted in a series of fifty-four pastel drawings documenting and illustrating my stormy inner process (see figures 11.a, 11.b, and 11.c). In 1995, I had my first breakthrough, when Salvation Army Missing Person's Service discovered my maternal grandmother and uncles who were living in Sydney and subsequently my birth mother who was living in New Zealand. However, my relatives refused to have anything to do with me, which was devastating.

Finally, six months later, my birth mother wrote, reluctantly. Her letter was brief but brought unexpected validation for my experiences. It described my conception as a rape at the hands of an Italian man who spoke no English. At the time, my birth mother was a teenager from a small town in far north Queensland. She was not only brutally traumatized by the rape but also shamed and blamed by her family. After two unsuccessful attempts at abortion, she was sent to a home for unmarried mothers in Brisbane. Following my birth that she described as a "traumatic forceps delivery," my birth mother was put on a boat to New Zealand without ever seeing or touching me. She had done her best to put the past behind her and start anew. In her letter she wished me well and blocked future attempts to contact her. Instead of bringing a sense of resolution, my experiences in Holotropic Breathwork continued with renewed intensity.

In one of my sessions, I identified experientially with a traditional Aboriginal woman who appeared in a historical context related to the end of the nineteenth century. This woman was tied, raped, and beaten at the hands of two uniformed men who appeared on horseback. The taking of her two children by force seemed to be the focus of the experience; to prevent her following them, her legs were doused in petrol, set ablaze, and badly burnt. I continued to document these episodes through drawing and journaling in an attempt to maintain my sanity. One day, following a therapy session that had again featured an Indigenous theme, I called, at Mary Madden's suggestion, the international directory enquiries and made a long distance call to New Zealand. I desperately hoped to make verbal contact with my birth mother and this attempt was successful.

In the conversation that followed, my birth mother disclosed my great-great-grandmother was a traditional Aboriginal woman and she graphically described a lineage of sexual, emotional, physical, and spiritual abuse. A history where, generation after generation, a daughter had been conceived in a rape and then stolen. I felt hopeful and inspired; the mystery seemed to be unfolding at last. However, following this conversation, my birth mother withdrew and refused further contact. In desperation, I approached an Aboriginal organization, Link Up, to assist me in verifying my Indigenous status. They couldn't offer support without my birth mother's permission and this was not forthcoming. My frustration grew.

My adoptive parents had staunchly supported this journey and one day my father found by chance a phone number that broke the story wide open. I made contact with an agency called Community and Personal Histories, who were willing to investigate my case. Some months later, I was called to a meeting with a social worker who presented me with pages of documentation from 1895 to 1918, detailing the history of my great-grandmother, the illegitimate daughter of an elderly Irish landowner in far north Queensland. He was seeking an exemption from the Aboriginal Protection Act, so this half-caste daughter could be returned from domestic service to care for him.

This man referred to "taking a full-blood Aboriginal woman Nuninja, as his mistress, resulting in two half-caste children." There was also the police report concerning two officers sent on horseback to capture "the gin and her children" who were subsequently sent into service and to the "nigger camp." It confirmed "the gin" didn't return due to an accident and injuries involving the campfire. This was astonishing confirmation of the experiences in my breathwork session. I was referred to a Stolen Generations counselor which was a rich, validating, and transformative experience. I reconnected with Link Up, an organization responsible for reuniting Indigenous families affected by the Stolen Generations. I flew to Sydney with an Indigenous counselor Robert Sturrman, for a three-day reunion with my grandmother and Uncle Robbie. Words will never adequately express the emotion experienced when I walked into my grandmother's unit. A tiny woman, she grasped me in her arms, sobbing and turning to her son to say: "At last our baby is home!"

I discovered that when the Salvation Army had made contact with my grandmother years prior, she had just suffered a stroke. Her eldest son had sent them away wanting to protect his mother. As she recovered and was told I had tried to make contact, they had no idea which agency had contacted them or how to reconnect. My uncle since died of a heart attack, and my grandmother, a deeply spiritual person, prayed every day that I would find my way back to her. There continues to be no contact between myself and my birth mother, however, my connection with my uncle Robbie has flourished. He wrote in a letter following our reunion, "I was trying to think of why you have made such a difference in our lives. Then it hit me that you completed our family when you arrived at Grandma's door. It was as if finally the circle was closed. We love you dearly." My grandmother passed away the year following our reunion; I feel in my heart she waited to meet me. I will be forever grateful to those who supported my tumultuous journey home.

We asked Marianne to sum up for us the changes in her life that she attributes to her experiences in Holotropic Breathwork training. We received from her the following letter:

The legacy of my devastating inherited and perinatal experiences left me imprinted with a relentlessly corrupted and intensely negative orientation to life. For over three decades, I felt increasingly powerless to arrest the inevitable sabotaging of my health, personal and professional relationships, compounded by the loss of connection to my culture, spirituality, family and community. My Holotropic Breathwork experiences, midwifed with extraordinary skill and sensitivity, resulted in relief of debilitating migraines, the resolution of chronic addiction issues, including bulimia, substance abuse, debilitating depression with suicidal tendencies, and concurrent abusive relationships.

The benefits I have experienced due to the process of Holotropic Breathwork have been profoundly life-changing. I consider it to be responsible for transforming my life on every level—spiritually, emotionally, intellectually, physiologically and socially. I feel a passionate commitment to promote Holotropic Breathwork within the Indigenous community as it embodies the potential to transform the legacy inherited by those who have survived the holocaust of the post-colonial invasion. I believe that—as a sacred technology—it offers a contemporary solution that reconnects us to our history, embracing tens of thousands of years when Aboriginal Australians performed powerful ceremonies to support the evolution of conscious awareness and maintain well-being. I am infinitely grateful for Holotropic Breathwork and those who midwife this process with such commitment and integrity.

Hope this or at least some of it is helpful.

All my love, Marianne

When we asked Marianne for permission to include her moving story in our book, she wanted to make sure that we mention the deep gratitude she feels to Tav Sparks, head of the staff of Grof Transpersonal Training, and to Mary Madden, her therapist and certified Holotropic Breathwork practitioner, for the crucial role these two extraordinary human beings played in her healing process. She is convinced that without their expert guidance and loving support she would not have been able to face the challenges and emotional pain of her difficult inner journey and bring it to successful completion. Marianne captured her moving story in a short film entitled *Nuninja: Nightmares from a Stolen Past*, which is now available for purchase (mwobcke@bigpond.com).

CHAPTER EIGHT

Therapeutic Mechanisms Operating in Holotropic Breathwork

Considering the powerful healing effect that Holotropic Breathwork can have on a large spectrum of emotional, psychosomatic, and sometimes even physical disorders, the question naturally arises about the nature of the therapeutic mechanisms involved. Only a small fraction of the wide range of mechanisms of healing and personality transformation that become available in holotropic states is known to traditional psychiatrists; many of them have been discovered in the last several decades by modern consciousness research and various avenues of experiential therapy.

On the superficial level of the holotropic experience, we can observe the traditional therapeutic mechanisms, such as the emergence of repressed memories, transference phenomena, important intellectual and emotional insights, and others, but in a modified and greatly intensified form. Significant changes can occur as a result of dynamic shifts in the governing systems of the psyche (COEX systems) described earlier in this book (pages 15f). Reliving of the biological birth trauma and experience of psychospiritual death and rebirth can positively influence a rich spectrum of emotional and psychosomatic disorders. There are also important therapeutic mechanisms associated with various transpersonal phenomena, such as past life experiences, encounters with archetypal figures, and experiences of cosmic unity. In the most general sense, healing can be understood as a movement toward wholeness.

1. Intensification of conventional therapeutic mechanisms

On the most superficial level, Holotropic Breathwork sessions engage all of the therapeutic mechanisms known from verbal psychotherapy. However,

these are greatly augmented and deepened by the non-ordinary state of consciousness the breathers are in, which dramatically changes the relationship
between the unconscious and conscious dynamics of the psyche. It lowers
an individual's psychological defenses and decreases the resistance against
facing memories of painful events from the past.

In holotropic states of consciousness, old memories from childhood
and infancy—including those that have been repressed—can become easily
available and spontaneously emerge into consciousness. This is accompanied
by intellectual and emotional insights that bring a new understanding of
the biographical roots of various emotional and psychosomatic disorders and
problems in interpersonal relationships. However, unlike in verbal therapy,
these memories can not only be remembered, but also relived in full age
regression, with all the original emotions and physical sensations associated
with them. This includes changes in the body image and the perception
of the world corresponding to the individual's stage of development at the
time when the traumas occurred.

Surprisingly, the traumatic memories that spontaneously emerge for
processing are not limited to events that caused psychological pain. In
Holotropic Breathwork sessions people commonly relive memories of physical traumas, such as painful and otherwise uncomfortable diseases, surgical
interventions, and injuries. Particularly frequent are memories of episodes
that involved interference with breathing, such as near drowning, whooping
cough, diphtheria, or strangulation. It seems to have escaped the attention of
mainstream professionals that physical traumas are also psychotraumas with a
significant impact on the victim's psyche and that reliving them can have a
profound healing effect on various emotional and psychosomatic disorders.

Let us now take a closer look at the mechanisms responsible for the therapeutic effect of reliving traumatic episodes from our early life. Psychogenic
symptoms seem to draw their dynamic power from deep-seated repositories
of difficult emotions and pent-up physical energies associated with various
psychotraumas. This was first described by Sigmund Freud and Joseph Breuer
in their book *Studies in Hysteria* (Freud and Breuer 1936). These authors
suggested that psychoneuroses were caused by traumatic situations in early
life that, because of their nature or due to external circumstances, did not
allow the victim a full emotional and physical reaction. This produced what
they called "jammed affect" (*abgeklemmter Affekt*), which then became the
source of future psychoneurotic problems.

Therapy consisted in bringing the patients into a holotropic state
of consciousness—in Freud and Breuer's case a hypnotic or autohypnotic
trance—which would make it possible for them to regress into childhood,
relive the repressed memory, and release the jammed affect and the energetic charge in a process Freud called *abreaction*. The name used for more

generalized and less focused emotional release, where the specific source of the emotions could not be identified, was *catharsis*, a term coined originally by Aristotle in the fourth century BC. Freud later abandoned this concept of the etiology of psychoneuroses and saw their cause in the clients' infantile fantasies rather than actual traumas. He also replaced the work with hypnosis, age regression, and abreaction by the method of free association and his original emphasis on making the unconscious conscious by the analysis of transference.

Abreaction and catharsis deserve a brief notice in this context, because their therapeutic potential has to be reevaluated in the light of the observations from holotropic therapy. Under Freud's influence, traditional psychiatrists and psychotherapists do not see abreaction as a mechanism capable of inducing lasting therapeutic changes, with one exception. Abreactive techniques using hypnosis or administration of Sodium Pentathol or Amytal (narcoanalysis) have been widely used in the treatment of emotional disorders caused by massive psychotraumas, such as acute traumatic neuroses, particularly those resulting from exposure to war situations.

Official handbooks of psychiatry usually recommend abreaction as a method of choice in the treatment of war neuroses (PTSD), but claim that it is ineffective in the therapy of any other emotional disorders. Surprisingly, they do not offer any explanation for this remarkable fact. The second half of the twentieth century saw emergence and increasing popularity of experiential therapies that replaced talking (as the primary approach) by direct expression of emotions and bodywork. Many practitioners of these new approaches came to the conclusion that Freud's decision to replace his abreactive technique by talking therapy was a mistake that took psychotherapy in the wrong direction for at least half a century (Ross 1989).

As Wilhelm Reich demonstrated very clearly, exclusively verbal therapy is inadequate to cope with the bioenergetic blockages underlying emotional and psychosomatic disorders. For therapy to be successful, the therapist needs to find effective ways of releasing them. For this purpose, Reich pioneered methods combining breathing and bodywork. The reason that abreaction did not bring satisfactory results was that in most instances it remained superficial. Therapists were not prepared to deal with the extreme forms abreaction can take when it reaches memories of life-threatening situations, such as near drowning, diseases interfering with breathing, or biological birth, and did not allow the process to go far enough.

The reliving of such situations can be very dramatic and involve various frightening manifestations, such as temporary loss of control, an experience of suffocation, panic, fear of death, vomiting, and lapse of consciousness. The therapist has to feel comfortable working with such extreme emotions and behaviors for abreaction to reach a good closure and be therapeutically successful. This seems to explain why abreaction has been effective in treating post-traumatic stress disorders (PTSDs) resulting from exposure to life-threatening situations in war, during natural disasters, or severe traumas due to abuse. Knowing that their clients were exposed to drastic circumstances that were far beyond the ordinary, therapists were prepared to deal with extreme forms of emotional expression. Without such a logical explanation, therapists witnessing manifestations of extreme intensity tend to conclude that the patient is entering psychologically dangerous psychotic territory and they discontinue the process.

Holotropic therapists are in the same situation as therapists treating traumatic war neuroses, or other forms of PTSD, but for a different reason. Their cartography of the psyche is not limited to the psychological aspects of postnatal biography and the Freudian individual unconscious. It includes memories of physical traumas, perinatal and prenatal events, as well as collective and karmic memories. Another potential source of extreme emotions and physical manifestations is the archetypal domain, a salient example being the work with demonic energy. The extended map of the psyche thus provides many logical reasons for extreme forms of abreaction and allows the therapist to feel comfortable working with them.

Frequently asked questions about reliving of childhood traumas are: What makes this process therapeutic? Why does it not represent retraumatization rather than being conducive to healing? The unique nature of the holotropic state allows the breather to simultaneously play two very different roles. A person, who is experiencing full age regression to the period of childhood when the traumatic event took place, identifies in a very authentic and convincing way with the child or the infant involved. At the same time, he or she retains the stamina and reasoning capacity of a mature adult. This situation makes it possible to fully experience the original event with the primitive emotions and sensations of the small child and, at the same time, process and evaluate it from the position of an adult. It is obvious that an adult is capable of coping with many experiences that during childhood were incomprehensible, confusing, and intolerable. In addition, the therapeutic context and support from people whom the breather trusts makes this situation vastly different from the circumstances under which the original trauma occurred.

This might be an adequate explanation for the healing impact that the conscious reliving has on some less extreme traumas. However, the healing of major traumas—particularly those that threatened survival and body integrity of the individual—seems to involve yet another therapeutic mechanism. It is very likely that in situations of this kind, the original traumatic event was recorded in the organism, but its impact was not fully experienced at the time when it happened. On occasion, massive psychological shock can lead to blacking out and fainting. It is conceivable that the experience can also be shut off partially, rather than completely; the individual then does not lose consciousness, yet does not sense the full impact of the trauma. As a result, the traumatic event cannot be fully psychologically "digested" and integrated; it is dissociated and remains in the unconscious as a foreign element. This does not prevent it from having a disturbing influence on the person's emotional and psychosomatic condition and behavior.

When such a traumatic memory emerges into consciousness, people do not simply relive the original event, they fully and consciously experience it for the first time. This makes it possible for them to reach completion, closure, and integration. This problem was discussed at some length in an interesting paper by the Irish psychiatrist Ivor Browne and his colleagues, entitled "Unexperienced Experience: A Clinical Reappraisal of the Theory of Repression and Traumatic Neurosis" (McGee et al. 1984). Once a traumatic memory is fully consciously experienced, processed, and integrated, it ceases to exert a negative impact on the individual's everyday life.

Another mechanism that can be greatly intensified in Holotropic Breathwork is transference. However, contrary to traditional psychoanalysis, it is not considered a useful therapeutic occurrence, but an untoward complication interfering with deep self-exploration. After Freud rejected and abandoned the work with regression and abreaction and started to use the method of free association, he shifted his attention to the phenomenon of transference. He noticed that in the course of psychoanalysis, patients projected on him various emotional reactions and attitudes that they had experienced as children in relation to their parents. Eventually, they developed what Freud called *transference neurosis* in which he, as the therapist, became the main focus of all their emotional energy. He considered *transference analysis*, a process clarifying these distortions, to be the principal therapeutic mechanism.

Unlike the verbal approaches, Holotropic Breathwork—and deep experiential therapy, in general—has the potential to take the client in a very short time to the original traumatic situations and thus to the source of the emotional or psychosomatic disorder. Development of transference diverts the attention of the clients from a serious quest for important answers deep inside to a horizontal pseudosituation, an artificial melodrama that they create in relation to the facilitator (or sitter). The task of the facilitators is to redirect the attention of the breathers to the introspective process, which alone promises to bring answers and healing. When Holotropic Breathwork uses this strategy, it becomes obvious that transference is a manifestation of psychological defense and resistance rather than a useful therapeutic mechanism. It is an attempt to avoid facing a very painful problem from the past by creating a less threatening, more manageable pseudoproblem in the present.

The drive to change the relationship with the therapist into an intimate one—a common aspect of the transference dynamics—has to be differentiated from anaclitic needs experienced by the breathers during age regression to early infancy. This deep craving for emotional and even physical closeness reflects a history of severe abandonment and emotional deprivation in infancy and childhood. It is genuine and legitimate and is not a result of psychological resistance. The best way to heal this "trauma by omission" is the use of supportive physical contact while the regressed breather is experiencing these anaclitic needs. The responsible and judicious use of this approach was discussed at some length earlier in this book (pages 40ff.).

The healing potential of Holotropic Breathwork is not limited to intensification and deepening of conventional therapeutic mechanisms. An exciting aspect of the work with holotropic states is that they offer many additional highly effective mechanisms of healing and personality transformation that have not yet been discovered and acknowledged by mainstream psychiatrists. In the following sections, we will describe and discuss these important new therapeutic perspectives.

2. Dynamic shifts in the psyche's governing systems

Many radical changes resulting from Holotropic Breathwork sessions can be explained in terms of dynamic interplay of unconscious constellations—systems of condensed experience (COEX systems). As we discussed earlier (see pages 15f.), these systems consist of multiple layers; the more superficial layers contain memories of emotionally important events from various periods of postnatal life and the deeper layers records of different stages of the biological birth process and periods of prenatal life. The deepest roots of the COEX systems reach to various transpersonal matrices: ancestral, karmic, racial, phylogenetic, or archetypal.

During a holotropic state of consciousness, the COEX system that becomes activated determines the content of the experience. Many instances of sudden improvement after a Holotropic Breathwork session can be explained as a shift from a negative COEX system (consisting of traumatic memories) to a positive one (containing memories associated with pleasant emotions). Such a dynamic shift can be referred to as *positive COEX transmodulation*. This does not necessarily mean that all of the unconscious material underlying the presenting symptoms has been worked through. It simply means that an inner shift occurred from the dominance of one governing system to another.

A typical positive transmodulation has two phases. It begins by an intensification of the emotional charge of the dominant negative COEX system;

after a period of variable duration, the emotions reach a culmination point and the positive COEX systems dominate the experiential field. However, if a strong positive system is readily available, it can govern the session from the very beginning. In this case, the negative system simply recedes into the background. A shift from one system to another does not necessarily have to be beneficial; it could be a shift from a positive system to a negative one (*negative COEX transmodulation*). When this happens, symptoms can emerge that were previously latent and may persist after the session.

A particularly interesting dynamic change is *substitutive transmodulation*, which involves a shift from one negative COEX system to another one, which is also negative. This results in a remarkable change in emotional and psychosomatic symptoms. Occasionally, this transformation is so dramatic that, from a traditional clinical perspective, it would move the breather into a different diagnostic category. Although the resulting condition might appear entirely new, careful analysis reveals that all its elements preexisted in the unconscious psyche before the shift occurred.

Dynamic shifts can happen on different levels of the COEX systems—biographical, perinatal, and transpersonal. This determines the nature and the depth of the changes that result. The shifts that involve the perinatal level and engage one of the BPMs tend to cause more radical and profound changes than those that happen on the level of various biographical layers of the COEXes. Possible exceptions in this regard are COEX systems that comprise memories of situations that seriously threatened the individual's survival or body integrity.

The COEX system that dominates the experience during the final period of the session determines the outcome of the session. Such a system continues to shape the everyday experience of the breathers in the post-session period. It colors their perception of themselves and of the world, their emotional and psychosomatic condition, system of values, and attitudes. A general strategy in Holotropic Breathwork sessions is therefore to make the negative systems conscious, reduce their emotional charge, work through and integrate their content, and facilitate experiential access to positive COEX systems. It is essential that the facilitators stay with the breathers as long as it takes to complete and integrate the material that was made available on the day of the session.

3. The therapeutic potential of the death-rebirth process

The therapeutic mechanisms operating on the biographical level do not present any theoretical challenge for academic psychiatry, because they involve memories for which there is a known material substrate—the brain of the infant, child, or individual in a later stage of development. The same is true for therapeutic mechanisms connected with the perinatal level, contrary to the official position of mainstream psychiatrists, who do not consider birth to be a psychotrauma and deny the possibility of birth memory. However, this is a remarkable misconception that can easily be corrected.

The usual reason for denying the possibility of a birth memory is that the cerebral cortex of the newborn is not mature enough to experience and record this event. More specifically, the cortical neurons are not yet completely covered with protective sheaths of a fatty substance called *myelin*. Surprisingly, the same argument is not used to deny the existence and importance of memories from the time of nursing, a period that immediately follows birth. The psychological significance of the experiences in the oral period and even "bonding"—the exchange of looks and physical contact between the mother and child immediately after birth—is generally recognized and acknowledged by mainstream psychiatrists, obstetricians, and pediatricians (Klaus, Kennell, and Klaus 1995; Kennel and Klaus 1998).

The myelinization argument makes no sense and is in conflict with scientific evidence of various kinds. It is well known that memory exists in organisms that do not have a cerebral cortex at all, let alone a myelinized one. In 2001, American neuroscientist of Austrian origin Erik Kandel received a Nobel Prize in physiology for his research of memory mechanisms of the sea slug Aplysia, an organism incomparably more primitive than the newborn child. The assertion that the newborn is not aware of being born and is not capable of forming a memory of this event is also in sharp conflict with extensive fetal research showing the extreme sensitivity of the fetus already in the prenatal stage (Tomatis 1991; Whitwell 1999).

Our life begins with a major traumatic experience—the potentially life-threatening passage through the birth canal, typically lasting many hours or even days. The memory of birth is a prime example of an "unexperienced experience" that we all harbor in our unconscious psyche. Experiential work involving age regression has shown that it is associated with intense vital anxiety, feelings of inadequacy and hopelessness mixed with rage, and extreme physical discomfort—choking, pressures and pains in various part of the body. The memories of prenatal disturbances and of the discomfort experienced during birth constitute a major repository of difficult emotions and sensations of all kinds and constitute a potential source of a wide variety of emotional and psychosomatic symptoms and syndromes. It is therefore not surprising that reliving and integration of the memory of birth can significantly alleviate many different disorders—from claustrophobia, suicidal depression, and destructive and self-destructive tendencies to psychogenic asthma, psychosomatic pains, and migraine headaches. It can also improve the rapport with one's mother and have positive influence on other interpersonal relationships.

Certain physical changes that typically accompany the reliving of birth deserve special notice because they have a profound beneficial effect on the breathers' psychological and physical condition. The first of these is release of any respiratory blockage caused by birth, which leads to significant improvement of breathing. This elevates the mood, "cleanses the doors of perception," brings a sense of emotional and physical well-being, increases zest, and engenders a sense of *joi de vivre*. The change in the quality of life following opening of respiratory pathways is often remarkable.

Another major physical change associated with the reliving of birth is the release of muscular tension, dissolution of what Wilhelm Reich called the *character armor*. This tension was generated as a reaction to the hours of painful and stressful passage through the birth canal under circumstances that did not allow any emotional or physical expression. After powerful and well-resolved perinatal experiences, breathers often report that they are more relaxed than they have ever been in their life. This can be also accompanied by clearing of various psychosomatic pains. With the relaxation and relief from pain comes a feeling of greater physical comfort, increased energy and vitality, a sense of rejuvenation, and an enhanced ability to enjoy the present moment.

4. The therapeutic mechanisms on the transpersonal level

While therapeutic mechanisms associated with postnatal, perinatal, and prenatal memories have a material substrate, the situation is quite different concerning the therapeutic mechanisms operating on the transpersonal level of the unconscious. The very existence of the transpersonal domain represents a formidable challenge for materialistic science. The only conceivable material substrates that exist for a small number of transpersonal experiences (ancestral, racial, phylogenetic) are the nuclei of the egg and the spermatozoid with their DNA. A rich array of the remaining transpersonal experiences urge us to accept the existence of memory without a material substrate, a concept alien to mainstream science. David Bohm's concept of the implicate order, Rupert Sheldrake's idea of morphogenetic fields, and Ervin Laszlo's hypothesis of the psi or Akashic field are promising steps in developing a theory accounting for and incorporating these fascinating phenomena (Bohm 1980; Sheldrake 1981; Laszlo 1993, 2004).

In spite of the major theoretical challenge involved, there can be little doubt that transpersonal experiences are genuine phenomena and that many of them have a remarkable therapeutic potential. Thus, occasionally, breathers can trace certain aspects of their problems to specific episodes in the lives of their ancestors and resolve them by reliving and integrating these ancestral memories. In some instances what initially seemed to be intrapsychic conflicts of the breathers turn out to be internalized conflicts between the ancestral lineages of their parents (when, for example, one of them is Catholic and the other Jewish, one white American and the other African American, one German and the other Jewish, and so on).

Particularly strong therapeutic changes are associated with what breathers experience as past life memories. These are highly emotionally charged experiential sequences that seem to take place in other historical periods and other countries. They are typically associated with a strong sense of *déjà vu* and *déjà vecu*—a strong sense that what they are experiencing is not happening to them for the first time, that they have seen or experienced it before. Past life experiences often seem to provide explanations for otherwise obscure aspects of the breather's current life—emotional and psychosomatic symptoms, difficulties in interpersonal relationships, passionate interests, preferences, prejudices, and idiosyncrasies.

The full conscious experience of these episodes, the expression of the emotions and physical energies associated with them, and reaching a sense of forgiveness can have remarkable therapeutic effect. It can bring the resolution of a wide array of symptoms and disorders that previously resisted all attempts at treatment. People who have these experiences typically discover that situations that happened in other historical periods and in various parts of the world seem to have left deep imprints in some unknown medium and have played an instrumental role in the genesis of their difficulties in the present lifetime.

The archetypal realm of the collective unconscious is an additional source of important therapeutic opportunities. Thus experiences of various archetypal motifs and encounters with mythological figures from the pantheons of different cultures of the world can often have an unexpected beneficial influence on the emotional and psychosomatic condition of the breathers. However, for a positive outcome it is important to avoid the danger of ego inflation associated with the numinosity of such experiences and to reach a good integration. Of particular interest are situations where the archetypal energy underlying various disorders has the form of a dark, demonic entity. Emergence into consciousness and the full experience of this personified energy often resembles an exorcism and can have profound therapeutic impact (see pages 194ff.).

The transpersonal domain offers an abundance of further healing mechanisms, some of which can be puzzling, perplexing, and mystifying. They can be, for example, associated with experiential identification with various animals or even plants, talking in tongues or foreign languages, and vocalizing or moving in a way that resembles art forms of foreign cultures, such as Japanese Kabuki, Balinese monkey chant (*ketjak*), Inuit Eskimo throat music, hocketing of the pygmies, Javanese dance, and others. For example, in one of our Holotropic Breathwork sessions at Esalen, we saw a painful chronic tension of the trapezius muscle dissolve after the breather had experienced a convincing identification with a crab. She felt that her painfully tense trapezius muscle became a carapace and kept moving with great determination and strength sideways on the floor. Since the two of us were doing bodywork on her "carapace," she dragged us along several times across the room until all the blocked energy was released from the muscle. Another time, we witnessed a depression that had lasted several years disappear after the participant repeatedly chanted a prayer in Sephardic (Ladino), a language which she did not know (pages 109ff.).

The most powerful healing and transformation seems to be associated with mystical experiences—union with other people, with nature, with the Cosmos, and with God. It is important to emphasize that these experiences need to be allowed to reach completion and be well integrated into everyday life to be healing. Ironically, contemporary psychiatrists consider them to be manifestations of serious mental diseases—psychoses—and try to suppress them with all possible means. Modern psychiatry does not have a category of "spiritual experience" or "mystical experience." If mystical experiences receive a psychopathological label and are truncated by suppressive medication, they can lead to long-term problems in the life of the individual.

5. Healing as a movement toward wholeness

As we have seen, the therapeutic mechanisms operating in Holotropic Breathwork cover a very wide range. As the psyche gets activated and symptoms become converted into a flow of experience, significant therapeutic changes occur when the individual relives emotionally important memories from childhood and infancy, from biological birth, and from prenatal existence. Therapeutic mechanisms on the transpersonal level involve widely diverse types of experiences—ancestral, racial, collective, karmic, and phylogenetic memories, identification with animals, encounters with mythological beings, visits to archetypal realms, and union with other people, with nature, with the universe, and with God.

This raises an interesting question: Can the healing mechanisms associated with such a rich array of experiences, originating on different levels of the psyche, be reduced to a common denominator? It is clear that the effective mechanism that would account for phenomena of such diversity would have to be extraordinarily general and universal. Finding such a general healing mechanism requires a radically new understanding of consciousness, of the psyche, and of human nature, as well as a fundamental revision of the basic metaphysical assumptions underlying the current scientific worldview.

Modern consciousness research has revealed the remarkable paradoxical nature of human beings. In the context of mechanistic science, it seems appropriate and logical to think about human beings as Newtonian objects, as material bodies made of organs, tissues, and cells. More specifically, humans can be seen as highly developed animals and complex biological thinking machines. However, the discoveries of consciousness research confirm the claims of Eastern spiritual philosophies and various mystical traditions that human beings can also function as infinite fields of consciousness transcending the limitations of space, time, and linear causality. This paradoxical definition has its distant parallel on the subatomic level in the famous wave-particle paradox involved in the description of the nature of matter and light, known as Niels Bohr's *principle of complementarity*.

These two complementary aspects of human nature are connected with two different modes of consciousness that can be referred to as *hylotropic* and *holotropic*. The first of these, *hylotropic consciousness*, means, literally, "matter-oriented consciousness" (from the Greek *hyle* = matter and *trepein* = oriented toward or moving toward something). It is the state of consciousness that most of us experience in everyday life and that Western psychiatry considers to be the only one that correctly reflects objective reality.

In the *hylotropic mode of consciousness*, we experience ourselves as solid material bodies operating in a world of separate objects that has distinct Newtonian properties: space is three-dimensional, time is linear, and everything seems to be governed by chains of cause and effect. Experiences in this mode support systematically a number of basic assumptions, such as: matter is solid; our senses have a limited range; two objects cannot occupy the same space; past events are irretrievably lost; future events are not experientially available; we cannot be in more than one place at the same time and be simultaneously in more than one historical period; objects have fixed sizes that can be situated on a continuous metric scale; a whole is larger than a part; and so on.

As we mentioned earlier, *holotropic consciousness* literally means consciousness moving toward wholeness. In contrast with the narrow and restricted hylotropic mode, holotropic consciousness has access to the entire material world without the mediation of sensory organs and also to normally hidden dimensions of reality that our physical senses cannot reach. Experiences in this mode of consciousness offer many interesting alternatives to the Newtonian world of matter with its rigid restrictions and limitations.

They systematically support a set of assumptions that are diametrically different from those characterizing the hylotropic mode: the universe represents essentially a virtual reality; the solidity and discontinuity of matter is an illusion generated by a particular orchestration of experiences; linear time and three-dimensional space are not absolute but ultimately arbitrary; the same space can be simultaneously occupied by many objects; the past and future are always available and can be brought experientially into the present moment; we can experience ourselves in several places at the same time; we can be simultaneously in more than one temporal framework; being a part is not incompatible with being a whole; something can exist and not exist at the same time; form and emptiness are interchangeable; and more.

For example, we can have a Holotropic Breathwork session at the Esalen Institute and—while we are physically in Big Sur, California—have a convincing experience of being also in the house where we spent our infancy and childhood, in the birth canal struggling to be born, in the womb during our prenatal life, or in Paris during the French Revolution. We can experience ourselves as a fetus and simultaneously as a single cell, the ocean, or the entire universe. In the holotropic mode of consciousness being a cell, a fetus, the ocean, and the entire universe are easily exchangeable experiences that can coincide or effortlessly morph into one another.

In the human psyche, these two modes seem to be in dynamic interplay: while we are in the hylotropic mode, we have a deep-seated need for holotropic experiences, for transcendence (Weil 1972), and experiences from the holotropic realms show a strong propensity to emerge into consciousness. An average individual, who is "healthy" by current psychiatric norms, has a sufficiently developed system of psychological defenses to prevent holotropic experiences from emerging into consciousness. Strong defenses are a mixed blessing, since the emergence of the holotropic material typically represents an effort of the organism to heal itself and simplify its functioning. While a strong defense system helps us to function undisturbed in everyday reality, it also prevents various traumatic memories to surface for processing.

There are individuals whose defense system is so permeable that it allows holotropic experiences to emerge into their field of consciousness on an ongoing basis and disturb their daily life. C. G. Jung's extended spiritual crisis during which he was flooded with the material from the collective unconscious can be used here as a prime example (Jung 1961, 2009). While these individuals are in desperate need of grounding, there are others who are so deeply entrenched in material reality that they have great difficulties entering the holotropic state of consciousness, despite their repeated participation in various spiritual retreats and workshops using powerful experiential techniques.

Emotional and psychosomatic symptoms of psychogenic origin can be seen as amalgams or hybrids between the hylotropic and holotropic mode that compete for the experiential field. They appear when some outer or inner influences weaken the defense system or increase the energetic charge (cathexis) of the unconscious material. In this unfortunate "betwixt and between" situation, the defense system is not strong enough to keep the material in the unconscious, but strong enough to prevent it from full emergence, conscious processing, and integration.

This understanding of the dynamics underlying symptoms then suggests a new therapeutic strategy. We outline for the clients the expanded cartography of the psyche describing the terrain they might traverse in this work, create a supportive environment, and teach them how to enter a holotropic state of consciousness. Once that happens, the unconscious material that is ready for processing automatically emerges into consciousness. By full experience and expression of the emotions and physical energies tied to the symptoms, the symptoms are transformed into a stream of experiential sequences (biographical, perinatal, and transpersonal) and cease to have a disturbing influence on the individual's conscious life.

An important characteristic of the holotropic strategy of therapy and self-exploration is that sooner or later it turns into a philosophical and spiritual quest. As soon as our experiences reach the perinatal level, they become numinous and provide for us overwhelming evidence that spirituality is a genuine, vital, and legitimate dimension of the psyche and of the universal scheme of things. On the transpersonal level, we can experience ourselves as other people, animals, and plants and even as various archetypal beings. It becomes clear to us that we are not body/egos, and that we do not have a fixed identity. We discover that our true identity is cosmic and that it stretches from our everyday self to the cosmic creative principle itself.

Unlike therapy that focuses on pharmacological suppression of symptoms, this uncovering strategy leads to self-discovery, self-realization, and spiritual opening. In the last analysis, it is a journey toward wholeness, toward the recognition of our true nature. It is probably not an accident that the word *healing* is related to the Old English and Anglo-Saxon *haelan*, meaning to make whole, sound, and well. *Healing* means to make whole, to bring something that is fragmented and impaired back to a state of wholeness.

CHAPTER NINE

Physiological Mechanisms Involved in Holotropic Breathwork

In view of the powerful effect Holotropic Breathwork has on the psyche, it is interesting to consider the physiological and biochemical mechanisms that might be involved in this process. Another relevant topic related to the physiology of Holotropic Breathwork is the concept of the "hyperventilation syndrome" and "carpopedal spasms" described in medical handbooks as mandatory reactions to faster breathing. This myth of respiratory physiology has been disproved by daily observations from Holotropic Breathwork sessions and other methods using accelerated breathing. Self-exploration using holotropic states has also brought some new insights into the nature and psychodynamics of psychosomatic disorders, a subject of many conflicting theories in academic circles.

1. Biochemical and physiological changes

Many people assume that when we breathe faster, we simply bring more oxygen into the body and into the brain; they believe that this is the mechanism responsible for the experiences in Holotropic Breathwork sessions. But—due to intricate homeostatic mechanisms operating in the human body—the situation is actually much more complicated. It is true that faster breathing brings more air and thus oxygen into the lungs, but it also eliminates carbon dioxide (CO_2). Since CO_2 is acidic, reducing its content in blood increases the alkalinity of the blood, more specifically the alkalinity/acidity index called pH. The blood pigment hemoglobin binds more oxygen in an acidic milieu and less in an alkaline milieu. This is a compensatory homeostatic mechanism that guarantees effective oxygen supply during physical exertion, which is typically associated with increased production of acidic metabolic products. The alkalosis during rapid breathing thus leads to reduced oxygen transfer to the tissues. This in turn triggers a homeostatic mechanism that works in the opposite direction: the kidneys excrete urine that is more alkaline to compensate for this change.

The situation is further complicated by the fact that certain areas in the body, including he brain, can respond to faster breathing by vasoconstriction, which naturally causes a reduction of the oxygen supply. Observations in Holotropic Breathwork sessions have shown that this is not a mandatory built-in response of these organs to faster breathing. Where this vasoconstriction occurs and how intense it will be reflects the involvement of these organs in traumatic situations in the individual's past. It tends to disappear when a person relives and works through the memory of these events. The physiological changes also depend on the type of breathing involved. Deep breathing leads to a more complete exchange of gasses in the lungs, while shallow breathing leaves a significant part of the gases in the "dead space," so that less oxygen reaches the pulmonary capillaries and less carbon dioxide (CO_2) is expelled from the lungs.

As we have seen, the physiological mechanisms activated by faster breathing are quite complex and it is not easy to evaluate the overall biochemical situation in an individual case without a battery of specific laboratory examinations. However, if we take all the aforementioned physiological mechanisms into consideration, the situation of people during Holotropic Breathwork very likely resembles that of being in high mountains, where there is less oxygen and the CO_2 level is decreased by compensatory faster breathing. The cerebral cortex, being the youngest part of the brain from an evolutionary point of view, is generally more sensitive to a variety of influences (such as alcohol and anoxia) than the older parts of the brain. This situation would thus cause inhibition of the cortical functions and intensified activity in the archaic parts of the brain, making the unconscious processes more available.

Many individuals, as well as entire cultures, that live in extreme altitudes are known for their advanced spirituality. Examples are the yogis in the Himalayas, the Tibetan Buddhists, and the Peruvian Incas. It is therefore tempting to attribute their advanced spirituality to the fact that, in an atmosphere with lower content of oxygen, they have easier access to holotropic experiences. However, we again have to take into consideration the intricate homeostatic mechanisms operating in the human body. While short-term exposure to high altitude might be comparable to Holotropic Breathwork, an extended stay in high elevations triggers physiological adaptations, such as increased production of red blood cells. The acute situation during Holotropic Breathwork might, therefore, not be directly comparable to an extended stay in high mountains.

In any case, there is a long way from the description of the physiological changes in the brain to the extremely rich array of phenomena that Holotropic Breathwork induces, such as authentic experiential identification with animals, archetypal visions, or past life memories. This situation is similar to the problem of explaining the psychological effects of LSD and other psychedelics. The fact that both of these methods can induce transpersonal experiences in which there is access to accurate new information about the universe through extrasensory channels shows that the matrices for these experiences are not contained in the brain.

Aldous Huxley, after having experienced psychedelic states with mescaline and LSD-25, came to the conclusion that our brain cannot possibly be the source of these experiences. He suggested that it functions more like a reducing valve that shields us from an infinitely larger cosmic input. The concepts, such as "memory without a material substrate" (von Foerster 1965), Sheldrake's "morphogenetic fields" (Sheldrake 1981), and Laszlo's "psi or Akashic field" (Laszlo 1993, 2004) bring important support for Huxley's idea and make it increasingly plausible.

2. Holotropic Breathwork and the "hyperventilation syndrome"

As we have shown earlier, therapeutic approaches and spiritual practices using various breathing techniques for inducing holotropic states of consciousness represent effective methods of treating psychosomatic disorders. However, they also bring important new insights regarding the response of the human body to an increased rate of breathing. They have amassed impressive empirical evidence correcting the deeply ingrained misconception concerning faster breathing found in traditional medical handbooks on respiratory physiology.

More specifically, they have dispelled the persistent myth passed among clinicians from generation to generation asserting that the mandatory physiological reaction to rapid breathing is the "hyperventilation syndrome." This syndrome is described as a stereotypical pattern of physiological responses, involving tetany of the hands and feet (carpopedal spasms), coldness of the extremities, and sweating. This is accompanied by certain neuromuscular changes that can be objectively detected. Here belong Chvostek's reflex (hyperexcitability of facial muscles) and Trousseau's reflex (spasm of muscles in the forearm and hand after compression of the upper arm artery with a tourniquet). Typical emotional reaction allegedly involves anxiety and agitation.

The relationship between hyperventilation and various medical conditions

Robert Fried, one of the most dedicated researchers of the relationship between breathing and various medical conditions, wrote a book called *The Hyperventilation Syndrome* (Fried 1982). According to him, physicians should pay much more attention to breathing. Stressed and distressed human beings hyperventilate; hyperventilation can be found in 50 to 70 percent of people with medical complaints, and in 90 percent of cases the development of hypertension is preceded by disruptions of breathing. Faulty breathing can be seen as a common etiological pathway for many problems. It is well known in academic circles that hyperventilation is closely related to anxiety, but there is no agreement as to whether hyperventilation causes anxiety or vice versa; it is clearly a "chicken-or-egg" problem.

Anxiety-prone people hyperventilate when they are exposed to stress; panic sufferers often have a respiratory alkalosis. According to G. J. Goldberg, "hyperventilation is one aspect of the anxiety reaction and it causes psychosomatic symptoms" (Goldberg 1958). Hyperventilation plays an important role in all anxiety disorders and possibly emotional disorders in general. In the first half of the twentieth century, spontaneous hyperventilation was often observed in hysterical patients. R. V. Christie called hysteria and anxiety neurosis "respiratory neuroses" (Christie 1935). Spontaneous episodes of hyperventilation occur in about 10 to 15 percent of the general population and with much greater frequency in psychiatric patients, particularly those who suffer from hysteria. The usual approach to episodes of spontaneous hyperventilation is to administer intravenous calcium to increase the level of ionized calcium in blood, give patients an injection of Librium or Valium to calm them down, and place a paper bag over their faces to keep CO_2 in their system and to reduce alkalosis.

These observations disprove the original idea expressed in W. B. Cannon's book, *The Wisdom of the Body*. Cannon believed that breathing, being so fundamental to life, is so strongly protected by homeostatic mechanisms that it can take care of itself (Cannon 1932). It has since become clear that, in spite of its apparent automaticity, breathing is not excluded from the influence of many pathophysiological and psychopathological processes that can interfere with it. In turn, abnormalities of the breathing patterns can cause physiological and psychological problems.

Medical literature on the hyperventilation syndrome lacks clarity and is full of confusion and controversy. Fried, who conducted systematic research of the effects of rapid breathing, pointed out that the stereotypical reaction described in the handbooks of respiratory physiology is in sharp contrast with clinical reports about the unusually broad range of phenomena that can occur in hyperventilating persons. These vary widely from person to person and also from episode to episode (Fried 1982). The range of possible reactions to faster breathing is so great that hyperventilating patients have been called "clients with the fat folder syndrome" (Lum 1987), because they make frequent fruitless visits to physicians. Traditionally, hyperventilation is seen as a symptom of some other disorder, rather than a factor responsible for generating symptoms. Clinicians usually do not believe that something as simple as hyperventilation can cause such intense and variegated changes; they tend to look for other causes.

According to S. R. Huey and L. Sechrest, who studied 150 hyperventilating persons, hyperventilation was able to mimic in otherwise healthy individuals a large array of medical conditions so successfully that these people were misdiagnosed and received a long list of false diagnoses (Huey and Sechrest 1981). These included diseases of the cardiovascular system, respiratory system, gastrointestinal system, musculoskeletal system, nervous system, endocrine system, immune system, and of the skin. Some of these individuals also received psychiatric diagnoses. This brings medical understanding closer to the observations from Holotropic Breathwork, but is still far from the recognition that the "hyperventilation syndrome," rather than being a pathological reaction requiring symptomatic suppression, represents a great therapeutic opportunity.

Hyperventilation in psychiatric patients and observations from
Holotropic Breathwork

As we mentioned earlier, spontaneous episodes of hyperventilation often occur in neurotics, particularly hysterical patients. Freud described in several case histories the extreme feelings of suffocation and marked respiratory distress occurring in panic attacks. That was the reason why he for some time entertained the idea that the birth trauma, being associated with suffocation, could be the source and prototype of all future anxieties (Freud 1953). Klein, Zitrin, and Woerner called the feelings of suffocation that accompany panic attacks "false suffocation alarm" (Klein, Zitrin, and Woerner1978). This panic cannot be alleviated by breathing oxygen with 5 percent of carbon dioxide that should prevent any respiratory alkalosis.

It has been noted that in psychiatric patients the symptoms induced by rapid breathing are more intense, colorful, and variegated. Patients with abnormalities of the central nervous system show a greater diversity of symptoms and persons suffering from pain have a lower threshold for hyperventilation. In psychiatric patients, hyperventilation tends to produce what has been described as an astonishing array of sensory, emotional, and psychosomatic symptoms. According to Fried, this long list includes dizziness, faintness, apprehension, depression, anxiety, panic, phobia, chest pain, muscle spasms, various physical sensations, headaches, tremors, twitches, blurred vision, nausea, vomiting, "lump in the throat," and many others (Fried 1982). These symptoms are not explainable in traditional medical terms and can mimic a variety of organic diseases. Fried also found that the mean breathing rate of control groups is lower (twelve breaths per minute) than of psychiatric patients (seventeen breaths per minute) and seizure patients (seventeen breaths per minute).

Hyperventilation tends to aggravate many symptoms and disorders, such as Raynaud's disease, migraine headache, angina pectoris, and the panic anxiety syndrome. Fried therefore suggested an approach to these disorders that teaches these clients slower breathing exercises as a "therapeutic measure." This is exactly opposite to the practice of Holotropic Breathwork based on the observation that the continuation of hyperventilation can resolve emotional and psychosomatic problems by accentuating them temporarily, exteriorizing them, and bringing them into consciousness for processing.

The practitioners of Holotropic Breathwork have a unique opportunity to study the psychological and somatic effects of rapid breathing, since they observe them regularly *in statu nascendi* as these emerge in the process of their clients. In Holotropic Breathwork workshops and training, only a small portion of the participants experience a response that the handbooks of respiratory physiology describe as typical and in a sense mandatory (carpopedal spasms, coldness of the feet, etc.) The observations from this work show that faster breathing produces an extraordinarily rich spectrum of emotional and psychosomatic symptoms. They thus support Fried's critique of a simplistic understanding of the hyperventilation syndrome.

For Fried, who views this amazing array of symptoms triggered by faster breathing from the point of view of traditional medicine, "it remains a mystery how such a simple physiological function as breathing can produce such a broad spectrum of symptoms." The practice of Holotropic Breathwork provides deep insights into the dynamics of the hyperventilation syndrome and offers a simple solution for this "mystery." It shows that the richness of the response to faster breathing cannot be understood in simple physiological terms because it is a complex psychosomatic phenomenon that reflects the entire psychobiological and even spiritual history of the individual.

The symptoms induced by rapid breathing can appear in all areas of the body and in all possible combinations. The systematic study of these reactions shows that they represent the intensification of preexisting psychosomatic symptoms or exteriorization of various latent symptoms. The continuation of accelerated breathing makes it possible to trace these symptoms to their sources in the unconscious—to memories of traumatic biographical events, biological birth, prenatal traumas, and even various transpersonal themes (e.g., phylogenetic memories, past life experiences, and archetypal motifs).

This is true even for some extreme physical phenomena that can occasionally be observed during Holotropic Breathwork, such as seizure-like activity, apnea, cyanosis, asthmatic attacks, or various dramatic skin manifestations. These phenomena represent exteriorization of historically determined imprints that are associated with specific events, such as near drowning episodes, serious accidents, operations, childhood diphtheria, whooping cough, biological birth, prenatal crises, or past life experiences. As precarious as they might appear, they are not dangerous if we are working with physically healthy people, who can tolerate the emotional and physical stress involved in such reliving. Naturally, it is important to respect the contraindications for deep experiential work and screen out persons with serious problems, particularly various cardiovascular disorders.

A surprising but consistent observation from Holotropic Breathwork is that the symptoms induced by hyperventilation initially increase in intensity, but continued breathing brings about their resolution and permanent disappearance. This fact is in direct conflict with the assumption that the psychosomatic symptoms are a mandatory physiochemical response to hyperventilation. Permanent disappearance of these symptoms after full emergence of the unconscious material with which they are connected shows that they are psychodynamic in nature and not simple physiological manifestations. In our work we see many people who do not develop any tensions during several hours of intense breathing. This type of reaction increases with the number of holotropic sessions and eventually becomes a rule rather than an exception.

Even the vasoconstriction occurring in various parts of the body as a result of faster breathing is not an invariable and mandatory effect of hyperventilation. The observations from Holotropic Breathwork show that bioenergetic blockage in a certain area typically causes vasoconstriction. The origin of this blockage can be psychological or physical traumas from postnatal history, the trauma of birth, prenatal crises, or various difficult transpersonal experiences. Faster breathing tends to bring the unconscious material to the surface and release this blockage after its temporary intensification. This is typically followed by the opening of circulation in the afflicted area.

An extreme example is Raynaud's disease, a severe disturbance of peripheral circulation in the hands associated with feelings of cold and even trophic changes of the skin (damage to the skin due to lack of oxygen and of nourishment). We have had the opportunity to work with a number of persons suffering from this condition, who were able to heal this disorder by doing Holotropic Breathwork. In their initial holotropic sessions, they all showed extreme and painful tetany in their hands and forearms. With continued hyperventilation, these cramps were suddenly released and were replaced by powerful flow of warm energy through the hands and experience of force fields enveloping the hands like giant gloves. After these experiences, the peripheral circulation remained permanently opened.

As we have already mentioned, the same mechanism can play a critical role in many chronic infections, such as sinusitis, pharyngitis, tonsillitis, bronchitis, or cystitis, which are traditionally considered to be purely medical problems. If we succeed in releasing the bioenergetic blockage, the circulation opens up and these "chronic infections" tend to clear. It is also conceivable that the same mechanism plays an important role in the genesis of peptic or duodenal ulcers and ulcerous colitis. The vitality of the gastric or intestinal mucous membranes that do not have good circulation might be compromised to such an extent that they cannot protect themselves against the bacteria implied in this disorder (*Helicobacter pylori*) and the effects of hydrochloric acid and digestive enzymes.

These observations show that in many instances diseases are related to blocked emotional or physical energy and resulting fragmentation, while healthy functioning is associated with a free flow of energy and wholeness. This is related to one aspect of the term *holotropic*, which literally means "moving toward wholeness" or "aiming for wholeness." These findings are consistent with the basic principles of Chinese medicine and of homeopathy. They are also related to the modern concept of *energy medicine*. The representatives of this orientation assert that medicine would become much more effective if it complemented or in some instances even replaced its organ-pathological strategy with an approach based on understanding and use of the bioenergetic dynamics of the body.

"The hyperventilation syndrome": Fact or fiction?

In summary, the experiences and observations from Holotropic Breathwork show that the traditional concept of the *hyperventilation syndrome* is obsolete and has to be revised. The muscular tensions that develop as a result of rapid breathing do not have to involve the hands and feet, but can occur anywhere in the body. Their source is the pent-up emotional and physical energy generated by traumatic events in the breather's history. Continued breathing typically leads to intensification, culmination, and resolution of such tensions. They can also be easily removed by emotional and physical abreaction. Repeated sessions tend to eliminate the occurrence of these tensions. Some people can breathe faster for several hours without showing any signs of tension; they actually become progressively more relaxed and ecstatic.

What seems to happen is that faster breathing creates a biochemical situation in the body that facilitates the emergence of old emotional and physical tensions associated with unresolved psychological and physical traumas. The fact that during rapid breathing symptoms surface and become manifest is not a pathological phenomenon, as it is traditionally understood. This situation actually represents a unique opportunity for healing. What emerges under these circumstances is unconscious material with strong emotional charge that is most ready for processing. This understanding of the symptoms of hyperventilation accounts for the enormous inter- and intra-individual variability of the responses to hyperventilation. That seems to be analogous to the situation concerning the extraordinary richness and variability of the experiential content of psychedelic sessions.

In the light of the observations from Holotropic Breathwork, spontaneous episodes of hyperventilation occurring in psychiatric patients and the normal population are attempts of the organism to heal itself and should be supported rather than suppressed. With correct understanding and skillful guidance, the emergence of symptoms during hyperventilation can result in the healing of emotional and psychosomatic problems, positive personality transformation, and consciousness evolution. Conversely, the current practice of suppressing the symptoms can be seen as interference with an important spontaneous healing process involving the psyche and the body.

3. Psychodynamics of psychosomatic disorders

The observations from Holotropic Breathwork also throw an interesting light on the genesis of psychosomatic symptoms, a topic that has elicited much controversy in medical and psychiatric academic circles. It is well known that many emotional disorders, such as psychoneuroses, depressions, and psychoses, have distinct physical manifestations—headaches, breathing difficulties, nausea, loss of appetite, constipation or diarrhea, heart palpitations, excessive sweating, tremors, tics, muscular pains, vasomotor disturbances, skin afflictions, amenorrhea, menstrual cramps, pain during intercourse (*dyspareunia*), orgastic inability, and erectile dysfunction. The sexual manifestations can also represent primary problems *sui generis*, which are serious and long lasting, rather than being transitory concomitants of neurotic reactions.

In some psychoneuroses, the physical symptoms are very specific and characteristic and represent the predominant feature of the disorder. This is certainly true for conversion hysteria, a psychoneurosis that can have a wide range of physical manifestations—hysterical paralysis, anesthesia, loss of voice (*aphonia*), inability to stand on one's own feet (*astasia*), temporary blindness, vomiting, hysterical attack with forceful arching back (*arc de cercle*) and muscular convulsions, false pregnancy (*pseudokyesis*), and even stigmata. Here belongs also a group of disorders that classical psychoanalysts called *pregenital neuroses*; it includes various tics, stammering, and psychogenic asthma. They are characterized by an obsessive-compulsive personality structure, but the basic defense mechanism involved in symptom formation is conversion of psychological conflicts into physical manifestations as is the case in hysteria.

There also exists a group of disorders with striking physical manifestations, in which the psychological component is so obvious and important that even the medical model refers to them as *psychosomatic diseases*. The term *psychosomatic* reflects the recognition of the importance of psychological factors in the genesis of these conditions and, over the years, it has gained considerable popularity. It is being used for a large variety of medical disorders of psychogenic origin, including migraine headaches, psychogenic asthma, peptic ulcers, colitis, certain forms of hypertension, psoriasis, various eczemas, and possibly some forms of arthritis.

In 1935, psychoanalyst Franz Alexander, considered to be the founder of psychosomatic medicine, proposed a theoretical model explaining the mechanism of psychosomatic disorders that underlies much of the clinical work and research in this area until this day (Alexander 1950). His key contribution was the recognition that psychosomatic symptoms result from the physiological concomitants of psychological conflicts and traumas. Emotional arousal during acute anxiety, grief, or rage gives rise to intense physiological reactions, which can cause psychosomatic symptoms and disease. However, according to Alexander, this happens only in those individuals who are organically predisposed, not in healthy ones. This predisposition is a crucial but variable factor in the genesis of psychosomatic diseases. There are considerable disagreements among psychoanalysts as to the nature of this predisposition.

Alexander differentiated between conversion reactions and psychosomatic disorders, which were previously considered to be similar to neurotic reactions. Although the source of the emotions underlying these disorders can be traced to psychological trauma, neurotic conflicts, and pathological interpersonal relationships, the symptoms do not have symbolic significance and do not serve as a defense against anxiety, which is characteristic of psychoneurotic symptoms. It is actually a failure of psychological defense mechanisms to protect the individual against excessive affective arousal.

In 1952, the American Psychiatric Association recognized in its standard nomenclature the ambiguity in the use of the word *psychosomatic* and coined the designation "psychophysiological autonomic and visceral disorder." The symptoms of these disorders are attributed to chronic intensification of the normal physiological expression of emotions. Such long-lasting physiological and visceral states may eventually lead to structural changes in various organs. The field of psychosomatic medicine is characterized by fundamental lack of agreement considering the nature of the predisposition for psychosomatic disorders and the specific vulnerability that determines the choice of the organ. The models fall into the following three categories: specificity models, non-specificity models, and individual response specificity models.

Specificity models of psychosomatic disorders

The theoretical models that belong to this category assert that various psychosomatic symptoms and diseases can be traced to specific psychotraumatic events and emotional states. In their interpretations, Franz Alexander and other psychoanalysts used the common analytic concepts, such as unconscious dynamics, fixation on various stages of development of the libido and of the ego, regression, psychological defense mechanisms, problems in object relationships, and so forth. According to this view, various traumatic events cause anxiety and psychological regression to emotionally strongly charged areas. For example, patients with peptic ulcers show a fixation on the oral period of libidinal development and have serious unresolved unconscious conflicts about dependency. Regression then leads to hypersecretion of gastric juices.

This category also includes various attempts to define the "personality profiles" of people who are prone to specific psychosomatic disorders. Search for personal characteristics of these individuals is a trend of research started by Flanders Dunbar (Dunbar 1954). For example, these studies distinguished A and B personality types. Type A personality refers to hard-driving executives and high-achieving workaholics who are preoccupied with schedules and the speed of their performance, are impatient, insecure about their status, highly competitive, hostile and aggressive, and incapable of relaxation. The Type B personality, in contrast, is patient, relaxed, and easy-going and usually more creative, imaginative, and philosophical (Friedman and Rosenman 1974). Type A has been shown to have a higher risk for developing heart disease.

Stewart Wolff and Harold Wolff developed techniques for studying psycho-physiological correlations, for example, between emotional holding on and constipation and between emotional letting go and diarrhea (Wolff and Wolff 1947). Similar concepts have become very popular in psychotherapeutic circles, implying that psychological issues and conflicts can be expressed in symbolic body language: pain in the neck and shoulder muscles in people who carry too much responsibility, stomach problems in people who are unable to "swallow" or "stomach" something, breathing difficulties caused by a mother who is "smothering" her offspring, oppressive feelings on the chest resulting from "heavy grief," and so forth.

Objections have been raised against the "specificity theories." Patients with various psychosomatic disorders can have a wide range of psychodynamic problems and psychiatric diagnoses that range from "normal" to psychotic. The psychological problems of the patients cannot be predicted from the nature of their psychosomatic symptoms and vice versa. The same "specific etiological variables" have been postulated for a wide range of psychosomatic disorders, for example pathological dependency needs and loss of a significant relationship for ulcerous colitis, ileitis, rheumatoid arthritis, psychogenic asthma, and some skin disorders. In addition, some psychosomatic disorders can be modeled in animals, such as gastric hypersecretion induced by non-specific stress. Naturally, here we cannot assume the role of unconscious fantasies, symbolic processes, interpersonal conflicts, among others.

Non-specificity models of psychosomatic disorders

The models that belong to this category reject the notion of specific psychopathological factors in the genesis of psychosomatic disorders. They argue that any stimulus capable of causing psychological distress may evoke a diffuse emotional state of chronic anxiety and lead to the development of a psychosomatic disorder. The nature of the disorder cannot be predicted from the psychological trigger. According to G. F. Mahl, the physiological concomitants could be the same, irrespective of the stressor, whether it is bombing during a war, highly competitive examination, or interpersonal conflict involving a sexual partner (Mahl 1949).

Hans Selye showed that there exist universal manifestations of chronic stress, such as gastric and cardiovascular activation and increase of adrenal steroid hormones (Selye 1950). However, the onset of psychosomatic disorders is often associated with a psychodynamically determined breakdown of psychological defenses that ordinarily protect the individual from intensive emotional arousal. Organ susceptibility can be a combination of constitutional factors and early experiences. This model, although too general, is consistent with clinical and research data.

Individual response specificity models of psychosomatic disorders

The models in this category suggest that the type of psychosomatic disorder the individual develops depends primarily on his or her specific response pattern rather than on the nature of the stimulus. Various individuals show highly characteristic and consistent patterns of emotional arousal, which may be evoked by a wide range of stimuli and lead to specific psychosomatic disorders. There are "gastric reactors," "cardiac reactors," "hypertensive reactors," among others. The emotional reactions of adults with psychosomatic disorders tend to show specific areas of activation, in contrast to the diffuse and immature reactions of infants. The characteristic response pattern is developed early in childhood and is highly consistent over time. This theory is very popular in academic circles.

Current situation in the field

It is generally accepted that no single model satisfactorily explains all psychosomatic disorders and the opinion leans toward multicausality. Psychological factors play a significant role but are not the exclusive causative determinants. In addition, we have to take into consideration constitution, heredity, organ pathology, nutritional status, environment, and social and cultural determinants. Psychological and somatic phenomena that were earlier seen as separate discrete processes are now seen as representing different aspects of a unitary phenomenon of affect engaged in reciprocal interaction. In addition, the brain structures that control emotions and visceral functions are identical or closely related. Fear, anger, sexuality, and the functioning of viscera and glands are all regulated by the limbic system and hypothalamic structures; they are also linked to cortical and subcortical levels of organization. The precise nature of these interrelationships has not yet been established.

Insights from Holotropic Breathwork and other experiential therapies

The explanations of psychosomatic symptoms and diseases offered by most schools of depth psychology are generally unconvincing. They attribute a causal role to memories of events witnessed in childhood or traumatic experiences from later life. They interpret psychogenic asthma as a cry for the mother or result of a restrictive "choking influence" of the mother and explain hysterical paralysis as reflecting a conflict about doing something forbidden. Similarly, stammering is seen as resulting from suppression of verbal aggression and struggle with an urge to utter obscenities, a sense of being burdened can lead to severe shoulder pains, the difficulty to "stomach" something can produce gastric disorders, and severe skin disorders can serve as a protection against sexual temptation.

More convincing insights concerning the nature and psychogenesis of psychosomatic disorders came from the work of the brilliant and controversial pioneer of psychoanalysis, Wilhelm Reich. He showed that the traumatic psychological events discussed in psychoanalysis are not sufficient to explain the development of emotional and particularly psychosomatic symptoms. According to him, the main factor underlying such symptoms is a bioenergetic blockage in the muscles and viscera ("character armor") (Reich 1949).

Reich attributed this blockage to a jamming of libido due to the fact that repressive moralistic society does not allow full satisfaction of our sexual needs. Blocked sexual energy then finds deviant expression in the form of neuroses, psychosomatic disorders, and perversions. On a large scale, it leads to destructive sociopolitical movements. Reich realized that psychotherapy

limited to verbal exchange could not, in and of itself, change the energetic situation in the organism. He introduced into therapy revolutionary
approaches, such as breathing techniques and bodywork aimed at release
of pent-up energies. However, according to him, full emotional and sexual
liberation required a revolution in human society. Reich became a Communist and after publishing his book *The Mass Psychology of Fascism* (Reich
1970), he was excommunicated from both the Psychoanalytic Association
and the Communist Party.

The work with holotropic states of consciousness, such as Holotropic
Breathwork, Primal Therapy, Rebirthing, or psychedelic therapy, reveals
enormous amounts of blocked and jammed emotional and physical energy
(bioenergy) underlying various psychosomatic disorders (and also emotional
disorders in general). This observation thus confirms the Reichian theory,
but only in the most general sense, not in specifics. While Reich believed
that the pent-up energy was suppressed libido, the new observations reveal
that much of this energy is of perinatal origin. It is the result of the excessive neuronal impulses generated during the passage through the birth
canal and stored in the organism. In addition, much of this energy seems
to be of transpersonal origin and can be traced back to the archetypal and
historical domains of the collective unconscious and to ancestral, karmic,
and phylogenetic memories.

An important contribution of experiential psychotherapy to the understanding of psychosomatic manifestations is the discovery of the critical
role that unassimilated and unintegrated physical traumas play in their
genesis. The psychodynamic schools tend to see psychosomatic symptoms
as results of somatization of psychological conflicts and traumas and fail to
see the critical role psychotraumas of physical origin play in their genesis.
Experiential work using holotropic states of consciousness leaves no doubt
that the most significant sources of psychosomatic symptoms are events that
involved physical insults.

For example, holotropic work on psychogenic asthma will inevitably
lead to unassimilated memories of situations that involved the experience
of suffocation, such as near drowning, being strangled by a parent or sibling, choking on a foreign object, inspiration of blood during tonsillectomy,
whooping cough, childhood pneumonia, birth, or a past life experience of
being hanged or strangled. Similarly, the material underlying psychosomatic
pains consists of memories of painful accidents, operations, or diseases, pain
experienced during the birth process, and physical suffering connected with
a past life injury or death.

The powerful psychotraumatic impact of physical insults has been recognized in Ron Hubbard's system, Dianetics, which represents the ideological
basis of the Church of Scientology (Hubbard 1950). While in traditional

verbal forms of psychotherapy the assessment of the emotional significance of traumas reflects the theoretical concept of the respective schools, in Dianetics its relevance is measured objectively in a process called *auditing*. Psychological exploration and therapy is guided by the use of an E-meter, a galvanoscope measuring the skin resistance of the client in a way similar to a lie detector.

The theoretical system of scientology does not include only physical traumas in postnatal life, but also somatic traumatization during birth, prenatal existence, and in past lives. Hubbard referred to imprints of physical traumatizations as *engrams* and saw them as primary sources of emotional problems. In his terminology, the usual psychological traumas are called *secondaries*; in a sense, they borrow their emotional power from their associations with engrams. Unfortunately, Hubbard's excursions into wild galactic fantasies; abuse of scientological knowledge for pursuit of power, money, and control; and the reckless practices of his organization have discredited Hubbard's important theoretical contributions.

We can now summarize the observations from consciousness research concerning psychosomatic disorders and use these findings to clarify some of the inconsistencies and disagreements about their nature and origin. According to our experience, the psychodynamic structure underlying these disorders has the form of COEX systems (systems of condensed experience), multilevel constellations of memories and other unconscious material (pages 15f.). The most superficial layers of COEX systems involve episodes from postnatal biography, in this case memories of both physical and psychological traumas. A deeper layer of these systems is formed by memories related to biological birth, an event that by its very nature is both physical and psychological. The recognition of the pathogenic impact of birth thus helps to resolve the conflict between psychological and biological theories of psychiatry. The deepest layers of the COEX systems are then matrices of a transpersonal nature, such as past life experiences, archetypal motifs, or phylogenetic elements.

The postnatal psychological traumatizations have specific links to developmental stages of the libido and the ego, specific parts of the body, and problems in interpersonal relations. They are also connected with various psychological defense mechanisms and symbolic elaborations. While postnatal physical traumatizations and particularly birth afflict various specific organs, they also represent an extreme form of raw and undifferentiated stress. This certainly seems to be relevant for the disagreements concerning the specific and unspecific triggers of psychosomatic disorders, as well as the difference between psychosomatic disorders and neurotic conversion reactions emphasized by Franz Alexander.

It could explain why both specific and non-specific stress can induce psychosomatic symptoms and also the fact that non-specific stressors of various kinds can induce the same symptoms in a particular individual. Birth is a major psychophysiological trauma and involves the first major loss of a love object—separation from the mother, followed by a situation of extreme dependency. Its involvement in the genesis of psychosomatic disorders could thus account for the fact that the loss of an important relationship and extreme dependency needs are factors that play a significant role in psychosomatic disorders of various kinds.

The observations from Holotropic Breathwork showing the depth of the roots of psychosomatic disorders and the paramount role physical traumas play in their genesis make it clear that psychotherapy limited to verbal means has very little chance to achieve positive results. Words alone are not very effective if we work with people who suffer from psychogenic asthma, painful muscular spasms, or migraine headaches. These symptoms require deep experiential work that involves reliving of the underlying memories and abreaction of the emotional and physical energies associated with them. Since the deep roots of psychosomatic diseases reach to the perinatal and transpersonal domains of the psyche, effective treatment of these disorders calls for a conceptual framework that provides a plausible and non-pathological explanation for intense experiences from these levels of the unconscious. The extended cartography of the psyche that includes the perinatal and transpersonal levels serves this purpose.

Without understanding that these experiences have natural sources, both the therapists and the clients would be afraid and reluctant to enter this experiential territory and to allow the material from the deep levels of the unconscious to emerge into consciousness. We have already mentioned that abreaction in sessions using hypnosis and narcoanalysis was found to be useful in the treatment of war neuroses (PTSD), but not psychoneuroses. Therapists knowing that their clients had been exposed to drastic situations were able and willing to tolerate these clients' emotional and physical reactions of extreme intensity without fear that they were entering a psychotic terrain.

CHAPTER TEN

Past, Present, and Future of Holotropic Breathwork

We first started using Holotropic Breathwork in its present form at the Esalen Institute in the year 1976. For more than ten years, we were the only two persons offering this new method of self-exploration in our workshops at Esalen and various parts of the world—North America, Mexico, South America, Australia, India, Japan, and various countries of Europe. On occasion, we received assistance from people who had become seriously interested in our work and wanted to apprentice with us. Several of them were Esalen residents and others were individuals who had participated in our Esalen month-long workshops and had considerable experience with the breathwork.

1. Training of Holotropic Breathwork facilitators

By 1987, the number and interest of these people increased to such an extent that a group of them approached us asking us to offer a training program for facilitators. Responding to their request, we decided to launch a one-time facilitator training for seventy highly motivated former participants in our workshops, who over the years had done a significant amount of work with us. It was followed by three-year training programs, in which participants met twice a year for two-week sessions. Two groups with this format met on the West Coast of North America, and the third one was a German-speaking group with participants from Switzerland, Germany, and Austria that took place in Europe.

In the next phase, we developed a training program that consisted of seven six-day units or "modules." Four of these modules were considered mandatory (The Healing Potential of Non-Ordinary States of Consciousness, Architecture of Emotional and Psychosomatic Disorders, Spiritual Emergency, and The Practice of Holotropic Breathwork). The remaining three modules were optional; here participants could choose a subject of their interest from a large selection of topics exploring the connection between Holotropic Breathwork and a variety of other fields—Vipassana Buddhism, shamanism, alcoholism and other forms of addiction, ecstatic chanting, fantastic art, cosmology and ontology, death and dying, and others. After the trainees had attended these seven modules, they completed their training by taking part in a two-week certification program.

This form of the training has continued with some minor modifications until today. Since 1971, Grof Transpersonal Training (GTT) has been run by Cary and Tav Sparks, with Cary in the role of the chief coordinator and Tav as the principal teacher. We continue to participate in the GTT as visiting lecturers in some of the modules and in large public introductory workshops. Much of the training is now conducted by senior staff members and takes place in different countries of the world. The trainees can choose in which countries they want to take the individual modules and how they want to space them. We recommend that the trainees do not complete the modules in less than two years, since the training involves much intense inner work and enough time is needed for adequate processing and integration. The basic information about the training can be found on the Internet (holotropic.com or stanislavgrof.com). As of today, more than a thousand people from different parts of the world have completed the training and an additional few hundred are currently in training.

Our training for facilitators radically changed the perspectives for Holotropic Breathwork. It made it possible for us to conduct breathwork workshops on a much larger scale. We had discovered in our early workshops that the intensity of participants' experiences tended to increase with the size of the group. We had also learned that the number of people in the processing groups had to be limited to about fourteen to eighteen for the sharing to be completed in one session. When we were working alone, with occasional apprentices, we were able to conduct workshops with up to thirty-six participants—weekend workshops in which each participant had one breathwork session or five-day workshops in which each had two sessions.

Once the number of participants exceeded this limit, we were not able to lead personally the sharing with every single person in the group. While the breathwork sessions could be conducted with all the group members at the same time (alternating as sitters and breathers), for the processing sessions the group had to be divided into smaller units. Beyond this point, the only limits for the number of participants were the size of the breathwork space, the availability of breakout rooms for the processing groups, and the number of experienced facilitators capable to support the breathers and lead the sharing sessions. Using this format, several of our large groups had over three hundred participants.

2. Holotropic Breathwork and the academic community

The increasing popularity of Holotropic Breathwork in paraprofessional circles and among laypeople has not so far been matched by equally keen interest in the academic community and among clinicians working in mainstream facilities. To our knowledge, only in Austria, Brazil, and Russia has Holotropic Breathwork been accepted as an official treatment modality. The reasons are easily understandable; both the practice and theory of this new form of self-exploration and therapy represent a significant departure from current therapeutic practices and conceptual frameworks. Work with Holotropic Breathwork and with holotropic states of consciousness, in general, requires radical changes of some basic premises and metaphysical assumptions, which professionals committed to traditional ways of viewing the world and the human psyche are not ready to make.

For most mainstream clinicians, it is not easy to accept that intense emotional states and the concomitant physical manifestations that they are used to diagnose and treat as psychopathology represent a self-healing process that should be supported rather than suppressed or truncated. Many traditional psychotherapists find it difficult to move from talking therapy to experiential therapies, particularly the more effective ones that induce holotropic states of consciousness. An additional challenge is the use of bodywork and of supportive physical contact, which belong to extremely useful and important components of Holotropic Breathwork.

Probably the most important challenge that the practice of Holotropic Breathwork represents for psychotherapists is the redefinition of the nature of therapeutic intervention and of the role of the therapist. This involves a radical departure from the concept of the therapist as an active agent ("doer"), who tries to reach intellectual understanding of the client's problems and derive from it an appropriate intervention—interpretation, analysis of transference, use of silence, among others. In Holotropic Breathwork, the guiding principle is the inner healing intelligence of the breather, and the role of the facilitator is to support the process that is spontaneously unfolding. The ability to trust the self-healing potential of the psyche and to refrain from judgment of any kind is among the most important prerequisites for successful and productive work with holotropic states of consciousness.

Equally challenging as the changes that Holotropic Breathwork introduces into therapeutic practice are some of its basic theoretical and metaphysical premises. The first of these is a radically different understanding of the nature of consciousness and of the human psyche. From the holotropic perspective, consciousness and psyche are seen as primary attributes of the universe (*anima mundi*) rather than products of the neurophysiological processes in the human brain and thus epiphenomena of otherwise inanimate and inert matter. Observations from various avenues of modern consciousness research have brought convincing evidence that consciousness can operate independently of the human brain; they lead to the conclusion that the brain mediates consciousness, but does not generate it (Goswami 1995; Ring and Valarino 1998; Ring and Cooper 1999; Cárdenas, Lynn, and Krippner 2000; Grof 2000 and 2006b).

The second major theoretical revision necessary for productive work with holotropic states is the addition of two large domains to the model of the psyche currently used by mainstream psychiatrists, psychologists, and psychotherapists, which is limited to postnatal biography and the Freudian individual unconscious. The two new domains—perinatal and transpersonal—expand the image of the human psyche to such an extent that it shows a deep resemblance with the concepts found in the great spiritual philosophies of the East and in various native cultures. This is a humbling realization for the members of the Western academic community who are taught that their own worldview and understanding of the human psyche are far superior to that of pre-industrial societies.

The observations from the research of holotropic states also radically change our understanding of the origin and nature of emotional and psychosomatic disorders, which are not organic in nature. They reveal that these conditions do not originate in infancy and childhood but have additional roots that reach to much deeper levels of the psyche—to perinatal, prenatal, ancestral, racial, collective, phylogenetic, karmic, and archetypal experiential matrices. The development of symptoms can be understood as an effort and attempt of the client's psyche to free itself from traumatic imprints on these different levels of the psyche.

This perspective can be applied even to some conditions currently seen as manifestations of serious mental disease. The extended cartography of the psyche makes it possible to view an important subcategory of spontaneous episodes of non-ordinary states of consciousness, currently diagnosed and treated as psychoses, as psychospiritual crises ("spiritual emergencies") that have great healing, transformational, and even evolutionary potential. Since the training of Holotropic Breathwork facilitators involves a large number of personal sessions, extensive experience in supporting their peers in holotropic states of consciousness, and lectures on transpersonal theory, certified facilitators are well prepared and equipped to support individuals undergoing spiritual emergencies.

The concept of symptoms as opportunities for healing and transformation also requires a major adjustment for traditionally trained professionals, since much of their routine treatment efforts focus on suppression of symptoms. In current clinical practice, the alleviation of symptoms is seen as a clinical improvement and the intensification of symptoms as worsening of the clinical condition. Symptomatic treatment is often mistakenly referred to as therapy, although it does not address the underlying problem. In somatic medicine, there is a clear distinction between causal therapy that targets the etiological factor and symptomatic therapy that makes the condition more tolerable for the client.

3. Benefits of the holotropic perspective

The aforementioned changes in practice and theory introduced into psychiatry and psychology by research of holotropic states of consciousness are radical and challenging. However, those who are able to accept them and apply them—either in their own self-exploration and healing or in their work with others—will be able to benefit greatly from this far-reaching conceptual reorientation. They will gain a deeper understanding of the nature and dynamics of emotional and psychosomatic disorders—phobias, depression, suicidal tendencies, sexual dysfunctions and deviations, psychogenic asthma, and many others—by recognizing their perinatal and transpersonal roots. They will also be able to obtain better and faster therapeutic results by engaging therapeutic mechanisms that become available on these deeper levels of the unconscious (Grof 1985 and 2000).

The new expanded cartography of the psyche brings clarity into the confusing array of psychotherapeutic schools with vastly different perspectives on fundamental issues related to the human psyche in health and disease. It includes, synthesizes, and integrates the views of Sigmund Freud, Melanie Klein, Otto Rank, Wilhelm Reich, Sandor Ferenczi, C. G. Jung, and the representatives of ego psychology and gives each of them a place in a comprehensive model of the psyche (Grof 1985). From this perspective, each of the founders of these schools put selective focus on a specific level of the psyche and neglected others or misrepresented them by reducing them to his or her own idiosyncratic point of view.

Holotropic Breathwork has important practical and economic advantages. It can reach roots of emotional and psychosomatic problems on levels of the psyche that are not available for verbal therapy and greatly accelerates the access to unconscious material. It also allows the processing of physical traumas underlying various psychosomatic disorders, such as those associated with near drowning or biological birth, which cannot be accomplished by talking. Another advantage is the favorable ratio between trained facilita-tors and clients. Holotropic Breathwork is commonly conducted in groups, in which one trained facilitator is needed for eight to ten participants and significant support can be provided by untrained sitters. In addition, our experience has shown that many people who experience the role of the sitter develop so much interest in this work that they want to enroll in the training for facilitators. This thus provides an opportunity for exponential growth of a support system for people experiencing spontaneous or induced holotropic states.

Another important aspect of the new psychology that has emerged from the study of holotropic states is the correction of the distorted view of spiri-tuality and religion found in Western scientific circles. Modern consciousness research has shown that spirituality is an important dimension of the human psyche and of the universal order. Genuine understanding of such phenomena as shamanism, mythology and ritual life of native cultures, mysticism, and the great religions of the world is impossible without expanding the map of the psyche by adding the perinatal and transpersonal dimensions. This is also necessary if we want to understand spiritual experiences—our own or those of others—and provide intelligent support to people struggling with chal-lenges of their inner journey. It is a serious error to dismiss and pathologize spirituality of any kind and form just because its existence is incompatible with the basic metaphysical assumptions of Western science or because it has often found deviant and distorted expression in organized religions.

The holotropic perspective also offers new insights into the psychology and psychopathology of art, which are much deeper and more revealing than previous efforts by Freud, Marie Bonaparte, Otto Rank, and others (Grof 2010). The strong emotional impact of many great works of art—novels, paintings, movies, and musical compositions—cannot be accounted for without the recognition that their sources are not just in the biography of their authors, but also in the perinatal and transpersonal domains of the psyche. In the highest forms of creativity, the artist becomes a channel for inspiration coming directly from transpersonal sources (Harman 1984).

4. Holotropic states of consciousness and the current global crisis

One aspect of systematic self-exploration using Holotropic Breathwork and other forms of responsible use of holotropic states of consciousness deserves special notice. This practice does more than alleviate emotional and psycho-somatic disorders and make the life of people involved in it more comfortable and fulfilling. The resulting changes in the worldview, hierarchy of values, and life strategy that follow the processing of biographical, perinatal, and transpersonal material have important implications that reach beyond the personal benefit for those who do intensive inner work. This transformation involves a significant reduction of aggression and the development of racial, gender, cultural, and ideological tolerance and compassion, ecological sensitivity, and a sense of planetary citizenship.

We are currently experiencing a dangerous global crisis that threatens the survival of our species and life on this planet. In the last analysis, the common denominator of many different aspects of this crisis is the level of consciousness evolution of humanity. If it could be raised to a higher standard, if we could tame the propensity to violence and insatiable greed, many of the current problems in the world could be alleviated or solved. It seems that the changes regularly observed in people who have undergone the transformation described earlier would greatly increase our chances for survival if they could happen on a sufficiently large scale. We hope that the information in this book concerning the potential of holotropic states of consciousness, in general, and Holotropic Breathwork, in particular, will provide useful guidance for those who decide to take this journey as well as those who have already chosen it.

Special Situations and Interventions in Holotropic Breathwork Sessions

While it is easy to understand and apply the general strategy of body-work used in Holotropic Breathwork, there are certain situations that deserve brief notice. As we will be describing a variety of situations and different forms of interventions, it is important to keep in mind that they all have one common denominator—to intensify the emotions and physical energies underlying the symptoms and bring them to conscious experience and full expression. This is highly specialized information that might be of interest for some general readers, but is of practical relevance only for certified facilitators of Holotropic Breathwork who have completed the GTT training and are thus permitted to use it in their work. We highly recommend as additional reading Tav Sparks' booklet entitled *Doing Not Doing: A Facilitator's Guide to Holotropic Breathwork*, an exposé of the basic strategy of holotropic work written in a clear and easily readable, humorous style (Sparks 1989).

1. The experience of choking and of pressure on the chest

A very common occurrence in holotropic sessions is the experience of constriction in the throat associated with choking. It has its source in the memories of situations that involved interference with breathing, such as near drowning, attempts at strangulation, diphtheria, whooping cough, and a difficult birth. Because of the fragility of the larynx and of the adjacent nerves and arteries, it is not possible to intensify this feeling by squeezing the throat. A very effective way of resolving this situation is to offer the breather a rolled-up towel and ask him or her to identify with the strangling force and demonstrate its effect by twisting the towel as strongly as possible. It will increase the power of this exercise if the towel is stretched across the upper body of the breather and its ends are held by assisting persons (usually the sitter and one of the facilitators or apprentices). It is necessary to hold the stretched towel in sufficient distance from the breather's body, so that it does not exert pressure on his or her throat.

While this is happening, we ask the breather to express any emotions and physical reactions that this situation evokes. An individual experiencing choking typically identifies with only the role of the victim and perceives the strangling force as alien rather than an intrinsic part of his or her personality. While this was the case in the original situation, it is not true at the time when the memory of it is surfacing in the breathwork session. By this time, the entire situation has been internalized and the experiences of choking and strangling are two different aspects of the breather's own personality. Using the towel in the way just described, the breather acknowledges and owes this fact by identifying with both the strangler and the strangled.

The same principle can be used when the breather experiences extreme pressure on the chest and constriction of the entire rib cage, a frequent concomitant of the birth experience. In this situation, the crushing force is the internalized and introjected pressure of the uterine contractions. Without recognizing and acknowledging it, the breather is the "crusher," as well as the victim of the constricting force. The best way of resolving constriction of this kind is for the facilitator and the breather to assume a reclining position on the mattress with their bodies parallel to each other; they then embrace and squeeze each other using considerable strength. While this is happening, the breather is encouraged to express fully the emotions evoked by this situation. Having a pillow or a cushion between the two bodies reduces the degree of physical closeness that might otherwise be experienced as too intimate or invasive.

2. Experience of muscular tensions and spasms

A very effective way of releasing blocked energy in the breather's hand and arm (tetany) is to stage a situation known as "Mexican arm wrestling." We ask breathers, who are lying on their backs, to put their forearms in a vertical position with the elbow resting on the floor and deliberately increase the tension in the muscles of that arm. Facilitators then position their bodies parallel to those of the breathers and grasp the breathers' hand. This is followed by an effort to push each other's forearm to the floor as it is done in the test of strength. However, the purpose here is not to win, but to maintain consistent tension for an extended period of time, while breathers express all the emotions and physical feelings that this situation evokes.

On occasion, the tension is not located in any particular part of the body, but is generalized; in this case the blockage of energy involves the entire body. This condition can reach various degrees of intensity from strong muscular tension to painful tetany. It is important to emphasize that we are not dealing here with a simple physiological reaction to faster breathing (hyperventilation syndrome), but a complex psychosomatic response. The source of this tension is unprocessed memory of an extremely traumatic situation or, more commonly, a layered constellation of such memories (a COEX system). These traumatic situations generated large amounts of emotional and physical energy that has remained unexpressed.

In some instances, the traumatization is so extreme that consciousness splits off from the hurting body; the breather reports that he or she "is not connected with the body" and is not feeling anything. This dissociation of consciousness from the body seems to be the same mechanism that is responsible for out-of-body experiences (OBEs) in near-death situations described in thanatological literature. Splitting off makes it possible for consciousness to avoid the experience of pain. In Holotropic Breathwork, such splitting of consciousness from the body tends to be associated with difficulties in "coming back" and with prolongation of the session.

What we are seeing in the two situations described here—tetany of the body that is fully consciously experienced and tetany leading to splitting of consciousness from the body—is a dynamic equilibrium between a strong energetic charge associated with the traumatic memories emerging from the unconscious and the psychological defenses that hold it down and prevent it from surfacing. The task of the helpers in this situation is to perturb this dynamic equilibrium and facilitate the emergence of the unconscious material.

The most effective way of achieving this is to ask the breather to lie on his or her back, flex the arms at the elbows, and accentuate the tension in the arms and in the rest of the body, imagining that the entire body is made of steel or granite. Two helpers, one on either side, then grasp the breather's wrists and lift the upper part of the body about two feet above the ground. The instruction for the breather is to hang in this position as long as he or she can and fully express the natural reaction to this situation without judging or censoring it.

This exercise tends to weaken the psychological defenses and set the experiential process in motion. Instead of seeming inertia and stagnation, we now see an intense reaction from the breather in the form of motor activity, outpouring of emotions, loud screams, coughing, and other manifestations. It now becomes obvious that the rigidity of the body and the lack of feelings in it were the result of a dynamic equilibrium between intense emotions and physical energies and equally strong psychological defenses that prevented them from surfacing. This exercise is a very effective way to break the energetic gridlock and expedite the completion of the session.

As we mentioned earlier, the dissociation of consciousness from the body is the reaction to very painful traumatic events in the breather's past. The underlying unconscious material, which surfaces under these circumstances, typically includes memories associated with extreme physical suffering, such as severe emotional, physical, and sexual abuse, difficult birth, and various life-threatening situations. When the memory of the trauma is brought to consciousness and the emotions associated with it fully expressed, the breather typically reaches a state of relaxation and feels connected to his or her body. We often hear under these circumstances: "I feel for the first time in my life that I really live in my body."

3. Problems related to blockages in the genital area, sex, and nudity

Specific problems associated with the release of blocked energy arise when its sites are the genital area, the anal region, or adjacent parts of the body. For obvious reasons, it is not possible to intensify the tension in these areas by applying direct manual pressure. Fortunately, there exists a very effective alternative. We ask the breather to flex his or her legs, tense them up, and hold the knees tightly together, while the facilitator and the sitter are pulling them apart. By experimenting with different angles of flexion in the hips, the breather can find a position that makes it possible to intensify the tension in the blocked area. The breather then fully expresses all the emotions that this situation evokes. Occasionally, the opposite arrangement can prove more effective; here the breather is trying to abduct the legs, while the facilitator and the sitter are pushing the knees together.

This form of bodywork can bring to consciousness traumatic memories, particularly those involving sexual abuse, and evoke very intense emotions. We always warn the breathers about the power of this exercise and ask for permission before we do it. We also remind them that they will be in full control of the situation the entire time we will be working with them and that they can interrupt or terminate this procedure whenever they want to by saying "stop." When we do this work with women, particularly those that do not have much experience with Holotropic Breathwork, it is preferable that only women assist them in this process. Touching the genital area and women's breasts is not permissible, even if the breather explicitly asks for it. It is always possible to find an indirect alternative.

In one of our workshops at the Esalen Institute, a young woman came to us seeking our advice: "My breather asked me to squeeze his balls; do you do that kind of thing?" When something like this happens, an experienced facilitator needs to intervene and take over the situation, offering an appropriate nonsexual alternative. Facilitators use a similar approach if they notice that the breather and sitter are violating our injunction that, in the course of Holotropic Breathwork sessions, sexual contact is not allowed, whether or not this involves mutual consent. It is imperative that the supportive physical contact is aimed at satisfying anaclitic needs of the breather and does not involve elements of adult sexuality.

On occasion, the breather can make attempts to change a supportive anaclitic situation into an overtly sexual one. This happens more frequently when the breather is male and the facilitator female. In most instances, this seems to happen when deep age regression is taking the breather to a situation in early childhood when he experienced painful and frightening dependence on a feminine figure or was exposed by her to some form of abuse. Changing the anaclitic situation into an adult sexual situation then functions as psychological defense and avoidance, since in adult male-female interaction the male is traditionally dominant.

When this happens, the task of the facilitator is to encourage the breather to focus his attention within, let himself regress to the period when the trauma occurred, and fully experience the original feelings. She has to make it clear to the breather that attempts to introduce adult sexual elements into a therapeutic situation, where they do not belong, would be counterproductive and that he would waste an important opportunity for a corrective and healing experience on a very deep level. This is much easier to do if the possibility of this happening has been discussed before the session. The facilitator can then simply refer to this conversation rather than trying to introduce this theme while the breather is in a holotropic state of consciousness.

Mixing sexual activity with Holotropic Breathwork is not only inappropriate in the usual ethical and social sense, but emotionally tricky and potentially dangerous for the breather. Many of the breathers are in deep age regression and their perception of the situation and reaction to it is not that of an adult, but that of an infant or child, depending on the depth of the regression. Under these circumstances, sexual interaction can be experienced as profoundly invasive, confusing, and traumatic. The importance to maintain clean sexual boundaries becomes even more important when Holotropic Breathwork is conducted on a one-to-one basis, behind closed doors rather than in the transparent public atmosphere of the group.

The situation is somewhat different if the sexual activity is autoerotic and does not involve other people. It is not uncommon that breathers experiencing regression to various periods of their personal history touch their private parts, responding to either sexual feelings or painful sensations. In rare instances this can take the form of explicit masturbation. Our policy has been not to interfere and discreetly cover the individual with a sheet. Intervening and interrupting the process when the person is in deep regression can be very disturbing. In this situation, it can also replicate a situation from childhood when strict parents caught the individual masturbating and incurred severe punishment.

Another situation we sometimes have to deal with in the breathwork is nudity. The motives for undressing during the session vary. In sessions with perinatal elements, it can reflect the breather's feeling that it is inappropriate to deal with issues related to birth and death while one is fully dressed. In individuals who experienced in their childhood severe sexual repression, stripping naked can represent a gesture of rebellion and liberation. We have seen this also on occasion in former nuns, priests, and individuals who spent many years in a seminary. Removing all clothes can also be an expression of overcoming the alienation from one's body and from nature characteristic of industrial societies. On rare occasions, the breathwork session can provide context for expressing latent or even manifest exhibitionistic tendencies.

The most important consideration concerning this situation is its impact on public relations and the image of Holotropic Breathwork. At the Esalen Institute, where we developed this method, it was not of much relevance if participants took off their clothes during the sessions. Esalen is known for its fabulous hot springs and integrated nude bathing. Following the breathwork sessions, most—if not all—group members typically headed for the baths. Wearing bathing suits was also optional around the Esalen swimming pool. Similarly, nudity has not been of much concern in our training for breathwork facilitators when we had the entire facility for ourselves, as was the case in White Sulphur Springs, Pocket Ranch, or Hollyhock Farm. Having shared deep emotional processes, participants knew one another well and felt comfortable with each other. Although the use of bathing suits in the hot tubs and in the swimming pool was always considered optional, participants usually preferred nudity.

The situation is different in large introductory workshops, which often take place in hotels and include many participants who are less open-minded than Esalen residents or our trainees. Under these circumstances, it is more likely that some people in the group or the hotel personnel could get upset and offended when confronted with nudity. In addition, according to our experience, when somebody takes off his or her clothes during breathwork, vivid descriptions of this event will figure prominently in the stories people will tell their friends about the workshop and in articles written about it. Naturally, this has an adverse effect on the image of Holotropic Breathwork in academic circles and in the general population.

In 1991, French certified facilitators subjected the public image of Holotropic Breathwork to a challenging test when they developed a nude variety of Holotropic Breathwork that they call Aquanima. During their breathing sessions, the breathers are floating on their backs in a swimming pool, supported by their partners. The pool is about five feet deep, of even depth in all its parts, and the water in the pool is lukewarm, close to body temperature. The potential of nudity and the water environment to trigger powerful emotional reactions was explored and described in the 1960s by Hollywood psychologist Paul Bindrim, the creator of the nude marathon and of the process he called aqua-energetics. This radical form of psychotherapy combined nudity, sleep deprivation, and fasting with experiential group work in water (Bindrim 1968, 1969).

Bernadette Blin-Lery, one of the originators of Aquanima, advanced in her book co-written with Brigitte Chavas a powerful argument for bringing the element of water into the Holotropic Breathwork process (Blin-Lery and Chavas 2009). Water forms 70 percent of our planet and 75 percent of our bodies. Life started in the primeval ocean and we begin our individual existence in the aquatic milieu of the maternal womb. Water is absolutely essential for life; no organism can exist without it. It is an element with extraordinary purifying properties, both in the physical and physiological sense and as a powerful spiritual symbol.

The work in water facilitates regression to archaic levels, both phylo-genetic—to the origins of life in the primeval ocean—and ontogenetic—to prenatal amniotic existence. The fact that the water in the pool is heated to body temperature eliminates the interface with the external world and is conducive to the dissolution of boundaries and feelings of unity. According to the reports of workshop participants, Holotropic Breathwork sessions in water seem to often feature experiences from early infancy, episodes of pre-natal life, and identification with various aquatic life forms. Some of them experienced the water as a sacred space or referred to it as the "ocean of love." The water also seemed to have a soothing effect and to facilitate good integration of the experiences. According to the originators, Aquanima is a particularly effective method of treating individuals suffering from hydropho-bia—pathological fear of water and inability to learn how to swim.

Blin-Lery and Chavas also addressed in their book the advantages of optional nudity during the Aquanima sessions. They emphasized that nudity liberates participants from irrational societal taboos and removes a wide range of unnecessary psychological defenses that have outlived their developmental necessity and usefulness. Since we all came into the world naked, nudity also facilitates regression to early infancy and to the perinatal and prenatal periods. Being seen and accepted by others as one is and seeing the naked bodies of others—both genders, different ages, and physical types, with all their imperfections—can greatly enhance one's self-acceptance. The rigorous prohibition of sexual contact actually makes this situation surprisingly safe.

Aquanima is conducted in groups of twenty to twenty-four with four to five trained facilitators. Participants work in triads, rather than dyads, as is the case with "dry" Holotropic Breathwork; each breather is supported by two peers. That introduces some interesting elements into the process; it can facilitate emergence of Oedipal issues and provide a corrective experience for those who had traumatic experiences in this regard. This arrangement can also precipitate some other issues related to triangular situations, such as sibling rivalry and problems with jealousy. This is the same situation that occasionally occurs in sessions of "dry" Holotropic Breathwork in groups with an odd number of participants that require double-sitting.

All of the aforementioned factors make Aquanima a very interesting psychotherapeutic experiment. Unfortunately, journalists and critics are seldom able to be mature and objective about this form of work and to refrain from sensationalizing and moralizing. The shadow side of this interesting innovation of French Holotropic Breathwork facilitators is thus its adverse effect on the public image of Holotropic Breathwork. The articles in newspapers and magazines covering this form of work tend to focus on nudity rather than the efficacy and transformative power of breathwork.

4. Overactive, erratic, and aggressive behavior

One of the most difficult challenges for the facilitators and sitters is to contain breathers who are extremely active and threaten to invade the space of other breathers. If a session starts going in that direction, the task of the helpers is to prevent the overactive breathers from interfering with the process of their peers and from hurting themselves and others. They can do this by using pillows, extra mattresses, and their own bodies. A particularly effective way of containing overly energetic or agitated breathers is to place them on a large blanket and create a cradle for them by lifting and firmly holding its edges.

This technique makes it possible to control even extreme forms of hectic activity. The wildest displays of erratic behavior are most frequently associated with the reliving of situations that involve interference with breathing. Examples include memories of near drowning, inhalation of foreign objects, childhood diphtheria, and difficult birth. Breathers reliving traumatic memories of this kind feel that they are suffocating and that their life is threatened. They become terrified and disoriented, desperately struggle for air, and chaotically kick and flail around. This can be associated with loss of awareness that they are in a workshop or a therapeutic situation;

under these circumstances, they might actually perceive their helpers as enemies threatening their life.

The basic rule of working with aggressive individuals is not to become identified as the target of the breathers' rage, but be perceived as a friend offering them help in expressing their violent feelings. Sometimes, in the course of this work, breathers can mistake us for enemies; to prevent this from happening, it might be necessary to reaffirm our role as helpers by asking such questions as: How are you doing? Is this helping? Are you feeling some relief? If the roles are not clear to the breather, disciplined inner work can turn into a dangerous fight.

If the breathers manifest frantic activity that is difficult to control by mattresses and pillows, but are fully conscious and cooperative, we can try another very effective alternative. We ask them to lie face down on the mattress and then stabilize and immobilize their lumbar area by pressing down with our hands or using the weight of our body. We encourage them to completely suspend control over the rest of the body and allow full expression of any physical movements and emotions that spontaneously emerge.

If the breather is willing to cooperate, we can use yet another useful strategy that makes it possible for the sitters and facilitators to work with aggressive individuals, including those who are much stronger than these helpers. In this form of work, the breather lies spread-eagle on his or her back and two helpers position themselves parallel to his or her body in such a way that they lie across the upper arms of this person and hold down the shoulders. The breather is then encouraged to suspend all control and give free expression to the full range of emotions and physical manifestations that spontaneously emerge. He or she can now fully unleash the anger without hurting anybody or destroying anything. In this way, the breather would have to elicit extraordinary strength to overpower the helpers. In our experience, women who were not particularly athletic have been able to work with strong men using this approach to contain them.

On occasion, the aggressive impulses can be aimed toward the breathers themselves and lead to self-destructive behavior: pummeling various parts of one's own body, beating the head against the floor or wall, exposing one's neck to pressure at dangerous angles and to risky torques, squeezing one's own throat, or sticking the fingers into one's eyes. This seems to happen particularly in individuals who in the course of their individual history have internalized anger because they were taught, explicitly or implicitly, that it was not acceptable or permissible to display it. Whenever the breathers behave in a way that might result in self-inflicted injury, the facilitators have to intervene and protect them.

Self-destructive actions usually reflect the effort of the breather to exteriorize and accentuate the sensations that are part of an unconscious gestalt. In spite of their dangerous nature, they are essentially expressions of a self-healing impulse. The strategy of the facilitators under these circumstances reflects the understanding of this dynamic. It consists in providing the stimulation that the breathers are seeking and in helping them augment the underlying sensations in a way that is safe and effective. For example, they put pressure on the areas of the body or the part of the head that the breather tries to hurt, find a safe pressure point on the bone of the orbit close to the eye, or apply pressure on certain regions of the neck without exposing it to potentially dangerous positions. The place and nature of this intervention mimics the self-destructive activity and represents its harmless alternative.

5. Working with demonic energy

The ultimate challenge for facilitators of Holotropic Breathwork is supporting the process of breathers who are experiencing manifestations of energy that has a distinctly demonic quality. It is usually associated with reliving of memories of severe emotional and physical abuse or of traumas that brought the individual to the threshold of death, such as a very difficult birth. As the emotional and physical expression of the breathers increase in intensity, they suddenly undergo a profound qualitative change. The first indication that this might be happening is a change of the breathers' facial and vocal expression, which become strange and uncanny. Their voice is deep and raspy, their eyes assume an indescribably evil expression, their face cramps up into a "mask of evil," spastic contractions make their hands look like claws, and their entire body tenses.

Subjectively, breathers experience within themselves alien dark energy that feels ominous and evil. It also seems to have definite personal characteristics or can even be visualized. Breathers in this condition usually find it difficult to admit that they harbor this entity because they are afraid that they will themselves be considered evil by their helpers. This concern is not completely unjustified. We have seen repeatedly that sitters and less experienced facilitators tend to withdraw from breathers who manifest demonic energy because of strong moral judgment, their own metaphysical fear, or both. This is particularly common in people brought up in a rigid fundamentalist setting.

Once it is understood that we are dealing with demonic energy, we reassure the breather that we feel comfortable working with it and that we have had ample experience doing it. The general strategy in this situation is to encourage the breather to fully express the alien energy with grimaces, sounds, and body movements. We do it with exhortations, such as: "Show us what it looks like! Show us what it sounds like! Express it fully, really fully, with your whole body!"

The emotions and physical energies released during this work can reach an extraordinary intensity. The breathers can muster physical strength that by far exceeds their everyday muscular power. This unusual phenomenon can also be observed during grand mal epileptic seizures occurring after the application of electroshocks or spontaneously. However, the demonic energy is not stereotypical and robotic, as is the case in grand mal epileptic seizures, but acts in a versatile, intelligent, and goal-oriented fashion. Its actions are wicked and aggressive; they are aimed at the breathers' helpers or against the breathers themselves.

The only way this situation can be effectively controlled is to use the aforementioned spread-eagle arrangement. Using this strategy might be complicated by the fact that the hands and nails of the "possessed" breathers often assault the helpers' backs, scratching, pinching, and otherwise hurting their skin. Additional people might be necessary to prevent this from happening. To provide for situations like this, it is useful to have extra people in breathwork sessions who help to "cover the floor," as we call it. Apprentices from our training have proved extremely valuable in this regard.

The actions of this evil energy are not only insidious and vicious, but also cunning. After a raging outburst, it often quiets down and nothing seems to be happening. If the helpers let down their guards and release the grip on the breather, his or her hand suddenly strikes and aims for one of the helper's eyes. We have to be aware that this is the nature of this energy and approach it accordingly. Once we encourage the breather to let the energy take over, it becomes autonomous and we cannot expect cooperation or help from the person with whom we are working. On occasion, the individuals with whom we had good rapport have actually warned us, saying something like: "Okay, I will let go of control, but you will be on your own. Be careful, it is sneaky!"

As difficult as working with demonic energy might be, it is well worth it. Episodes that were subjectively experienced as liberation from an evil entity and externally resembled an exorcism resulted in some of the most profound healing and transformation we have seen during the years of our practice. This phenomenon deserves special attention during the training of Holotropic Breathwork facilitators. They must have sufficient theoretical understanding and enough practical experience to be able to face demonic energy with calm, equanimity, and without moral judgment, like any other manifestation occurring in the course of breathwork sessions.

6. Excessive self-control and inability to let go

The idea of surrendering self-control and letting go can be very challenging for many people. The degree of fear of abandoning control typically reflects the nature of the unconscious material that is trying to emerge and the intensity of the emotional and physical energy that is associated with it. If the tension between the unconscious forces and the system of psychological defenses is strong, the individual can be afraid that the loss of control would not be just a temporary episode in the breathwork session, but a permanent condition extending into everyday life.

The fear of loss of control is typically associated with fantasies of what would happen if the unconscious energies took over. Different people have specific fearful anticipations as to what would ensue. Some imagine that it would result in unleashing of aggressive energy and "running amok"—indiscriminate violent attacks against others. An alternative fantasy involves violent life-threatening impulses of self-destructive rather than destructive nature. Yet another variety is the fear of indiscriminate sexual acting out, such as exposing oneself, becoming promiscuous, or indulging in aberrant forms of sex. The source of these aggressive and sexual impulses is often the third perinatal matrix (BPM III).

When the fear of letting go becomes an issue in Holotropic Breathwork, the first step is to convince the breather that the fantasies associated with it are unsubstantiated. Actually, what a temporary loss of control would lead to—considering that it happens in a protected environment and with expert help—is exactly the opposite of what the breather anticipates and is afraid of. Since the unconscious material and the associated energies that caused the fear of letting go would be released and leave the system, the breather would now be truly in control—not because he or she is able to prevent the unconscious elements from surfacing, but because these have ceased to exist as dynamic forces in the psyche.

Once the breather understands the nature of this process and is willing to let go, it helps to provide external containment. The sense that the energies are under external control makes the process of surrendering less scary for the breather. Effective techniques of containing breathers who are overtaken by elemental energies—the spread-eagle arrangement, the use of a blanket cradle, and the grounding the middle part of the body—were described earlier (pages 192ff.). Under these circumstances, giving up control and unconditional letting go can be a very liberating experience that can lead to remarkable healing and transformation.

7. Working with nausea and the tendency to vomit

Reliving memories of repulsive or disgusting situations or of medical interventions associated with anesthesia (including its use in childbirth) can result in residual feelings of intense nausea. The best way of working with this problem is to ask the breathers to imagine that they are actors in a pantomime and that their task is to express without words—just by grimaces, movements, gagging, and sounds—how they feel. This process, which starts as playacting and exaggeration, tends to very quickly become profound and authentic and often leads to purging through vomiting. Facilitators, assisting the breather with a bowl or a plastic bag, encourage him or her to continue until the nausea is cleared. In a short time, this form of purging can often transform feelings of severe malaise into a state of profound relief and relaxation.

8. Standing and dancing in the sessions

As part of the preparation, we ask breathers in workshops and training to remain in a reclining position throughout the session. Having to maintain a vertical position and to keep balance tends to detract the breather's attention from the inner process, particularly in an environment filled with mattresses, pillows, and blankets and little space between the breathers. Standing and especially jumping and dancing also represent danger for other breathers and, for this reason, are generally discouraged. The reclining position also facilitates regression to early infancy where kneeling or standing was not yet possible.

However, there are certain specific situations where leaving the reclining position and standing up or dancing is very appropriate and represents a meaningful part of the process. It can be an expression of a newly found freedom of the body, discovery of one's ability to dance, celebration of life after breaking out of a long-lasting depression, or affirmation of one's independence and ability to stand on one's own feet. Under these circumstances, the helpers might have to stand around the breather and keep the situation safe by preventing him or her from falling and invading other breathers' space.

9. Reliving the memory of biological birth

Much external intervention and support might be needed when breathers are reliving the memory of their biological birth. The range of appropriate or necessary actions is very broad and is guided by the momentary situation, experience, and intuition. Many people struggling to be born tend to move forcefully forward on the floor and need to be stopped with the use of pillows or skillfully maneuvered in such a way that they move in a circle in the space assigned to them.

Sometimes breathers need to push with their heads against resistance or receive bodywork in various parts of their bodies to facilitate expression of emotions, vocalization, or coughing. If a lot of energy seems to be blocked in the legs and lower part of the body, it can be very useful if two helpers form a cradle by placing their bodies parallel to that of the breather and, facing each other, join their arms under the breather's neck and under the knees of his or her flexed legs. The breather is then encouraged to push against this confinement and give full expression to any feelings that this situation evokes.

When a breather reliving birth begins to arch and flex the head backward, this is an indication that the process is reaching its final stage; it reflects the situation when the base of the fetus' skull is leaning against the mother's pubic bone and the perineum is being pulled over its face. Since this typically means encountering various forms of biological material, we can often see the breather grimacing, spitting, and attempting to wipe some imaginary material from his or her face. Here it might be very helpful to slide the palm of one's hand slowly over the breather's face from the forehead to the chin and with the other hand apply pressure at the base of the breather's skull. This can greatly facilitate the completion of the birth process.

Holotropic Breathwork and Other Breathing Techniques

During the discussion periods in our lectures and workshops, people often ask what characterizes Holotropic Breathwork and what distinguishes it from other approaches that work with breath. Various breathing techniques have been used since time immemorial in the context of shamanism, native rituals, and practices of various religious and spiritual groups. They also form an important part of many therapies developed in the course of the twentieth century—Johannes Schultz's autogenic training, various neo-Reichian approaches (Alexander Lowen's bioenergetics, John Pierrakos' core energy therapy, and Charles Kelley's Radix therapy), Leonard Orr's Rebirthing, and Gay and Kathleen Hendricks' Radiance Breathwork, to name just a few.

Like these other breathing practices, Holotropic Breathwork uses breath to initiate a process of psychosomatic self-exploration and healing, but with a different focus and emphasis. Unlike the practitioners of the aforementioned approaches, we do not give specific instructions for the way the breath should be used during the session—alternate fast breathing with withholding of breath, breathe from the tip of the lungs, engage in superficial and gentle "lizard breathing," use deep yogic breathing, inhale and exhale alternately through the right and left nostril, an so on. After a period of faster connected breathing, when participants enter a holotropic state of consciousness, we encourage them to let their breathing be guided by their inner healing intelligence and develop their own unique style of working with the breath.

Holotropic Breathwork has several other characteristics that distinguish it from approaches used by various spiritual systems and modern forms of experiential psychotherapy. The first of these is the use of carefully selected powerful evocative music, drawn from various spiritual traditions, aboriginal cultures, and classical and contemporary composers. This is an essential part of Holotropic Breathwork and facilitators spend much time and effort finding the most effective and appropriate pieces of music for various stages of the session. The second distinctive feature of the way we practice breathwork is working in pairs with participants alternating in the roles of breathers and sitters. We have also developed a unique form of energy-releasing bodywork that is not part of other breathwork methods. The way of conducting the processing groups and the use of mandalas are additional distinctive traits of Holotropic Breathwork.

However, what distinguishes Holotropic Breathwork from other respiratory methods more than anything else is its comprehensive theoretical framework based on decades of research of holotropic states of consciousness and anchored in transpersonal psychology and in the new paradigm in science (Grof 1985 and 2000). The attempts to bring some degree of intellectual rigor into an otherwise highly controversial field makes Holotropic Breathwork acceptable to open-minded professionals with academic training. This distinguishes Holotropic Breathwork particularly from Leonard Orr's Rebirthing. The inquiries about the similarities and differences between these two methods belong to the most frequent questions raised in discussions.

The practice of Rebirthing is without any question a very powerful and effective form of self-exploration and therapy. However, Leonard Orr's theoretical speculations are rather simplistic and his therapeutic slang has little chance of being embraced by professional circles. This can be illustrated by his famous "Five Biggies in Life," among which he counts: 1) the birth trauma, 2) specific negative thought structures, 3) the parental disapproval syndrome, 4) the unconscious death urge, and 5) influences from other lifetimes. Although participants in breathwork sessions certainly encounter all five of these themes, the list is painfully incomplete and can hardly be considered a comprehensive conceptual framework. Rebirthing has attracted many professionals because of its effectiveness as a powerful and innovative therapeutic tool; however, this happened in spite of Leonard Orr's excursions into psychiatric theory rather than because of them.

In conclusion, what the different breathing techniques have in common is more important than the differences between them. Since time immemorial, breathing has been seen not only as a vital body function, but also as an activity that connects the physical world (air) with the human body, psyche, and spirit. Its extraordinary potential as an important tool in the ritual and spiritual life of humanity, as well as various healing practices, has been repeatedly tested in a wide range of countries, cultures, and historical periods.

BIBLIOGRAPHY

Alexander, F. 1950. *Psychosomatic Medicine*. New York: W. W. Norton.

Aristotle. 2006. *Poetics*. Translated by Joe Sachs. Newbury Port, MA: Focus Philosophical Library, Pullins Press.

Bindrim, P. 1968. "A Report on a Nude Marathon." *Psychotherapy: Research and Practice* 5,3:180–188, Fall.

Bindrim, P. 1969. "Nudity as a Quick Grab for Intimacy in Group Therapy." *Psychology Today* 3,1:24–28, June.

Blanck, G., and Blanck, R. 1974. *Ego Psychology I: Theory and Practice*. New York: Columbia University Press.

Blanck G., and Blanck, R. 1979. *Ego Psychology II*: New York: Columbia University Press.

Blin-Lery, B., and Chavas, B. 2009. *Guérir l'ego, révéler l'être: le défi des thérapies transpersonnelles*. Paris: Edition Trédaniel.

Bohm, D. 1980. *Wholeness and the Implicate Order*. London: Routledge and Kegan Paul.

Browne, I. 1990. "Psychological Trauma, or Unexperienced Experience." *Re-Vision Journal* 12(4):21–34.

Bubeev, Y. A., and Kozlov. 2001a. "Experimental Psychophysiological and Neurophysiological Study of Intensive Breathing." In *Holotropic Breathwork: Theory, Practice, Researches, Clinical Applications* (V. Maykov and V. Kozlov, eds.). Moscow: Publications of the Institute of Transpersonal Psychology.

Bubeev, Y. A., and Kozlov. 2001b. "Experimental Studies of the Influence of Intensive Breathing on an Individual and Group." In *Holotropic Breathwork: Theory, Practice, Researches, Clinical Applications* (V. Maykov and V. Kozlov, eds.). Moscow: Publications of the Institute of Transpersonal Psychology.

Cannon, W. B. 1932. *The Wisdom of the Body*. New York: Norton.

Capra, F. 1975. *The Tao of Physics*. Berkeley, CA: Shambhala Publications.

Cárdenas, E., Lynn, S. J., and Krippner, S. (Eds.). (2000). *Varieties of Anomalous Experience: Examining the Scientific Evidence*. Washington, DC: American Psychological Association.

Cassoux, M., and Cubley, S. 1995. *Life, Paint, and Passion: Reclaiming the Magic of Spontaneous Expression*. New York: Putnam.

Christie, R. V. 1935. "Some Types of Respiration in Neuroses." *Quarterly Journal of Medicine* 16:427–432.

Cohen, S. 1965. "LSD and the Anguish of Dying." *Harper's Magazine* 231:69.

Corbin, H. 2000. "Mundus Imaginalis, Or the Imaginary and the Imaginal." In *Working with Images*, Edited by B. Sells. Woodstock, CT: Spring Publications, 2000. 71–89.

Dante, A. 1990. *Il Convivio*. Translated by R. H. Lansing. New York: Garland.

Dunbar, H. F. 1954. *Emotions and Bodily Changes*. New York: Columbia University Press.

Evans-Wentz, W. E. 1957. *The Tibetan Book of the Dead*. London: Oxford University Press.

Fenichel, O. 1945. *Psychoanalytic Theory of Neurosis*. New York: W. W. Norton.

Foerster, H. von. 1965. "Memory without a Record." In *The Anatomy of Memory*. Edited by D. P. Kimble. Palo Alto, CA: Science and Behavior Books.

Franz, M.-L. von. 1997. *Alchemical Active Imagination*. New York: C. G. Jung Foundation Books.

Freud, S. 1953. *The Interpretation of Dreams*. London: The Hogarth Press and the Institute of Psycho-Analysis, Vol. IV.

Freud, S. 1955a. *Totem and Taboo*. London: The Hogarth Press and the Institute of Psycho-Analysis, Vol. XIII.

Freud, S. 1955b. *Group Psychology and the Analysis of the Ego*. London: The Hogarth Press and the Institute of Psycho-Analysis, Vol. XVIII.

Freud, S. 1957a. *Dostoevsky and Parricide*. London: The Hogarth Press and the Institute of Psycho-Analysis, Vol. XI.

Freud, S. 1957b. *Leonardo da Vinci and a Memory of His Childhood*. London: The Hogarth Press and the Institute of Psycho-Analysis, Vol. XI.

Freud, S. 1960a. *The Psychopathology of Everyday Life*. London: The Hogarth Press and the Institute of Psycho-Analysis, Vol. VI.

Freud, S. 1960b. *Jokes and Their Relation to the Unconscious*. London: The Hogarth Press and the Institute of Psycho-Analysis, Vol. VIII.

Freud, S. 1962. *Three Essays on the Theory of Sexuality*. New York: Basic Books.

Freud, S. 1964a. *Future of an Illusion*. London: The Hogarth Press and the Institute of Psycho-Analysis, Vol. XXI.

Freud, S. 1964b. *Civilization and Its Discontents*. London: The Hogarth Press and the Institute of Psychoanalysis, Vol. XXI.

Freud, S., and Breuer, J. 1936. *Studies in Hysteria*. New York: Nervous and Mental Diseases.

Fried, R. 1982. *The Hyperventilation Syndrome: Research and Clinical Treatment*. Baltimore: Johns Hopkins University Press.

Friedman, M., and Rosenman, R. H. 1974. *Type A Behavior and Your Heart*. New York: Knopf.

Frost, S. B. 2001. *Soul Collage*. Santa Cruz, CA: Hanford Mead Publishers.

Goldberg, G. J. 1958. "Psychiatric Aspects of Hyperventilation." *South African Medical Journal* 32:447–449.

Goldman, D. 1952. "The Effect of Rhythmic Auditory Stimulation on the Human Electroencephalogram." *EEG and Clinical Neurophysiology* 4:370.

Goswami, A. 1995. *The Self-Aware Universe: How Consciousness Creates the Material World*. Los Angeles: J. P. Tarcher.

Grof, C., and Grof, S. 1990. *The Stormy Search for the Self: A Guide to Personal Growth Through Transformational Crises*. Los Angeles, CA: J. P. Tarcher.

Grof, S. 1975. *Realms of the Human Unconscious: Observations from LSD Research*. New York: Viking Press. Republished in 2009 as *LSD: Doorway to the Numinous: The Ground-Breaking Psychedelic Research into Realms of the Human Unconscious*. Rochester, VT: Park Street Press.

Grof, S. 1980. *LSD Psychotherapy*. Pomona, CA: Hunter House. Republished in 2001 by Multidisciplinary Association for Psychedelic Studies (MAPS) Publications in Sarasota, Florida.

Grof, S. 1985. *Beyond the Brain: Birth, Death, and Transcendence in Psychotherapy*. Albany: State University of New York Press.

Grof, S. 1987. *The Adventure of Self-Discovery*. Albany: State University of New York Press.

Grof, S. (with Hal Zina Bennett). 1992. *The Holotropic Mind: The Three Levels of Consciousness and How They Shape Our Lives*. San Francisco, CA: Harper Collins.

Grof, S. 1998. *The Cosmic Game: Explorations of the Frontiers of Human Consciousness*. Albany: State University of New York Press.

Grof, S. 2000. *Psychology of the Future: Lessons from Modern Consciousness Research*. Albany: State University of New York Press.

Grof, S. 2006a. *When the Impossible Happens: Adventures in Non-Ordinary Realities*. Louisville, CO: Sounds True.

Grof, S. 2006b. *The Ultimate Journey: Consciousness and the Mystery of Death*. Sarasota, FL: MAPS Publications.

Grof, S. 2006c. *LSD Psychotherapy*. Ben Lomond, CA: MAPS Publications.

Grof, S. 2010. *The Visionary World of H. R. Giger*. New York: Scapegoat Publishing.

Grof, S., and Grof, C. 1989. *Spiritual Emergency: When Personal Transformation Becomes a Crisis*. Los Angeles, CA: J. P. Tarcher.

Harman, W. 1984. *Higher Creativity: Liberating the Unconscious for Breakthrough Insights*. Los Angeles, CA: J. P. Tarcher.

Harner, M. 1980. *The Way of the Shaman: A Guide to Power and Healing*. New York: Harper and Row.

Hellinger, B. 2003. *Farewell: Family Constellations with Descendants of Victims and Perpetrators*. Heidelberg: Carl-Auer-Systeme Verlag.

Hines, B. 1996. *God's Whisper, Creation's Thunder: Ultimate Reality in the New Physics*. Brattleboro, VT: Threshold Publications.

Hubbard, L. R 1950. *Dianetics: The Modern Science of Mental Health*. East Grinstead, Sussex, England: Hubbard College of Scientology.

Huey, S. R., and Sechrest, L. 1981. *Hyperventilation Syndrome and Psychopathology*. Center for Research on the Utilization of Scientific Knowledge, Institute for Social Research, University of Michigan (manuscript).

Huxley, A. 1959. *The Doors of Perception and Heaven and Hell*. Harmondsworth, Middlesex, Great Britain: Penguin Books.

Huxley, A. 1945. *Perennial Philosophy*. New York and London: Harper and Brothers.

Jilek, W. J. 1974. *Salish Indian Mental Health and Culture Change: Psychohygienic and Therapeutic Aspects of the Guardian Spirit Ceremonial*. Toronto and Montreal: Holt, Rinehart, and Winston of Canada.

Jilek, W. J. 1982. "Altered States of Consciousness in North American Indian Ceremonials." *Ethos* 10:326–343.

Jung, C. G. 1959a. *The Archetypes of the Collective Unconscious*. Collective Works, Vol. 9.1. Bollingen Series 20. Princeton: Princeton University Press.

Jung, C. G. 1959b. *Mandala Symbolism*. Translated by R. F. C. Hull. Bollingen Series. Princeton: Princeton University Press.

Jung, C. G. 1961. *Memories, Dreams, Reflections*. New York: Pantheon.

Jung, C. G. 2009. *The Red Book*. New York: W. W. Norton and Company.

Kalff, D. 2003. *Sandplay: A Psychotherapeutic Approach to the Psyche*. Cloverdale, CA: Temenos Press.

Kamiya, J. 1969. "Operant Control of the EEG Alpha Rhythm and Some of Its Effects on Consciousness. In *Altered States of Consciousness*. Edited by C. T. Tart. New York: Wiley. 489–501.

Kast, E. C., and Collins, V. J. 1966. "LSD and the Dying Patient." *Chicago Medical School Quarterly* 26: 80.

Katz, R. 1976. *Boiling Energy: Community Healing Among the Kalahari Kung*. Cambridge, MA: Harvard University Press.

Kellogg, J. 1977a. "The Use of the Mandala in Psychological Evaluation and Treatment." *American Journal of Art Therapy* 16:123.

Kellogg, J. 1977b. "The Meaning of Color and Shape in Mandalas." *American Journal of Art Therapy* 16:123–126.

Kellogg, J. 1978. *Mandala: The Path of Beauty*. Baltimore, MD: Mandala Assessment and Research Institute.

Kennell, J. H., and Klaus, M. 1998. "Parental Bonding: Recent Observations That Alter Perinatal Care." *Pediatrics in Review* 19:4–2.

Klaus, M., Kennell, J. H., and Klaus, P. H. 1995. *Bonding: Building the Foundations of Secure Attachment and Independence*. Reading, MA: Addison Wesley.

Klaus, M. H. 1976. *The Impact of Early Separation: The Impact of Early Separation or Loss on Family Development*. St. Louis, MI: Mosby Publications.

Klein, D. F., Zitrin, C. M., and Woerner, M. 1978. "Antidepressants, Anxiety, Panic, and Phobia." In *Psychopharmacology: A Generation of Progress*. Edited by M. A. Lipton, A. DiMascio, and K. F. Killiam. New York: Raven Press.

Laszlo, E. 1993. *The Creative Cosmos*. Edinburgh: Floris Books.

Laszlo, E. 2004. *Science and the Akashic Field: An Integral Theory of Everything*. Rochester, VT: Inner Traditions.

Lee, R., and DeVore, I. 1999. *Kalahari Hunter-Gatherers: Studies of the !Kung San and Their Neighbors*. Cambridge, MA: Harvard University Press.

Lum, L. C. 1987. "Hyperventilation Syndrome in Medicine and Psychiatry: A Review." *Journal of the Royal Society of Medicine* 80,4:229–231.

Mahl, G. F. 1949. "The Effect of Chronic Fear on Gastric Secretion." *Psychosomatic Medicine* 11:30.

Mahr, A. 1999. *Das wissende Feld: Familienaufstellung als geistig energetisches Heilen (The Knowing Field: Family Constellation as Spiritual and Energetic Healing)*. Munich: Koesel Verlag.

Martin, J. 1965. "LSD Analysis." Lecture and film presented at the Second International Conference on the Use of LSD in Psychotherapy held on May 8–12, 1965, at South Oaks Hospital, Amityville, New York. Paper published in *The Use of LSD in Psychotherapy and Alcoholism*. Edited by H. A. Abramson. Indianapolis, IN: Bobbs-Merrill. 223–238.

Maslow, A. 1962. *Toward a Psychology of Being*. Princeton: Van Nostrand.

Maslow, A. 1964. *Religions, Values, and Peak Experiences*. Columbus: Ohio State University Press.

Maslow, A. 1969. "A Theory of Metamotivation: The Biological Rooting of the Value-Life." In *Readings in Humanistic Psychology*. Ed. A. J. Sutich and M. A. Vich. New York: The Free Press. 41–103.

Maxfield, M. C. 1990. "Effects of Rhythmic Drumming on EEG and Subjective Experience." Unpublished Doctoral Dissertation. Institute of Transpersonal Psychology, Menlo Park, CA.

Maxfield, M. C. 1994. "The Journey of the Drum." *Re-Vision Journal* 16:148–156.

McCririck, P. 1966. "The Importance of Fusion in Therapy and Maturation." Unpublished mimeographed manuscript.

McGee, D., Browne, I., Kenny, V., McGennis, A., and Pilot, J. 1984. "Unexperienced Experience: A Clinical Reappraisal of the Theory of Repression and Traumatic Neurosis." *Irish Journal of Psychotherapy* 3:7.

Moreno, J. L. 1973. *Gruppenpsychotherapie und Psychodrama (Group Psychotherapy and Psychodrama)*. Stuttgart: Thieme Verlag.

Moreno, J. L. 1976. "Psychodrama and Group Psychotherapy." *Annals of the New York Academy of Sciences* 49,6:902–903.

Neher, A. 1961. "Auditory Driving Observed with Scalp Electrodes in Normal Subjects." *Electroencephalography and Clinical Neurophysiology* 13:449–451.

Neher, A. 1962. "A Physiological Explanation of Unusual Behavior Involving Drums." *Human Biology* 14:151–160.

Orr, L., and Ray, S. 1977. *Rebirthing in the New Age*. Millbrae, CA: Celestial Arts.

Perls, F. 1973. *Gestalt Approach and Witness to Therapy*. Palo Alto, CA: Science and Behavior Books.

Perls, F. 1976. *Gestalt Therapy Verbatim*. New York: Bantam Books.

Perls, F., Hefferline, R. F., and Goodman, P. 1951. *Gestalt Therapy: Excitement and Growth in the Human Personality*. New York: Julian Press.

Pribram, K. 1971. *Languages of the Brain*. Englewood Cliffs, NJ: Prentice Hall.

Ramacharaka (William Walker Atkinson). 1903. *The Science of Breath*. London: L. N. Fowler and Company, Ltd.

Reich, W. 1949. *Character Analysis*. New York: Noonday Press.

Reich, W. 1961. *The Function of the Orgasm: Sex-Economic Problems of Biological Energy*. New York: Farrar, Strauss, and Giroux.

Reich, W. 1970. *The Mass Psychology of Fascism*. New York: Simon and Schuster.

Rider, M. 1985. "Entrainment Mechanisms Are Involved in Pain Reduction, Muscle Relaxation, and Music-Mediated Imagery." *Journal of Music Therapy* 22:183–192.

Ring, K., and Cooper, S. 1999. *Mindsight: Near-Death and Out-of-Body Experiences in the Blind.* Palo Alto, CA: William James Center for Consciousness Studies.

Ring, K., and Valarino, E. E. 1998. *Lessons from the Light: What We Can Learn from the Near-Death Experience.* New York: Plenum Press.

Ross, C. A. 1989. *Multiple Personality Disorder: Diagnosis, Clinical Features, and Treatment.* New York: John Wiley & Sons.

Sabom, M. 1982. *Recollections of Death: A Medical Investigation.* New York: Harper and Row Publications.

Sabom, M. 1998. *Light and Death: One Doctor's Fascinating Accounts of Near-Death Experiences.* Grand Rapids, MI: Zondervan Church Source.

Selye, H. 1950. *The Physiology and Pathology of Exposure to Stress.* Montreal: Acta.

Shapiro, F. 2001. *Eye Movement Desensitization and Reprocessing: Basic Principles, Protocols, and Procedures.* New York: Guilford Press.

Shapiro, F. 2002. *EMDR as an Integrative Psychotherapy Approach: Experts of Diverse Orientations Explore the Paradigm Prism.* Washington, DC: American Psychological Association Books.

Sheldrake, R. 1981. *A New Science of Life: The Hypothesis of Formative Causation.* Los Angeles, CA: J. P. Tarcher.

Sheldrake, R. 1988. *The Presence of the Past: Morphic Resonance and the Habits of Nature.* New York: Times Books.

Sparks, T. 1989. *Doing Not Doing: A Facilitator's Guide to Holotropic Breathwork.* Mill Valley, CA: Holotropic Books and Music.

Stoll, W. A. 1947. "LSD, ein Phantastikum aus der Mutterkorngruppe" (LSD, a Fantasticum from the Group of Ergot Alkaloids). *Schweizer Archiv für Neurologie und Psychiatrie* 60: 279.

Stone, H., and Stone, S. 1989. *Embracing Our Selves: The Voice Dialogue Manual.* Mill Valley, CA: Nataraj Publishing.

Sutich, A. 1976. "The Emergence of the Transpersonal Orientation: A Personal Account." *Journal of Transpersonal Psychology* 8: 5–19.

Taylor, K. 1991. *The Holotropic Breathwork Workshop: A Manual for Trained Facilitators.* Santa Cruz, CA: Hanford Mead Publishers.

Taylor, K. 1994. *The Breathwork Experience: Exploration and Healing in Non-Ordinary States of Consciousness.* Santa Cruz, CA: Hanford Mead Publishers.

Taylor, K. 1995. *Ethics of Caring: Honoring the Web of Life in Our Professional Healing Relationships.* Santa Cruz, CA: Hanford Mead Publishers.

Taylor, K. 2003. *Exploring Holotropic Breathwork: Selected Articles from a Decade of the Inner Door.* Santa Cruz, CA: Hanford Mead Publishers.

Teilhard de Chardin, P. 1964. *The Future of Man.* New York: Harper and Row.

Teilhard de Chardin, P. 1975. *The Human Phenomenon.* New York: Harper and Row.

Tomatis, A. A. 1991. *The Conscious Ear: My Life of Transformation through Listening.* Barrytown, NY: Station Hill Press.

Turner, V. W. 1969. *The Ritual Process: Structure and Anti-Structure.* Chicago: Aldine.

Turner, V. W. 1974. *Dramas, Fields, and Metaphors: Symbolic Action in Human Society.* Ithaca, NY: Cornell University Press.

Vithoulkas, G. 1980. *The Science of Homeopathy.* New York: Grove Press.

Weil, A. 1972. *The Natural Mind.* Boston: Houghton Mifflin.

Whitwell, G. E. 1999. "The Importance of Prenatal Sound and Music." *Journal of Prenatal and Perinatal Psychology and Health* 13,3–4:255–262.

Wilber, K. 1980. *The Atman Project: A Transpersonal View of Human Development.* Wheaton, IL: Theosophical Publishing House.

Wilber, K. 1982. *A Sociable God.* New York: McGraw-Hill.

Wolff, S., and Wolff, H. 1947. *Human Gastric Function.* London: Oxford University Press.

Zaritsky, M. G. 1998. "Complex Method of Treating Alcoholic Patients: Using Medichronal Microwave Resonance Therapy and Holotropic Breathwork." *Lik Sprava* 7:126–132.

Studies of Holotropic Breathwork

Ashauer, B., and Yensen, R. 1988. "Healing Potential of Non-Ordinary States: Observations from Holotropic Breathwork." Presented at the Ninth International Transpersonal Conference in Santa Rosa, CA, entitled "The Transpersonal Vision: Past, Present and Future," October 9–14.

Binarová, D. 2003. "The Effect of Holotropic Breathwork on Personality." *Česká a slovenská psychiatrie* 99:410–414.

Binns, S. 1997. "Grof's Perinatal Matrix Theory: Initial Empirical Verification." Honors Year Dissertation. Department of Psychology, Australian Catholic University. Victoria, Australia.

Brewerton, T., Eyerman, J., Capetta, P., and Mithoefer, M. C. 2008. "Long-Term Abstinence Following Breathwork as Adjunctive Treatment of Substance Dependence." Presented at the Tenth Annual Meeting of the International Society of Addiction Medicine in Cape Town, South Africa.

Brouillette, G. 1997. "Reported Effects of Holotropic Breathwork: An Integrative Technique for Healing and Personal Change." Doctoral dissertation. Proquest Dissertations and Theses 1997. Section 0669, Part 0622, 375 pages; United States—California: Institute of Transpersonal Psychology. Publication Number: AAT DP14336.

Byford, C. L. 1991. "Holotropic Breathwork: A Potential Therapeutic Intervention for Post-Traumatic Stress Disorder in Female Incest Victims." M.T.P. dissertation. Proquest Dissertations and Theses. Section 0669, Part 0621, 119 pages; United States—California: Institute of Transpersonal Psychology. Publication Number: AAT EP15296.

Cervelli, R. 2008. "Holotropic Breathwork, Mandala Artwork, and Archetypal Symbolism: The Potential for Self-Actualization." Doctoral dissertation. Institute of Transpersonal Psychology Palo Alto, California, January 21.

Crowley, N. 2005. "Holotropic Breathwork: Healing Through a Non-Ordinary State of Consciousness." Paper based on a talk delivered by Dr. Crowley on May 9,

2005, at a special interest group meeting of the Royal College of Psychiatrists, United Kingdom.

Edwards, L. 1999. "Use of Hypnosis and Non-Ordinary States of Consciousness in Facilitating Significant Psychotherapeutic Change." *The Australian Journal of Clinical Hypnotherapy and Hypnosis*. September issue.

Everett, G. 2001. "The Healing Potential of Non-Ordinary States of Consciousness." Doctoral dissertation, 251 pages. Australia–Norfolk Island. School of Psychology, College of Social Science, Greenwich University.

Grof, P., and Fox, A. 2010. "The Use of Holotropic Breathwork in the Integrated Treatment of Mood Disorders." *Canadian Journal of Psychotherapy and Counseling* (in press).

Hanratty, P. M. 2002. "Predicting the Outcome of Holotropic Breathwork Using the High-Risk Model of Threat Perception." Doctoral dissertation. Proquest Dissertations and Theses 2002. Section 0795, Part 0622, 171 pages; United States—California: Saybrook Graduate School and Research Center. Publication Number: AAT 3034572.

Henebry, J. T. 1991. "Sound Wisdom and the Transformational Experience: Explorations of Music, Consciousness, and the Potential for Healing." Doctoral dissertation. Proquest Dissertations and Theses. Section 1033, Part 0622, 329 pages; United States—Ohio: The Union Institute. Publication Number: AAT 9125061.

Holmes, S. W. 1993. "An Examination of the Comparative Effectiveness of Experientially and Verbally Oriented Psychotherapy in the Amelioration of Client-Identified Presenting Problems." Doctoral dissertation. Proquest Dissertations and Theses. Section 0079, Part 0622, 257 pages; United States—Georgia: Georgia State University. Publication Number: AAT 9409408.

Holmes, S. W., Morris, R., Clance, P. R., Thompson Putney, R. 1996. "Holotropic Breathwork: An Experiential Approach to Psychotherapy." *Psychotherapy: Theory, Research, Practice, Training* 33,1:114–120. Spring.

Jackson, P. A, 1996. "Stanislav Grof's Holotropic Therapy System." This fifty-page-paper is based on presentations Peter Jackson made at the Nelson Conference of the New Zealand Association of Psychotherapists in March 1996 and at the First World Congress of the World Council for Psychotherapy in Vienna, Austria, July 1996.

Jefferys, B. 2003. "Holotropic Work in Addictions Treatment." In *Exploring Holotropic Breathwork*. Edited by K. Taylor. Santa Cruz, CA: Hanford Mead Publishers.

La Flamme, D. M. 1994. "Holotropic Breathwork and Altered States of Consciousness." *Proquest Dissertations and Theses*. Doctoral dissertation. Section 0392, Part 0622, 264 pages; United States—California: California Institute of Integral Studies. Publication Number: AAT 9410355.

Lahood, G. 2007. "From 'Bad' Ritual to 'Good' Ritual: Transmutations of Childbearing Trauma in Holotropic Ritual." *Journal of Prenatal and Perinatal Psychology and Health* 22:81–112.

Lapham, J. A. 2000. "Holotropic Learning: The Language of Holotropic Light. Unpacking the Experience." Doctoral dissertation. Proquest Dissertations and

Theses. Section 1033, Part 0451, 171 pages; United States—Ohio: The Union Institute. Publication Number: AAT 9992717.

Lyons, C. 2003. "Somatic Memory in Non-Ordinary States of Consciousness." Master's thesis. 86 pages. United Kingdom–Merseyside. School of Psychology, Liverpool John Moores University.

Marquez, N. A. 1999. "Healing Through the Remembrance of the Pre- and Perinatal: A Phenomenological Investigation." Doctoral dissertation. Proquest Dissertations and Theses. Section 0669, Part 0622, 250 pages; United States—California: Institute of Transpersonal Psychology. Publication Number: AAT 9934567.

Metcalf, B. A 1995. "Examining the Effects of Holotropic Breathwork in the Recovery from Alcoholism and Drug Dependence." In *Exploring Holotropic Breathwork*. Edited by K. Taylor. Santa Cruz, CA: Hanford Mead Publishers.

Murray, M. 2001. "Deepening Presence: How Experiences of No-Self Shape the Self, an Organic Inquiry." Doctoral dissertation. Proquest Dissertations and Theses. Section 0392, Part 0620, 256 pages; United States—California: California Institute of Integral Studies. Publication Number: AAT 3016609.

Myerson, J. G. 1991. "Rising in the Golden Dawn: An Introduction to Acupuncture Breath Therapy." Doctoral dissertation. Proquest Dissertations and Theses. Section 1033, Part 0621, 76 pages; United States—Ohio: The Union Institute. Publication Number: AAT 9216532.

Nelms, C. A. 1995. "Supporting People During Spiritual Emergency: A Manual and Resource Guide for Non-Clinicians." M.T.P. dissertation. Proquest Dissertations and Theses. Section 0669, Part 0622, 95 pages; United States—California: Institute of Transpersonal Psychology. Publication Number: AAT EP15327.

Pressman, T. E. 1993. "The Psychological and Spiritual Effects of Stanislav Grof's Holotropic Breathwork Technique: An Exploratory Study." Doctoral dissertation. Proquest Dissertations and Theses. Section 0795, Part 0622, 152 pages; United States—California: Saybrook Graduate School and Research Center. Publication Number: AAT 9335165.

Rhinewine, J. P., Williams, O. J., 2007. "Holotropic Breathwork: The Potential Role of a Prolonged, Voluntary Hyperventilation Procedure as an Adjunct to Psychotherapy." *The Journal of Alternative and Complementary Medicine* 13,7:771–776. September 1.

Robedee, C. 2008. "From States to Stages: Exploring the Potential Evolutionary Efficacy of Holotropic Breathwork." Submitted in partial fulfillment of the requirements for the degree of Master of Arts in Conscious Evolution at the Graduate Institute in Millford, CT, July.

Selig, M. 2006. "Facilitating Breathwork at a Psychosomatic Clinic in Kassel, Germany." In *The Inner Door* 17:6–7.

Spivak, L. I., Kropotov, Y. D., Spivak, D. L., and Sevostyanov, A. V. 1994. "Evoked Potentials in Holotropic Breathing." *Human Physiology* 20,1:17–19. (An English translation of the Russian original.)

Terekhin, P. I. 1966. "The Role of Hypocapnia in Inducing Altered States of Consciousness." *Human Physiology* 22,6:730–735, 1996. (An English translation of the Russian original.)

Zaritsky, M. G. 1998. "Complex Method of Treating Patients Sick with Alcoholism Utilizing Medichronal Microwave Resonance Therapy and Holotropic Breathwork." *Lik Sprava* 7:126–132.

INDEX

ABOUT GROF
TRANSPERSONAL TRAINING

Grof Transpersonal Training (GTT) offers workshops and certification in Holo-tropic Breathwork™ (see important section further on about trademark).

Our six-day workshops (modules) are designed both for those who wish to become certified Holotropic Breathwork practitioners and for people who may not want to be practitioners but would like to experience Holotropic Breathwork in the setting of a longer workshop combined with interesting related topics. It is also valuable for professionals, such as therapists, educa-tors, and clergy who wish to enhance their skills.

The certification program is a 600+ hour program that takes place over a minimum of two years, though there is no maximum time to complete the training. Requirements include seven six-day modules, a two-week closing intensive, personal consultations, workshop attendance, and apprenticeships. In addition, those completing the program agree to follow a set of ethical standards and the principles of Holotropic Breathwork.

Each six-day module is devoted to a specific practical and/or theoretical theme and features Holotropic Breathwork sessions, along with complementary experiential practices, such as meditation, dance, art, film, time in nature, and ritual. Examples of module themes include The Power Within; The Practice of Holotropic Breathwork; Music and Transcendence; New Understanding of Emotional and Psychosomatic Disorders; Spiritual Emergency; Transpersonal Approach to Alcoholism and Addiction; Psychological, Philosophical, and Spiritual Dimensions of Death and Dying; Psyche and Eros; The Cosmic Game; Ecstatic Remembrance: Kirtan Chanting; Shamanism; Movie Yoga; and The Power of Archetype.

More about modules:

- You can take any GTT retreat without making a commitment to the entire training or to becoming a certified practitioner.

- Participants can attend without previous experience of Holotropic Breathwork.

- Attending for the longer six-day period offers an opportunity for deeper and more thorough personal work.

- Art, music, dance, integration, and community are all important parts of the modules.

- You will meet people from all over the world who share your interests in exploring the deeper realms of the psyche, transpersonal psychology, and the holotropic perspective.

- Continuing Education (CE) hours are available for MFTs and social workers in California and reciprocal states.

Every year, GTT modules take place in various locations around the world. They have been offered in different parts of the United States, and in Argentina, Australia, Austria, Brazil, Chile, Denmark, Germany, Italy, Mexico, Norway, Russia, Spain, Sweden, Switzerland, and the United Kingdom.

For a current list of training locations, dates, and module topics, or for a complete description of the training, please visit our website, www.holotropic. com, e-mail gtt@holotropic.com, or telephone (U.S.): (415) 383-8779.

About the Trademarked Term Holotropic Breathwork

The practice of Holotropic Breathwork requires a committed, rigorous process of personal growth and extensive education in psychology and other related disciplines. It would be highly unethical to attempt to use this method with others without completing the certification program. Further, persons who are not certified through GTT do not have permission to call any work they do "Holotropic Breathwork." Grof Transpersonal Training is the only certifying organization for Holotropic Breathwork.

The Association for Holotropic Breathwork International

The Association for Holotropic Breathwork International is a membership organization that is open to anyone who is interested in exploring or supporting the practice of Holotropic Breathwork. AHBI works to make Holotropic Breathwork more available worldwide, to support the practice of facilitators and participants, to create communications and connections for people interested in Holotropic Breathwork, to promote awareness about

Holotropic Breathwork, and to support future multidisciplinary research of this method.

To find out more about Holotropic Breathwork, including current clinical research, upcoming workshops, and facilitators in your area, or talk with facilitators and other participants, visit the Association for Holotropic Breathwork International at www.ahbi.org.